STUDIES IN HISTORY, ECONOMICS AND PUBLIC LAW

EDITED BY THE FACULTY OF POLITICAL SCIENCE OF COLUMBIA UNIVERSITY

Number 289

LEGISLATIVE FUNCTIONS OF NATIONAL ADMINISTRATIVE AUTHORITIES

PREFACE

As early as 1919 the writer's attention was directed to the general problem of national administrative legislation. In 1920 he decided to write his dissertation in this field. Washington, D. C., was the logical place for securing information. This latter fact made it necessary for the writer to secure his information piecemeal. For this reason, it was not possible for him to complete his work until the spring of 1926.

In the meantime a few magazine articles and one or two books appeared having to do with some special phase of the subject or with all phases of it in connection with a particular department or agency of the National Government. The first general work dealing with national administrative legislation was James Hart, *The Ordinance Making Powers of the President of the United States.* This excellent treatise came to the writer's attention early in 1926. He at once consulted his adviser, Professor Howard Lee McBain of Columbia University, on the advisability of publishing the then almost completed dissertation. He was told that in as much as the work was his own, it should be carried through as planned. This was done. Mr. Hart's treatise was of value in dealing with the general legal features of this discussion, and he has been given due credit.

TABLE OF CONTENTS

PAGE

PREFACE 5

CHAPTER I

Introduction 9

CHAPTER II

Administrative Legislation: Distinctions and Classification . . . 21

CHAPTER III

The History of Administrative Legislation 50

CHAPTER IV

The Constitutional Aspects of Delegated Legislation 113

CHAPTER V

Interpretative Regulations: Their Place in Administrative Legislation 137

CHAPTER VI

Administrative Legislation: Safeguards 170

CHAPTER VII

Political Safeguards: Group Opinion in the Framing of Administrative Legislation 198

CHAPTER VIII

Political Safeguards; Group Opinion in the Framing of Administrative Legislation, Continued 239

INDEX 271

CHAPTER I

Introduction

I

In the summer of 1914, a joint committee of Congress was considering an important piece of federal legislation. Its report to both houses contained this illuminating sentence:

> Recognizing the dangers of our present tendency towards a government by rule and regulation instead of a government by law, our committee successfully endeavored to construct a bill without an authorization of departmental power to create rules and regulations which too frequently result in vetoeing of congressional action or the emasculation of the purposes intended by Congress.[1]

Three years later Lord Wrenbury of Great Britain, in the course of giving a legal opinion, made this observation:

> There is room for difference of opinion whether what I may call legislation by devolution is expedient; whether a statute ought not to be self-contained; whether it is desirable that a statute should provide that regulations made by a defined authority or in a defined matter shall themselves have the effect of a statute.[2]

Although the latter statement was expressed under a different polity, it brings up the same general problem that

[1] *Report of the Joint Committee on Postage on Second Class Mail Matter and Compensation for Transportation of Mail*, 63rd Cong., 2nd Sess., August 31, 1914.

[2] Rex *v.* Halliday, A. C. (1917), 260, 207.

was vexing the congressional committee, viz., the ever-increasing delegation of legislative functions to administrative authorities. It may be that on occasion this problem can easily be solved by simple and direct action of the legislature; yet taken generally, it is still one of the questions that both theoretical and practical students have been puzzling over in the central and state governments of the United States for almost half a century. Indeed, if this subordinate legislative function be combined with the semi-judicial power that is now being thrust upon the Executive by the legislature, one might think that all nations of Anglo-Saxon origin and inheritance are well on their way toward the continental system with its emphasis upon the activities of the executive department. Even if this were true, one would and should find each of these states developing the additional duties of the administrative agency in a manner all its own, blunderingly to be sure, but nevertheless steadily. Some say that the tendency is good, some insist that it is bad, but experience seems to show that neither those who approve nor those who disapprove can for any length of time resist its pressure.

In the early history of this country and even up to the Civil War period, the public was not thoroughly impressed with the idea that there should be much legislative activity on the part of government. Perhaps few persons realized that there was an overshadowing national Constitution or that there was a national legislature with a definitely enumerated set of indefinitely broad powers. Occasional crises brought out these facts, to be sure; but, for the most part, people went on their own way. Besides, the government, local and national, was supposed to function in accordance with the *laissez-faire* ideal of as little government as possible. Such an ideal would naturally keep the volume of legislation at a minimum with little need for additional law-making authorities, at least in domestic legislation. There was, in addition, an inheritance from England that had a marked influence upon American statesmen: whatever legislative power was to be exercised, should be exercised by the legislature. Consequently statutes had to be concrete and detailed, or loaded with provisos, and necessary generalities had to be interpreted by the Judiciary.[1] This left the Executive, in theory, with few or no legislative functions, much to the satisfaction of the citizens of the United States.[2] This country lived up to its English inheritance until the nineteenth century was well advanced. The departures therefrom in times of need were the exception rather than the rule.

The smugness with which the minimum-government theory fitted into early American economic and political de-

[1] Railroad Co. *v.* Smith, 9 Wall. 95, 99 (1869), held that the regulation of the Secretary of the Interior was not necessary to complete the law as to what swamp land was, since a jury could determine what such land was as well as he.

[2] See Hart, *The Ordinance Making Powers of the President*, p. 265 *et seq.* He quotes Gneist, *History of the English Constitution*, vol. ii, p. 22 *et seq.* and *Story on the Constitution*, secs. 1413, 1417. L. Oppenheim, *The Future of International Law*, pp. 26-36, says that different groups of people employ very different methods in drafting their laws; that if an Englishman, a Frenchman, and a German were given individually the task of drawing up a law with the same purpose to be accomplished, very different drafts would emerge. He continues as follows:

> The English draft would deal in the most concrete manner possible, with the situations to which it meant to apply; it would adduce as many particular cases as possible, and so would run the risk of forgetting some series of cases altogether.
>
> The German draft would be as abstract as possible and would entirely disregard individual cases . . . and would expose itself to the danger that in practice cases would be brought within the enactment which were outside the intention of the legislature.
>
> The French draft would attach more weight to the principles than to individual points, enunciating principles in a legislative manner and leaving it to practice to construct out of the principles the rule for the particular case.

velopment begot a complacency that extended far into the period following the Civil War. But eventually new demands began to be made upon government. State and local units set about increasing the volume of legislative output. The inevitable "slop-overs" from state jurisdictions bestirred the citizenry to utilize the legislative powers of Congress. To this demand Congress responded with the result that its capacity and power were sorely tried.

Despite the facts, only a few people, prior to the present century, recognized that conditions generally were calling for a change in the part that government had to play in the life of the nation. Native and foreign students of American political development began to inquire into the causes that were bringing about this change. All comments, it seems, indicated that much government was being substituted for little government because of the very complexity of modern society; that the machinery of such society compelled an increase in the scope of publicly-controlled matters, however delicate, intricate, or technical they might be; that what was once thought sacredly private had, through the converting power of modern forces, become public or semi-public; that the people had somehow come to realize that in most problems it was not the few but the many who were interested and that their interests had to be considered in settling a particular dispute or in solving a particular problem.[1] Professor Dicey of Great Britain, in discussing the growth of administrative law in America, said:[2]

The most striking thing in the growth of political organiza-

[1] See Woodrow Wilson, "Study of Administration," 2 *Pol. Sci. Quar.* 198 (1887); Elihu Root, "Public Service by the Bar," 2 *Amer. Bar Assn. Jl.* 747-750 (1916); A. A. Berle, Jr., "Expansion of American Administrative Law," 30 *Har. Law Rev.* 430-436 (1917); John B. Cheadle, "Delegation of Legislative Functions," 27 *Yale Law Jl.* 892 (1918).

[2] 31 *Har. Law Rev.* 644-646.

tion of the last half century is the rapidity with which, by sheer pressure of events, the state has been driven to assume a positive character. We talk less and less in the restrained terms of the nineteenth century individualism. The absence of governmental interference has ceased to seem the ultimate ideal. There is everywhere almost an anxiety for the further extension of governmental functions.

As it came to be known that the increase in governmental control was due chiefly to social and economic forces that were inevitably giving emphasis to group rather than to individual control, that this country was well on its way toward a practice, the philosophy of which was collectivistic rather than individualistic, attention was turned to the consideration of the agencies that were to participate in the determination and regulation of this control. It was but natural that the statesmen of this country should adhere to the Anglo-Saxon inheritance, i. e., to have the legislature undertake the entire task, supplemented by the Judiciary. This tendency, early planted in the habits of the people as a result, perhaps, of the practical fear of a strong executive, resulted in a fairly close application of the doctrine of the separation of powers in the national Constitution.

Congress could well assume the light burdens of legislation during the first sixty or seventy years of national life although even during this period there were exceptions.[1] With the extension of democracy and changing economic conditions, numerous subjects of social and industrial regulation, involving a great mass of legislation, fell under governmental control. The resulting strain of the added burdens constituted an exacting test of the honesty and capacity of legislators as a group. Law-making bodies of state and city fell into almost utter disrepute; their powers were legally limited; and in many cases the electorate set it-

[1] See chap. iii.

self up as the actual lawmaker or as the direct checking agency. In the meantime as a result of its failure to accomplish the will of the voters, Congress was struggling under a stigma. Under the leadership of strong mayors, governors and presidents, the floundering process of "muddling through" by means of decadent legislative methods gave way to the modern process of definite executive leadership in both legislation and administration.[1] In other words, there was a beginning of the redistribution of powers, with the executive branch in the ascendancy and well supported by public opinion.

The national legislature, in practice, has succumbed to this idea, whether because it felt that executive activity in law-making would lighten the pressure; because it realized its inadequacy for the task; because it wished to shift political responsibility; or because it realized that this was the only way to increase the productive law-making units for grinding out a legislative grist commensurate with the demands of the nation without formally changing the fundamental law. The earnestness with which Congress has set about delegating legislative power can be seen by reviewing the functions of the President, of the ten great departments, and of the ever-growing list of independent executive establishments such as the Interstate Commerce Commission, the Federal Reserve Board, the Shipping Board, the Federal Power Commission and the Veteran's Bureau.[2] Indeed government by law and rule has become, in large part, government by the wish and discretion of administrative officers. Whether Mr. Common Citizen is making commercial catsup in Oregon, or selling oleomargarine in Illinois, or shipping

[1] Hart, *op. cit.*, pp. 268-275.

[2] *Cf.* John A. Fairlie, "Administrative Legislation," 18 *Mich. Law Rev.* 181; and Roscoe Pound, "The Growth of Administrative Justice," 2 *Wis. Law Rev.* 321.

cotton from Texas or cattle from Oklahoma, or importing seed from Russia, or exporting munitions of war to Mexico, or sending shrubbery from New England, or fishing in the navigable waters of the United States, or paying federal income taxes, or buying interstate transportation, or prescribing habit-forming drugs, or securing sacramental wine —whatever he is doing under national law he is likely to be acting in accordance with, or contrary to, some rule, order or proclamation of the appropriate administrative officer of the United States.[1]

II

An influential portion of the American public is beginning to look the problem of administration squarely in the face. It has already begun to realize the truth of what Woodrow Wilson said nearly forty years ago, "It is getting harder to run a constitution than to frame one."[2] Hence students of Anglo-Saxon institutions have been considering the practice of delegated legislation with a view to evaluating it as a means of helping to run constitutions. Professor Ernst Freund endeavored to set forth the advantages and disadvantages resulting from the new administrative activities of a legislative character.[3] Cecil T. Carr presented the British viewpoint in 1921,[4] and James Hart has summarized the viewpoints of these and others in his excellent publication of 1925.[5] The advantages, in brief, are as follows:

[1] *Cf.* Judge Rosenberry's statement in his "Development of the Federal Idea," *No. Amer. Rev.*, Aug. 1923, p. 145.

[2] Woodrow Wilson, "The Study of Administration," 2 *Pol. Sci. Quar.* 198 (1887).

[3] Ernst Freund, "The Substitution of Rule for Discretion in Public Law," *Amer. Pol. Sci. Rev.*, November, 1915, and *Standards of American Legislation.*

[4] *Delegated Legislation*, especially chapter iii.

[5] Hart, *op. cit.*, especially chapter x. *Cf.* the following classification of

1. Neither Congress nor any of its working groups can have the intimate knowledge of social and industrial problems that inures to the administrative agency which, through some or all of its parts, learns the best means of enforcing a legislative policy by actually enforcing it. Legislative debates, committee hearings and junkets are no substitute for experience in knowing what " will work ".

2. Congress, like all other legislatures, is not organized for speed, nor is it at work eight hours a day for forty-five weeks of the year. Consequently, in inaugurating a scheme of regulation to carry out a new policy or in effecting an old policy under rapidly moving conditions, the administrator has the advantage in being able easily to correct his mistakes.

3. The law-making body in attempting to formulate legislative administration is, in almost all cases at least, leaving the Executive the task of fitting a square peg into a round hole. Where administrative legislation is permitted, there is opportunity for the Executive to use his own discretion as to how he shall peg the hole.

4. Administrative legislation, in the long run, has greater permanence, continuity and scientific value than legislative administration issuing from fickle popular bodies. The administrator is inclined to work out principles from numerous

the occasions for the delegation of legislation as enumerated by Sir Josiah Stamp, 2 *British Journal of Public Administration*, 22-25:

(a) Local variety and detail can best be handled by administrative officers under general rules of law.

(b) Unknown future conditions, subsequent to legislation, can be best applied to constantly moving sets of facts.

(c) Complex and technical affairs can only be handled by administrative experts.

(d) Urgency may require immediate action and only the administrative agency can respond.

(e) Political feeling may block detailed legislation, but the general principles may be got through and the details may later be applied by officials.

experiments in enforcement of policy and, of course, is little inclined to bend such principles to the whim of popular opinion.

5. If the legislature is organized and manned to do anything at all, it is to formulate general principles or policies. To do this well is a great undertaking. Details of such policies should be left either to the Executive or to juries. Since juries are in no way scientific, there is reason to believe that supplementary rule-making by administrative agencies is better.

The same authorities seem to agree, for the most part, that administrative legislation has its seamy side. The disadvantages are here set down:

1. Administrative action is less amenable to public opinion than action by a deliberative assembly. It seems not to matter whether the discretion of an officer has been exercised in the best or most scientific way so long as public opinion has not been satisfied; for in the last analysis the ideas of the public must control.[1]

2. Legislators have a keener sense than executive officers of what is politically expedient. It would do little good to have sound administrative rules that are far in advance of general political standards. Administrators are likely to kill a good legislative policy by disregarding political expediency.

3. The fact that legislators are still regarded as representatives *par excellence* of the will of the people and further the fact that executive officials, popularly elected or not, still retain traces of odium formerly attached to the rule of the one or the few, give to the measures of popular assemblies a higher moral authority than to rules and regulations of administrators.

[1] Chapters vii and viii indicate that much more public opinion, which, after all, is the opinion of groups interested and well organized, is brought to bear on administrative legislation than one might think.

4. Delegated legislation has dangers that are more or less inherent. In the days of Jackson and Grant the spoils system worked havoc in certain types of administrative action. The discretionary power granted to the Secretary of the Navy and to the Secretary of the Interior under a recent Administration indicates that it is unsafe to trust too much power to executive departments. Even the civil service may transform live discretion into tradition or red tape.

III

Although the following study of delegated legislation tends to give point to most of the above statements, it tends, above all, to emphasize the growing recognition of the worth of the expert in government. The over-burdened national legislature, made up of men not superhumanly capacitated, was made to realize that the electorate, or groups thereof, was earnest in its desire to have certain results flow from legislation. This popular body, without method and without technique in which it was adept, came to see that it could not accomplish alone the aims it was continuously visualizing. In some way or other Congress found that there were men within and without the administrative force who had, or could develop, the expertness necessary for reaching the goal it so much desired. On the heels of this discovery has come a conscious effort to delegate to the "expertise" a large portion of the burden which congressmen had been unable to carry because of impolicy or impracticability. It seems that the constitutional power of Congress to legislate effectively on many involved subjects will be no longer, of necessity, "as important and useless as a dead hand upon a ship's rudder in a storm"; the quick hand of the "expertise" will put new life into the exercise of the great powers vested in Congress by the Constitution.[1]

[1] *Cf.* John M. Gaus, "The New Problem of Administration," 8 *Minn. Law Rev.* 217-231; and Harold J. Laski, "The Growth of Administrative Discretion," 1 *British Journal of Public Administration* 92-98.

IV

The main purpose of this study is to present in a limited way the practice of Congress in shifting a large part of its functions to the Executive. The material studied is taken largely from periods in which the United States is at least nominally at peace with the world, though practices of the usual type, running on through actual warfare but little touched thereby, are brought in now and then. Even though periods of stress have their influence, normal practice in ordinary times better sets the norm of political actions. The first quarter-century of this nation's existence, too, indicates what the practice might well be in times of actual warfare. As it is impossible to avoid the legal aspects of this delegation occasional reference to the philosophy that lies behind it may be pardoned. No attempt is made, however, to analyze the practices with a view to fitting them into the Anglo-Saxon system of jurisprudence. This viewpoint has begun to appeal to those who have concluded that such practices must be unified and properly related. At least one political scientist who has become thoroughly convinced of the ripeness of the time for attacking such a problem has made a worthy effort towards its solution.[1]

The following brief summary indicates the lines along which the subject of federal administrative legislation is to be developed in this study: The formal law of the United States is divided into five parts. The fifth part, administrative legislation, is divided into two classes—complementary and contingent—based upon the particular manner of investment of delegation, with reasons given for designating the administrative functions discussed as legislative in character. The historical development of the law-making function of the executive branch of the government is then taken up and

[1] James Hart, *op. cit.*; see especially his viewpoint, pp. 25-26.

a number of court decisions are analyzed in connection with certain delegations. A chapter summarizing the more important constitutional aspects of such legislation follows. A brief discussion of so-called interpretative regulations shows the important bearing such regulations have upon the general subject under consideration. The remaining chapters deal with the various safeguards, judicial and political, that have been thrown around the Executive in its exercise of delegated legislative power.

CHAPTER II

Administrative Legislation: Distinctions and Classification

I

In an attempt to distinguish the law that results from delegations by Congress to the Executive from the remainder of the law of the national government,[1] it has been found convenient to divide the whole into the following formal parts: the Constitution, the statutes, the treaties, the independent law-making power of the President, and that part which includes rules and regulations, executive orders and proclamations. The Constitution, to be sure, is the legal basis for all the other parts. To it are referable all legislative powers of the national government. That which distinguishes the American system from that, e. g., of Great Britain lies in this, viz., that the authority for legislation, whatever form it may take, must be within the legal bounds of this Constitution. It purports to outline not only the content of legislative power but also the agencies that are to exercise this power. In Article Five is found a procedure by which its terms may be formally altered and in Article Three is located the agency which, by the force of logic and circumstance, may procure similar results without formal amendment.[2]

Next in weight and importance comes the statutory law.

[1] That is, formal law.

[2] C. G. Haines, *The American Doctrine of Judicial Supremacy*; Beard, *The National Government of the United States*, ch. v.

It consists of the formal legislation of the Senate and the House of Representatives in Congress assembled. Such legislation must have the approval of the President or an extraordinary majority of both houses.[1] By far the most valuable law subordinate to the Constitution is the statute. As it is the child of the fundamental law, so it is the parent of delegated legislation.[2] The Constitution points the path which the national legislature may take; the statute guides the makers of subordinate legislation.

Treaties,[3] although made by the President by and with the advice of the Senate, go to make up a not inconsiderable portion of the law. Although their source is the Constitution, and although apparently they have the power to some extent to reach into state jurisdiction where ordinary statutes cannot go,[4] yet they must yield to any law of Congress passed subsequently to and in conflict therewith.[5]

The independent law-making power of the President is that part of the national law which inures to the Chief Executive from the expressed or clearly-implied terms of the Constitution itself. This legislation although limited in

[1] However, the President's failure to return a bill within a specified time during a session of Congress, results in the bill's becoming law. Hind's *Precedents*, vol. iv, pars. 3482-3484 says: "Concurrent resolutions are by custom devoted to things not strictly law and do not require the signature of the President."

[2] Migratory Bird Treaty, 39 Stat. 1702 (1916). Articles II, par. 1, V, VI and X specifically sanction both laws and regulations for carrying out the terms of the treaty. If a self-executing treaty were to provide for regulations to be made by the Executive, such regulations might be as binding as those resulting from an enforcing act.

[3] The Constitution, Art. VI, par. 2; Willoughby, *Constitutional Law of the United States*, vol. i, secs. 190, 210.

[4] Missouri *v.* Holland, 252 U. S. 416 (1920).

[5] See 1 Stat. 578; The Cherokee Tobacco, 11 Wall. 621 (1870); see also Ward *v.* Race Horse, 163 U. S. 504, 516 (1896).

scope is significant. It falls to the President as a result of his acting as commander-in-chief of the Army and Navy;[1] of his pardoning power, i. e., his granting of amnesties;[2] of his recognition of foreign states;[3] and of his obligation faithfully to execute the laws of the United States.[4]

As head of the armed forces of the United States the Chief Executive can issue minor regulations governing such forces;[5] he can order the Army and Navy anywhere he wishes, provided funds are available;[6] he can establish military government in conquered territory and even set up a civil government, which is legal until Congress has made its own provisions therefor.[7] Under his pardoning power the President may issue a general pardon or an amnesty, as evidenced in Washington's amnesty proclamation in connection with the Pennsylvania Whiskey Rebellion,[8] or in Johnson's Civil War amnesty proclamation.[9] To the President

[1] The Constitution, Art. II, sec. 2, par. 1.

[2] *Ibid.*

[3] *Ibid.*, Art. II, sec. 2, par. 2 and sec. 3.

[4] *Ibid.*, Art. II, sec. 3. Mr. Hart, *op. cit.*, classifies this power, together with delegated legislation and the treaty-making power, as the ordinance-making power. The writer admits that the first two powers might well be subdivisions of the ordinance power, but for the purposes of his thesis he has chosen the separate classification.

[5] This power was exercised in the Code for the United States Revenue Cutter Service (1897), an agency similar to the Navy in organization and discipline. See G. Norman Lieber, *Remarks on the Army Regulations and the Executive Regulations in General*, p. 6 *et seq.* The strongest statement made by this writer is as follows: "These establish a federal system, including a code of penalties and a system of procedure. No other regulations have ever undertaken to go to this extreme and it may well be doubted whether the executive power may be carried so far."

[6] Taft, *Our Chief Magistrate and His Powers*, p. 94, cited in Hart, *op. cit.*, p. 243, note 118.

[7] Willoughby, *Constitutional Law of the United States.*

[8] Richardson, *Messages and Papers of the Presidents*, vol. i, p. 181.

[9] *Ibid.*, vol. ix, p. 3906.

alone belongs the function of recognition of foreign states, a function which results from his power to receive foreign representatives, to appoint diplomatic representatives and to initiate treaties. This, since legal rights and duties follow such recognition, is no mean legislative power.[1] Under his obligation to see that the laws are faithfully executed, the President has exercised a large, independent law-making power, which is potentially increased by statutes and treaties. For example, Mr. Taft cites a clause of the Constitution as the basis for his government of Cuba under the Platt Amendment contained in the treaty with Cuba.[2] Perhaps the famous Executive Order of President Grant, forbidding national civil officers, with certain exceptions, from holding state, territorial or local offices, falls under this "faithful execution" clause.[3] President Coolidge's amendment to this order, promulgated May 22, 1926, permitted the police forces of the various subdivisions of the United States to act as national prohibition officers. Although this order was recalled in the face of adverse public opinion, it indicates what the President may legally do in cases where there is a real demand for additional officers to enforce the internal laws of the United States.[4]

[1] Willoughby, *op. cit.*, vol. ii, secs. 194, 580; Hart, *op. cit.*, pp. 215-216.

[2] Taft, *op. cit.*, p. 88.

[3] Richardson, *Messages and Papers of the Presidents*, vol. ix, pp. 4172-4173. *Cf.* Submarine Cable Controversy, reviewed in the *Report of the House Com. on Interstate and Foreign Commerce*, 67th Cong., 1st Sess. (1921), on S. 535.

[4] *New York Times*, May 22, 1926, p. 2, gives this order as follows: "The executive order of January 17, 1873, is hereby amended by the addition of the following paragraph:

In order that they may more efficiently function in the enforcement of the National Prohibition Act, any state, county or municipal officer may be appointed, at a nominal rate of compensation, as prohibition officer of the Treasury Department to enforce the provisions of the National Prohibition Act, and acts supplemental thereto, in states and territories,

It is interesting to note that with few exceptions, such as " recognition ordinances ", practically all writers agree that Congress has either direct or indirect control over the independent law-making power of the President and can cover the field to the exclusion of the Executive. If Congress acts before or after the President, either in harmony with or against him, the will of that body is taken as the basis for action rather than that of the Chief Executive.[1]

The lowliest, yet by no means the least effectual, part of national legislation consists of rules and regulations, executive orders and proclamations, that have the force of law.[2] These terms are employed to indicate that part of federal legislation which results from statutory power explicitly or implicitly given to administrative officers for the purpose of carrying out the details of a statute or of putting into effect

except in those states having constitutional or statutory provision against state officers holding office under the Federal Government."

This order was considered valid by the Senate Committee on the Judiciary, June 7, 1926. *New York Times*, June 8, 1926, p. 2.

[1] Goodnow, *Administrative Law of the United States*, ch. iii; Wyman, *Administrative Law*, sec. 97; Lieber, *Remarks on the Army Regulations and Executive Regulations in General*; *Willoughby on the Constitution*, vol. ii, sec. 779; H. C. Black, *Relation of Executive Power to Legislation*, p. 36; George Melling, *Laws Relating to the Navy*, Annotated, pp. 81-89; Howard White, *Executive Influence in Determining Military Policy in the United States*; C. A. Berdahl, *War Powers of the Executive in the United States*; James Hart, *The Ordinance Making Powers of the President*.

[2] Decisions and instructions are many times nothing more than regulations or orders. Without the necessity of going into this matter further at present, it might be said that it is possible for any of the terms used not to have reference to subordinate legislation with the force of law; hence the qualification "having the force of law" is at times necessary. The usual Thanksgiving Proclamation, the proclaiming of Boy Scout Week (41 Stat. 1747) and of Forest Protection and Arbor Day Observance (March 5, 1923) are examples of proclamations without the force of law in so far as they serve to govern individual citizens. Hart, *op. cit.*, uses the term "ordinance" for all executive functions of a legislative character. His arguments for such use are convincing.

admittedly conditional statutes. Just as a large part of congressional legislation results directly from the "necessary and proper" clause of the Constitution, so this statutory delegated legislation is a direct result of the secondary "necessary and proper" clauses of the statutes under which it issues.

II

Two general classes of delegated legislation based upon the particular manner of investment appear from a study of the numerous delegations of legislative functions and of the judicial pronouncements thereon. The one may be called supplementary or detailed legislation, the other, contingent legislation. The former class was recognized in an opinion of a lower federal court where it was remarked that a legislative body may delegate power "to make and enforce regulations for the execution of a statute according to its terms".[1] This class involves discretion on the part of the Executive in framing legislation for perfecting or elaborating a policy stated in general terms. It may be defined as that class of delegated legislation which names, or adds to, the administrative law by which the more or less definitely stated purpose or policy of Congress is to be carried out.[2] Thus, one of the department heads is given the power "to

[1] St. Louis National Bridge Terminal Ry. Co. *v.* U. S., 188 Fed. 191, 195 (1911); also U. S. *v.* Moody, 164 Fed. 269 (1908).

[2] Administrative law may involve, in its broadest terms, not only mere procedural methods, such as the establishment of a method by which certain privileges or rights may be secured, but it may include as well some substantive elements, if they are necessary to putting the law into execution. This definition is made up from the form of investments of power and from remarks of the Court, such as those found in Wayman *v.* Southard, 10 Wheat. 1, 311, 315 (1825); U. S. *v.* Whiskey, 95 U. S. 571, 576 (1877); Buttfield *v.* Stranahan, 192 U. S. 470 (1904); U. S. *v.* Grimaud, 220 U. S. 506 (1911); Utah, etc., Co. *v.* U. S., 243 U. S. 389 (1917); National Lead Co. *v.* U. S., 252 U. S. 140 (1920).

make such rules and regulations . . . as will insure the objects of said [forest] reservations, viz., to regulate their occupancy and use and to preserve the forests thereon from destruction ".[1]

It has been indicated that this class of delegated legislation may manifest itself under different names. The difficulty constantly confronting the student in recognizing the supplementary legislative products of the executive agencies, by mere reference to the specific designations under which they appear, has been well indicated by Professor Fairlie in the following words:[2] " There is no approach to uniformity in nomenclature. Rules, Regulations, Instructions, General Orders, Circulars, Bulletins, Notices, Memoranda, and other terms are given to different series of publications by different government offices, with no clear distinction as to the meaning of these terms."

Proclamations and executive orders might also be added to this list.[3] The phrase " rules and regulations ", redundant and made up of substantives reciprocally interpretative, seems, however, to be the most common expression of investment although " regulations " takes precedence over " rules " when the twins are separated. In converting all the other terms into rules or regulations as the designation for executive acts known as supplementary legislation, it is at once necessary to limit their scope. The dictionaries insist that generality is one of the essential characteristics of a rule or of a regulation which purports to be a written or unwritten authoritative direction. "*Words and Phrases*"[4] makes

[1] 34 Stat. 35 (1897); see also chap. iii for additional examples.

[2] "Administrative Legislation," 18 *Mich. Law Rev.* 181, 199 (1920).

[3] E. g., *Migratory Bird Regulations*, promulgated by the President, July 31, 1918, May 21, 1919. See *Game Laws of* 1921, p. 67.

[4] Vol. vii. See also Wong Wai *v.* Williamson, 103 Fed. 384; Landrum *v.* U. S., 16 Ct. Cls. 74.

the validity of either one depend upon its being general in scope and undiscriminating in application. The Supreme Court has remarked that regulations must be uniform and applicable to all of a class.[1] The requirements of generality and explicit or clearly implied authority from Congress must be met by rules and regulations that are to be dignified with the name of " supplementary legislation ".

The requirement of generality eliminates many so-called rules and regulations from further consideration. Thus, most of the specific orders of administrative authorities, i. e., those applicable to particular cases, cannot be included. Their function is to execute or enforce a regulation previously made or to make a permitted exception to a general rule.[2] However, an apparently specific order may meet the required conditions when, in effect, it lays down a rule of future action for a specific individual and at the same time affects a class vitally related to that individual, as, e. g., a rate order of the Interstate Commerce Commission issued to the Pennsylvania Railroad.[3]

The greatest difficulty, however, appears in trying to distinguish between what are commonly called regulations which may meet the test of generality but can not meet that of authority, and those which can meet both tests. For purposes of clarity, the former are designated as interpreta-

[1] U. S. *v.* Ripley, 7 Pet. 18 (1833).

[2] Melling, *Laws Relating to the Navy*, p. 196; Harvey *v.* U. S., 3 Ct. Cls. 38, 42 (1867). Congress has recognized this distinction in law, e. g., 28 Stat. 209, sec. 12 (1894): "The Secretary of the Treasury shall prescribe suitable rules and regulations, and may make orders in particular cases, relaxing the requirement of mailing, or otherwise sending the accounts as aforesaid."

[3] Prentis *v.* Atlantic, etc., Co., 211 U. S. 210 (1908); So. Pac. Co. *v.* Bartina, 170 Fed. 725, 776 (1909); Erie R. R. Co. *v.* Commission, 254, U. S. 394, 413 (1920). See also Hart, *op. cit.*, p. 35, for the necessary exceptions from uniformity.

tive, the latter as administrative.[1] Administrative rules, the very essence of complementary or detailed legislation, are those that appreciably add to the procedural or enforcing provisions of substantive law and are enforceable; they involve the discretion of a lawmaker on the part of the Executive; and their source of authority is found in a general statutory delegation of rule-making power,[2] in a delegation of a general character for a particular law,[3] or in a specific delegation for a particular provision of a law.[4] Interpretative regulations supposedly express the true meaning of a statute or division thereof; they are not in themselves law.[5] The administrative official issuing them has the apparently simple task of acting as popular interpreter of the foreign language of the legislature. The relation of such regula-

[1] These two classes are taken from a discussion of Mr. Fred T. Field, found in *Columbia Income Tax Lectures*, pp. 96-98 (1921); also, Malley *v.* Baker Co., 281 Fed. 41, 46 (1922). Mr. Field names as a third class of regulations those having to do with the fixing of standards and apparently partaking of the nature of both of the main classes. For purposes of this discussion, this midway class is assimilated to that made up of administrative rules. See Oertel *v.* Gregory, 270 Fed. 789, 792 (1921); and Monroe Co. *v.* Riordan, 280 Fed. 624, 634 (1924).

[2] E. g., 1 Stat. 28 (1789): "The head of each Department is authorized to prescribe rules and regulations, not inconsistent with law, for the government of his Department, the conduct of its officers and clerks, the distribution and performance of its business, and the custody, use, and preservation of the records, papers, and property appertaining to it." See also Oertel *v.* Gregory, 270 Fed. 789, 792 (1921).

[3] E. g., U. S. Rev. Stat., Sec. 321, income tax; U. S. Rev. Stat., Sec. 4462, steamboat inspection; Revenue Act, June, 1924, Sec. 1001; 41 Stat. 1062, Sec. 4, (h) (1920), water power; 39 Stat. 482, Sec. 28 (1916), Warhouse Act; 41 Stat. 437, Sec. 32 (1920), public land mining.

[4] E. g., Income Tax, 1918, Sec, 204; U. S. Rev. Stat., Sec. 4480, steamboat inspection; 34 Stat. 229, Sec. 3, quarantine; 35 Stat. 1137, Sec. 241, interstate shipment of game (1909); 141 Stat. 1062, Sec. 4 (f)) (1920), water power.

[5] Logan *v.* Davis, 233 U. S. 613 (1914); Smith *v.* U. S., 170 U. S. 372, 380 (1898).

tions to administrative legislation will be considered in a later chapter.[1]

The contingent class of delegated legislation involves discretion on the part of administrative officials in putting on the active list quiescent or dormant statutes which express congressional policy. The judiciary has handed down a variety of definitions of this class. It is "putting legislation into force conditionally";[2] it is partially made up of "statutes that are in the alternative, depending on the discretion of some person or persons to whom is confided the duty of determining whether the proper occasion exists for putting them into effect";[3] it is the making of a "law to delegate a power to determine some fact or state of things upon which the law makes, or intends to make, its own action depend";[4] it is the "delegation of power to determine some fact or state of things upon which the enforcement of the act depends".[5] Its nature is thus explained outside of case books: ". . . a law may be enacted to go into effect at some future time, upon the happening of some contingency or upon the determination by some officer of the existence of a fact

[1] See chap. v. A letter from the Executive Secretary of the Federal Power Commission to the writer, dated February 1, 1926, gives his criticism of the above classifications: "With regard to classification of regulations as supplementary (administrative) or explanatory, I doubt whether this classification is particularly helpful. It seems to me a better classification would be—

(1) Those made pursuant to and in aid of a statute to carry out its purposes (administrative); and

(2) Those purely administrative for regulating the orderly conduct of public business (interpretative).

[2] Field *v.* Clark, 143 U. S. 649, 691 (1892), quoting from *Brig Aurora*, 7 Cranch 382 (1813).

[3] *Ibid.*, quoting from Moers *v.* Reading, 21 Penn. 202.

[4] *Ibid.*, quoting from Locke's *Appeal*, 72 Penn. 202.

[5] Union Bridge Co. *v.* U. S., 204 U. S. 364, 387 (1904); see also U. S. *v.* Penn. Co., 235 Fed. 961, 964 (1916).

or state of things, but the law must otherwise be complete as it leaves the hands of the legislators." [1] Under the first definition there is sufficient elasticity to satisfy the most inveterate bureaucrat; under the last there is rigidity enough to answer the purposes of the most ardent believer in the theory of separation of powers.

Contingent delegation, then, might be said to be that form of legislation which requires more or less discretion on the part of the Executive in determining stated conditions, simple or complex, upon which alternative laws, a law, or alternative parts of a law shall become operative or inoperative. For example, when the President has, in his judgment, arranged for "reciprocal and equivalent concessions" with a foreign country in favor of certain named American articles of commerce, an alternative duty is to be put into force upon articles coming into the United States from that country.[2] It might be added that when the laws or parts of laws, which are to be made effective in this manner, are incomplete, the Executive is given the power to complete the details. For illustration, a statute provides that when the President shall be satisfied that Canada has placed burdens of a reciprocally unjust and unreasonable character upon American commerce passing through certain waters under her control, he shall have power to deny free passage to Canadian commerce through waters controlled by the United States and to name the rates to be charged therefor within a maximum limit.[3] This combination of

[1] 6 *American and English Encyclopedia* 1023-1031.

[2] 30 Stat. 151, Sec. 3 (1890); 42 Stat. 1625, Sec. 6 (1922): "...whenever the President shall be of the opinion that the national emergency hereby declared has passed he shall by proclamation declare the same, and thereupon, except as to prosecutions for offences, this Act shall no longer be in force or effect, and in no event shall it continue in force and effect for longer than twelve months from the passage thereof." See also chap. iii for additional examples.

[3] 27 Stat. 267 (1892); see also chap. iii for additional examples.

the two classes of legislation gives the Executive at times a high degree of power.

The nomenclature applied to executive actions, putting into effect contingent legislation, varies almost as much as does that used in supplementary legislation. Proclamations, executive orders, treasury decisions, general orders, service orders, and others are found. In fact, almost all of the terms are identical. Whenever the President exercises such power his acts are designated as proclamations or executive orders. Thus, when he put into force section 3 of the Tariff Act of 1897, he made a proclamation to that effect.[1] In withdrawing public lands under the Act of 1910, he issued, for example, Executive Orders numbers 1640 and 1641.[2] When to the Secretary of the Treasury is delegated the power to raise the tariff upon more or less indefinite contingencies, he gives notice in the form of Treasury decisions.[3] The Interstate Commerce Commission sets provisions of the Commerce Act in motion by means of orders or service orders.[4] All these actions include not only the decision of the Executive that the time has arrived for putting the law into effect, but also the proper regulations of a supplementary nature which are contingent thereon. In other words, they represent a combination of supplementary

[1] 30 Stat. 151 and Proclamations, 31 Stat. 1974 and 34 Stat. 3231. Other examples are 17 Stat. 13 and Proclamation, 17 Stat. 951; 36 Stat. 11 and Proclamations, 36 Stat. 2524 and 2600; 42 Stat. 858 and Proclamations as to Oxalic Acid, Dec. 29, 1924, and as to Wheat, March 7, 1924.

[2] 36 Stat. 841. Additional Executive Orders, Nos. 1650, 1654.

[3] E. g., 42 Stat. 11, Secs. 201, 202 and Treas. Decs. 39177, 39208; 42 Stat. 858, Sec. 303 and Treas. Decs. 39541, 39789, 39812, 40001.

[4] E. g., Order No. 6790 (1917), *31st Annual Report of the I. C. C.*, page 7; General Order increasing passenger fares, freight rates, and pullman surcharges found in *35th Annual Report of I. C. C.*, pp. 7-8 (1921); Service Orders, Nos. 1-7, *34th Annual Report of I. C. C.*, p. 14 (1920).

and contingent legislative power. If reference is made to the sources of delegations or to the wording of the proclamations, executive orders, Treasury decisions or orders, there is little difficulty in distinguishing the character of such executive actions.

III

The question may well be asked why such functions of the Executive are considered legislative in character. The reasons therefor will be found in the nature of the acts performed, in the attitude of the courts in approving or disapproving such acts, in the specific declarations by the Judiciary that such functions are legislative in character and, finally, in the attitude which Congress itself takes toward such executive activities.

Legislation involves the "discretionary determination of the legal rights and duties of private persons generally, or private persons of a reasonably defined class, and the provision of means of enforcing these rights and duties". Discretion implies the exercise of a choice involving a "subjective evaluation of the advisability of alternatives". There are included in full discretion several elements, among which are the following: the decision as to the expediency of regulating a matter under the jurisdiction of the legislature; the determination of what legal rights and duties are to be created; the designation of the group or class of persons to which the rights and duties are to be applied; the naming of the time when, or the circumstances under which, the rights and duties are to become operative; and the laying down of the penal or administrative sanctions which shall be imposed for the violation of the rights and duties. An action of the Executive involving any one of these elements of discretion is to that extent legislative in character, provided it applies to persons generally or to persons of a class or to a person who has general powers.[1]

Under the interpretation of the Supreme Court it would be unconstitutional for Congress to delegate discretion as to the expediency of regulating any or all subjects that come under its jurisdiction.[2] As to the other phases of discretion, it might be said, although it is admitted that example is lacking in some cases, that they could be delegated. Discretion as to rights and duties is not at all uncommon. In order to carry out the legislative policy concerning the conservation of the National Forests, an administrative department really defines the right and the duty of live-stock grazers by making them secure permits and pay a prescribed fee.[3] Wholesalers who wish to exercise the right of dealing in oleomargarine must conform to administrative rules which provide for methods of book-keeping and for periodic returns.[4] The rights and duties connected with the interstate shipping of cattle,[5] cotton,[6] grain [7] and naval stores [8] are determined in large part by quarantine regulations or standards instituted by the Department of Agriculture. The rights and duties of those who import teas [9] and plants [10] are subject

[1] Hart, *op. cit.*, p. 28.

[2] See chap. iv.

[3] 34 Stat. 35 (1897); *Forest Regulations* No. 45; U. S. *v.* Grimaud, 220 U. S. 506 (1911).

[4] U. S. *v.* Lamson, 173 U. S. 673 (1909); law and regulation quoted therein.

[5] 32 Stat. 791 (1903); B. A. I. 231; U. S. *v.* Penn. Co., 235 Fed. 961 (1916).

[6] 42 Stat. 1517 (1923); *Official Cotton Standards*, Aug. 1, 1923.

[7] 39 Stat. 482 (1916); *U. S. Wheat Standards*, March 31, 1917.

[8] 42 Stat. 1435 (1923); *Naval Stores Standards*, 1924.

[9] See law and regulations in Buttfield *v.* Stranahan, 192 U. S. 470 (1904).

[10] 37 Stat. 315 (1912) and amendments, 37 Stat. 854 (1913) and 39 Stat. 1165 (1917); *Plant Quarantine* No. 37.

to the rules and regulations of the same department. The right to recover an excess tax payment is conditioned upon the duty of conforming to the rules of the Secretary of the Treasury.[1] It will be noticed that the persons who are to exercise the rights and duties in each of the above cases are, in effect, designated by the officers who make the rules and regulations that set forth the conditions of such exercise.

A very common investment of discretion is found in laws which delegate to the Executive the power completely or incompletely to put stated legislative policies into effect. Of course, where the putting of the law into action is based upon the ascertainment of a simple fact, there is no appreciable discretion present except that involved in " seeing but not recognizing " such fact. But where the situation is involved and demands a subjective evaluation, discretion may be very broad. Although a series of such delegations are found in the following chapter, for purposes of illustration a select number will be given here. " Whenever, in his opinion, the public safety shall require it," the President is endowed with power to lay an embargo on the commerce with a foreign state.[2] Whenever the President shall be satisfied that the discriminating or countervailing duties " of a foreign nation have been abolished he may reduce or remove certain tariff duties ".[3] " Whenever the President shall be satisfied that [*inter alia*] American fishing vessels [are] unjustly vexed or harassed " in the waters of the British Dominions, it shall be his duty, " in his discretion ", to deny entrance to Dominion vessels for the purpose of trading.[4] " Whenever during the existence of war in which the United States is not en-

[1] See law and regulations in Rock Island, etc., Ry. Co. *v.* U. S., 254 U. S. 141 (1920).

[2] 1 Stat. 372 (1794).

[3] 3 Stat. 224 (1815).

[4] 24 Stat. 475 (1887).

gaged, the President shall be satisfied that there is reasonable ground to believe that any state or subdivision thereof is preventing or restricting the importation of United States' products contrary to the law of nations," he is authorized to prohibit or restrict importation of the products of such country " as in his opinion the public interest may require ".[1] Whenever the Interstate Commerce Commission, after hearing, " shall be of the opinion that any of the rates " of a common carrier are " unjust and unreasonable ", it shall prescribe what will be just and reasonable rates.[2] Whenever the President, upon investigation, finds that the duties fixed in the law do not equal the difference between the cost of production of imported articles and like or similar domestic articles, he is given power to equalize this cost of production by raising or lowering the statutory norm by 50 per cent.[3] If the Postmaster-General finds that the statutory classification and rate of postage of fourth-class mail are not providing proper service to the public or paying for the cost of the service rendered, he may, with the consent of the Interstate Commerce Commission, reform the rates and classification.[4]

There have been few, if any, delegations of power to name penalties for the violation of rights and duties. There is one, however, in the Interstate Commerce Act, as amended,[5]

[1] 39 Stat. 799 (1916).

[2] 34 Stat. 589, Sec. 15 (1906).

[3] 42 Stat. 858, Sec. 15 (1922).

[4] 37 Stat. 557 (1912); *Postal Laws and Regulations*, Secs. 455, 457.

[5] 24 Stat. 379 (1887), as amended by 41 Stat. 456 (1920); see also chap. iii. Apparently Tennessee has delegated the power to impose criminal penalties for the breaking of administrative regulations. See O'Hoover *v.* Montgomery, 120 Tenn. 448. If successful experiments are made in the states along this line, it is possible that the Judiciary will be more likely to allow it to be done by the national Executive.

That this provision does give the Commission power to name penalties which, on its face, is a delegation of this power. It reads as follows:

> The Commission may, after hearing, on a complaint or upon its own initiative without complaint establish reasonable rules, regulations, and practices with respect to car service by carriers by railroad subject to this Act, *including* the compensation to be paid for the use of any locomotive, car, or other vehicle not owned by the carrier using it, *and the penalties or other sanctions for nonobservance of such rules, regulations, or practices.*[1]

The Executive, however, has been given the power to enforce policies of Congress which are in effect sanctions more direct than specific penalties. Thus in 1794 the President was authorized " to give such instructions to the revenue officers of the United States, as shall appear best adapted for carrying " out the law establishing the embargo.[2] A statute of the same year left to the discretion of the President the matter of placing an embargo, as well as the power " to give all such orders to the officers of the United States, as may be necessary to carry the same into full effect ".[3] Such administrative sanctions are left to executive discretion. Under Section 316 of the Tariff Act of 1922[4] unfair

is the opinion of the Director of the Bureau of Service. In a letter to the writer, dated August 9, 1926, he makes the following statement:

> So far the Commission has not found it necessary to require rules with respect to car service to be filed with it as tariffs. Consequently it has not passed upon the question of penalties or other sanctions for non-observance of such rules, regulations or practices.
>
> While, as indicated, the Commission has not passed upon the precise question referred to in your letter [of June 21, 1926], it is my personal opinion that the penalties or other sanctions for non-observance of such rules, regulations, or practices referred to in paragraph 14, refer to such reasonable rules, regulations, and practices as may be established by the Commission after hearing.

[1] The italics are the author's.

[2] 1 Stat. 400.

[3] 1 Stat. 372.

[4] 42 Stat. 853.

methods of competition and unfair acts in the importation of articles into the United States, or their sale therein, which will tend to injure or destroy domestic industry are declared unlawful. Once such unfair methods are established, the President has the discretion of imposing an additional duty upon the articles involved of from 10 to 50 per cent of their value or of prohibiting their entry altogether. These are the only methods by which the policy of Congress is to be enforced; they serve as a penalty for an unlawful act. It is in this way that the President is given discretion in naming the sanction. Likewise in Section 317 of the same Tariff Act, the President, by means of an additional duty ranging from 1 to 50 per cent *ad valorem* or by means of exclusion, is given discretionary power to penalize discriminations against American trade on the part of foreign countries. The Senate Majority Report looked upon this provision as penal in its character.[1]

The provision for penalizing discriminations against American trade covers discriminations in that sphere. The first step authorized is the very modest one of additional duties to be measured by the extent of injury done to this trade. If the foreign country does not then accord to American commerce that equality of treatment which it is the policy of the United States to extend to theirs, the President may take more drastic measures, which, under especially irritating conditions, may take the form of exclusion.

Rules and regulations and proclamations that involve some phase of discretion on the part of the issuing officers would seem to justify the title "delegated legislation". There is further reason for this designation, however, in that the Judiciary looks upon such administrative activities somewhat as it does upon the primary action of Congress. If discretion is exercised in accordance with the authority

[1] *Senate Report* No. 595, part 1, 67th Cong., 2nd Sess. (1922), p. 4.

delegated, the Supreme Court has usually held that there is no power to go back of it; i. e., there is finality in executive discretion, just as there is in congressional discretion. In a recent case [1] the President was accused of abusing his discretion in controlling telephone lines. The court said in reply:

> But as the contention at best concerns not a want of power, but a mere excess or abuse of discretion in exerting a power given, it is clear that it involves considerations which are beyond the reach of the judicial power. This must be, since, as the court has often pointed out, the judicial may not invade the legislative or executive departments so as to correct alleged mistakes or wrongs arising from asserted abuse of discretion.

Although this decision grew out of President Wilson's extensive war powers, the same principle has been applied under less disturbing conditions. It was said in 1842 that certain canal regulations made by the Secretary of War could not be "questioned or defied" because they might be thought "unwise or mistaken".[2] In passing judgment upon the exercise of discretion of a state commission, the Court remarked that a law could not be declared invalid because, in its opinion, it did not accord with sound policy; and that the law-making power was the ultimate appeal body.[3] In upholding a delegation to the Secretary of War, the Supreme Court said that in view of the assumption by Congress of full control over the subject of navigable waters and in view of the large powers delegated to that officer, the regulations made by him could not be considered "other-

[1] Dakota Central Telephone *v.* S. D., 250 U. S. 163 (1919). *Cf.* Philadelphia Co. *v.* Stimson, 223 U. S. 605 (1912), in which the Supreme Court remarks that it cannot interfere with executive discretion but that it can inquire into the validity of rules established, whether they are within the law or whether the law is constitutional or not.

[2] U. S. *v.* Eliason, 16 Peters 291, 301.

[3] Red "C" Oil Co. *v.* N. C., 222 U. S. 380 (1912).

wise than an authoritative determination of what was reasonably necessary to be done to insure free and safe passage ".[1] In Buttfield *v.* Stranahan,[2] it was said:

Whether or not the Secretary of the Treasury failed to carry into effect the expressed purpose of Congress and established standards which operated to exclude teas which would have been entitled to admission had proper standards been adopted, is a question we are not called upon to consider. The sufficiency of the standards adopted by the Secretary of the Treasury was committed to his judgment, to be honestly exercised, and if that were important, there is no assertion here of bad faith or malice on the part of that officer in fixing the standards, or on the part of the defendant in the performance of the duty resting on him.

Were it not for a decision rendered in 1920,[3] which went exactly counter to the principle brought out above, one might say that the Judiciary, in respect to review of discretion, treats administrative regulations or proclamations on an equal footing with laws. It is this case of rate fixing by a municipal authority, however, that makes one hesitant in affirming that the Court will, in all matters—especially industrial matters—refuse to review administrative discretion. Mr. Ray A. Brown, in a recent criticism of this decision,[4]

[1] So. Pac. Co. *v.* Olympian Dredging Co., 43 Sup. Ct. 26 (1922).

[2] 192 U. S. 470 (1904). The same idea is implied in this statement taken from McChord *v.* L. and N. R. Co., 183 U. S. 483, 495: "The fixing of rates is essentially legislative in its character and the general rule is that legislative action cannot be interfered with by injunction."

[3] Ohio Valley Water Co. *v.* Ben Avon Borough, 253 U. S. 473. See J. B. Cheadle, "Judicial Review of Administrative Determination," *Southwestern Political and Social Science Quarterly*, June, 1922.

"Functions of the Courts and Commissions in Public Utility Rate Regulations," 38 *Har. Law Rev.* 141 *et seq.* Perhaps the courts have determined to watch more carefully the discretion delegated to officers in matters of right than in matters of privilege, inasmuch as the risk of arbitrary action is greater in the former than in the latter. See E. F. Albertsworth, "Judicial Review of Administrative Action by the Federal Supreme Court," 35 *Har. Law Rev.* 127.

remarks that if it is adhered to or extended, the net result will be that the fixing of a rate by a commission is but useless expenditure of time and energy, as the courts will immediately afterwards be called upon to tread laboriously over the same field.

The typical attitude of federal rule-issuing officers toward the authoritativeness of their products is evidenced by the following statement of a legal expert of the Treasury: [1]

> Though the courts are very careful to state that the power delegated to the executive department to make rules and regulations is not a legislative power, the administrative rules so made are in many respects similar to statutes. Like statutes, e. g., they do not ordinarily have retroactive effect. Furthermore, they are noticed judicially by the courts.

This viewpoint is certainly correct as to all valid regulations and proclamations. The courts, high and low, hold themselves bound to accept them as authoritative acts, just as they would accept the complete enactments of Congress. They are interpreted as though they were statutes.[2] They bind the departments that promulgate them, as well as persons coming within their terms, and cannot be made retroactive where the interest of an individual is placed in jeopardy.[3] Expressions such as " lawful order ", " lawful

[1] Fred T. Field, "The Federal Income Tax," *Columbia University Income Tax Lectures*, p. 91 (1921).

[2] Boske *v.* Comingore, 177 U. S. 459 (1900): "In determining whether regulations promulgated by him [Secretary of the Treasury] are consistent with law, we must apply the rule of decision which controls when an act of Congress is assailed as not being within the powers conferred upon it by the Constitution." See also Cinn. etc. R. Co. *v.* I. C. C., 206 U. S. 142 (1906); I. C. C. *v.* I. C. R. Co., 215 U. S. 452, 470, 474 (1910); also, U. S. *v.* Molasses, 174 Fed. 325 (1909).

[3] Kwack Jan Fat *v.* White, 253 U. S. 454, 464 (1920); U. S. *v.* Davis, 132 U. S. 334, 336 (1889); U. S. *v.* Ala. Ry. Co., 142 U. S. 615, 621 (1892); U. S. *v.* McDaniel, 7 Pet. 1, 15; U. S. *v.* Dunton, 288 Fed. 959

duty", "force and effect of law", "as though embodied in the statute", and "efficacious and binding as though public law", give emphasis to this attitude of the courts.[1] The following excerpt from the Supreme Court itself is convincing:[2]

> Whenever, by express language of an act of Congress, power is entrusted to either of the principal departments of government to prescribe rules and regulations for transaction of business in which the public is interested, or in respect to which they have a right to participate, and by which they are to be controlled, the rules and regulations prescribed in pursuance of such authority become a mass of that body of public records of which the courts take judicial cognizance.

In enforcing Article VI, Clause 2, of the Constitution, which provides that the Constitution itself, the laws made in pursuance thereof, and the treaties of the United States shall

(1923). In this last case the lower court, while admitting that an alien had not legally entered the United States, held that the failure of the Department of Labor to follow its own rule was deporting him without due process of law. The Department was the victim of its own rules because it would not obey them.

[1] I. C. C. *v.* Ill. C. R. Co., 216 U. S. 452, 470 (1910); Haas *v.* Henkel, 216 U. S. 462, 479 (1910); Smith *v.* Whitney, 116 U. S. 167, 181 (1886); Gratiot *v.* U. S., 4 How. 81 (1846); *Ex parte* Reed, 100 U. S. 13, 22 (1879).

[2] Caha *v.* U. S., 152 U. S. 211, 218 (1894). See also Cosmos Co. *v.* Gray Eagle Co., 190 U. S. 301, 309 (1903); U. S. *v.* Morrison, 240 U. S. 192 (1916); National Lead Co. *v.* U. S., 252 U. S. 140 (1920). In passing upon the validity of inland water rules of the way made by the Board of Supervising Inspectors under authority of U. S. Rev. Stat., Sec. 4412, the Court in Belden *v.* Chase, 150 U. S. 674, 698, said:

> The rules laid down have the force of statutory enactment and their construction is for the court, whose duty is to apply them as a matter of law to the facts in the case. They are not mere prudential regulations, but binding enactments, obligatory from the time the necessity for precaution begins.

be the supreme law of the land, the courts have asserted that all valid rules and regulations that come into conflict with state laws take precedence over such laws. Section 13, paragraph 4, of the Interstate Commerce Act, as amended in 1920,[1] provides that the Interstate Commerce Commission shall have regulatory power over intra-state commerce under certain conditions and that the Commission's regulations shall take precedence over the "law of any State or the decision or order of any State authority" contrary thereto. This supremacy of federal administrative rules was indirectly given sanction by the Supreme Court in its approval of the principle laid down in this paragraph.[2] In Johnson *v.* Maryland[3] the Court held that the regulations of the Postmaster-General relative to mail-truck licenses take precedence over the Maryland license laws. The best presentation of a case for the Post Office Department is found in *Ex parte* Willman,[4] where regulations as to lighting equipment for trucks were held to supersede the Cincinnati ordinances dealing with the same police problem. The Court allowed the regulations of the Secretary of War to take precedence over a Pennsylvania law establishing property lines along port waters within that State.[5] This same principle has been applied not only to all laws of the various sub-

[1] 24 Stat. 379 (1887) as amended by 41 Stat. 484 (1920).

[2] R. Com. *v.* Chicago B. and Q. Ry. Co., 257 U. S. 563 (1922); N. Y. *v.* U. S., 257 U. S. 591 (1922); Tex. *v.* Eastern Tex. Ry. Co., 258 U. S. 204 (1922).

[3] 254 U. S. 51 (1920). Ohio *v.* Thomas, 173 U. S. 276 (1898) is cited, a case where the Court held that the regulations of the Board of Managers of the Old Soldiers Home took precedence over Ohio's police laws regulating oleomargarine. The decision is perhaps weakened by the statement that Congress had approved the regulations by granting an appropriation.

[4] 277 Fed. 819 (1921). U. S. *v.* Gurley, 279 Fed. 874 (1922) is a decision placing forest regulations above state grazing laws.

[5] Philadelphia Co. *v.* Stimson, 223 U. S. 605 (1912).

divisions of the United States, but also to all orders or decisions of authorities of such subdivisions.[1]

Perhaps the greatest strain to which the "no-delegation" rule has been subjected in placing regulations and proclamations on a par with statutes occurs in those cases where the administrative authorities have been given the power to define offenses. This discretion, which closely approaches that involved in naming penalties, has been termed by the federal courts the very quintessence of legislation.[2] Nevertheless, such delegations have been upheld. To swear falsely is made a crime; such a crime cannot be committed before an officer not named in law as capable of administering oath; and the content of an oath must be lawfully made. There are instances where the executive authority, with judicial approval, actually names the content of the oath, the officer who is to administer it, or both.[3] Where the violation of rules and regulations is specifically or impliedly made criminal by the terms of a statute, there is a broad field in which the subordinate authority can work. It can name the particular acts the violation of which subjects the individual to criminal penalties. A statute provides that the proper department head "may make such rules and regulations and establish such service as will insure the objects of such [national forest] regulations," viz., to regulate their occupancy and use and to preserve the forests from destruc-

[1] Boske *v.* Comingore, 177 U. S. 459 (1900); U. S. *v.* Eliason, 16 Pet. 289; U. S. *v.* Midwest Oil Co., 236 U. S. 459 (1915); Grisard *v.* U. S., 6 Wall. 363. See, also, In *re* Hirsch, 24 Fed. 928; In *re* Weeks, 82 Fed. 729; Stegall *v.* Thurman, 175 Fed. 813 (1910); Cassarello *v.* U. S., 271 Fed. 486 (1919).

[2] E. g., Stantenburg *v.* Hennick, 29 U. S. 141; U. S. *v.* Butler, 195 Fed. 657 (1912); St. Louis, etc., Co. *v.* U. S., 188 Fed. 191 (1911); U. S. *v.* Mossew, 261 Fed. 999 (1919).

[3] U. S. *v.* Baily, 9 Pet. 238 (1835); U. S. *v.* Smith, 236 U. S. 405 (1915); U. S. *v.* Morehead, 243 U. S. 607 (1917).

tion. It is further provided that a named punishment shall fall on those who violate such regulations. Whatever the department head thinks will accomplish the objects of the statute, is a very broad definition of a misdemeanor.[1] It would certainly be impossible to convict a person of a criminal offense against the United States because of the indefiniteness of the crime [2] were it not for the intermediate act of the Executive, which converts general principles from the static into the dynamic or chooses the specific content of the crime and brings it within the penal statute.[3] The Supreme Court gave its approval to such regulations, but only after a second hearing and after three new Justices had been appointed.[4]

What is more, a departmental regulation, written or un-

[1] 30 Stat. 35 (1897).

[2] International Harvester Co. *v.* Ky., 234 U. S. 216, 221 (1914); U. S. *v.* Cohen, 255 U. S. 81.

[3] *Cf.* Wilkins *v.* U. S., 96 Fed. 837 (1899), carried to the Supreme Court on appeal but denied without a record of reasons: "It would seem, therefore, that the regulations do not create the crime; the crime is the result of them but the most that can be said of them is that they call into being the evidence or indicia which render possible a commission of crime."

[4] U. S. *v.* Grimaud, 220 U. S. 506 (1911); 216 U. S. 614. This decision has been characterized as follows: "This is by far the broadest decision upon the subject [of delegation], in that the court sustained an authority to constitute a crime against the United States, delegated to the Secretary of Agriculture, without prescribing any elements, facts, or state of things controlling of (sic) the Secretary in that denouncement." *Cong. Rec.*, vol. 62, 67th Cong., 2nd Sess., p. 12201. The report of the Commsr. of the General Land Office, Aug. 1901, p. 130 *et seq.*, gives a most interesting account of the legal quarrel between Attorney-General John W. Griggs and Solicitor-General John K. Richards as to the power of Congress to penalize the violation of regulations of the Secretary of the Interior. The former upheld and the latter denounced this power. The Attorney-General advised, despite several adverse lower court decisions, the continuance of the efforts of the Secretary in all jurisdictions. The Supreme Court accepted his opinion thirteen years later, 1911. For a more recent case, see McKinley *v.* U. S., 249 U. S. 397 (1919).

written, and touching only the employees of that department in effect defines a particular crime, thereby naming the class of offenders. This result is produced by the combining of three elements—a general statute delegating powers to the Executive, regulations issued thereunder, and sections of the Federal Criminal Code. Thus, to the Secretary of Agriculture is delegated the general power to make regulations for his department by the Revised Statutes, Section 161; the giving out of cotton reports ahead of time is contrary to a rule of practice developed under the statute; the Penal Code, Revised Statutes, Section 5451, makes it a crime to offer to bribe any officer of the United States to induce him to do or not to do any act in violation of his lawful duty. A person charged with bribing an official of the Bureau of Statistics to divulge cotton reports before they are officially released is convicted of a crime in that he is bribing an official to act in violation of his lawful duty—a duty whose content is established by an unwritten rule.[1] The Supreme Court has given its sanction in more than one instance to this roundabout way of arriving at what is a crime, showing that it is possible for an insignificant, perhaps unwritten, intra-departmental rule to play a most important part in depriving an officer or layman of his liberty.[2]

The judiciary has, in a few instances, specified directly what it considers the nature of executive discretionary power to be. Especially has this been the case in regard to the power to make rates for common carriers and other public utilities. The fixing of rates is essentially legislative in character and an injunction will not interfere with legisla-

[1] Haas *v.* Henkel, 216 U. S. 462 (1910).

[2] E. g., U. S. *v.* Birdsall, 233 U. S. 223 (1914); Pakas *v.* U. S., 245 U. S. 467 (1918); U. S. *v.* McDaniel, 7 Pet. 1, 14. For additional comments upon this general subject, see 35 *Harvard Law Rev.* 952-956 (1922), and "Legislative Power to Penalize the Violation of Administrative Rules," *No. Car. Law Review*, June, 1922.

tive action.[1] The function of rate making is purely legislative in its character. This is true whether it is exercised directly by the legislature itself or by some subordinate or administrative body.[2] Mr. Justice Brandeis, in a recent case, says, "To determine what rate, rule or practice shall be deemed reasonable for the future is a legislative or administrative function." [3] The orders of the District of Columbia Public Utilities Commission are legislative in character and the court that can substitute its discretion for that of the Commission is legislating.[4] When a rate is fixed by a Commission, whether the rate be general or applicable to all carriers or to one, the nature of the act is the same, viz., legislative.[5] Mr. Justice Holmes characterized rate fixing as legislative for the reason that "it looks to the future and changes existing conditions by making a new rule to be applied thereafter to all or some part of those subject to its power".[6] Even a rate made by the carriers themselves, and merely approved by the Commerce Commission, is corrective legislation.[7]

[1] McChord *v.* Louisville Ry. Co., 183 U. S. 483 (1901); I. C. C. *v.* C. N. O. and T. P. R. Co., 167 U. S. 479 (1897).

[2] Knoxville *v.* Knoxville, 212 U. S. 1 (1909); Louisville, etc., Co. *v.* Garrett, 231 U. S. 298 (1913); R. R. Com. *v.* C. B. I. Ry. Co., 257 U. S. 563 (1922); Maximum Rate Cases, 167 U. S. 479 (1897).

[3] Great No. Railway *v.* Merchants Elevator Co., 259 U. S. 285 (1922). The opinion includes regulations governing railroads for the future.

[4] Pub. Util. Com. *v.* Potomac Elec. Power Co., 43 Sup. Ct. Rep. 405 (1923).

[5] So. Pac. Co. *v.* Bartina, 170 Fed. 725 (1909).

[6] Prentis *v.* Atlantic, etc., Co., 211 U. S. 210 (1908). This rule would include all regulations and proclamations which have been given the name "delegated legislation" in this discussion. In Terminal Railroad Association *v.* U. S., U. S. Sup. Ct. *Advanced Opinions*, Nov. 1, 1924, p. 5, the statement is made that "the making of rates is a legislative and not a judicial function." A review of several important cases dealing with this same attitude is here given.

[7] Keogh *v.* Chicago, etc., Ry. Co., 271 Fed. 444 (1921). For comment

Almost all acts of Congress are law, at least in the technical or formal sense. It therefore follows that those functions which when exercised by Congress are legislative, are likewise legislative when delegated to administrative officers. A reading of the laws shows that functions falling within the jurisdiction of Congress have been exercised directly by that body or have been delegated to the Executive. Policy, controlled by necessity or convenience, apparently determines which method shall be used. That this alternative exercise of congressional functions is consciously carried on by the national legislature is evidenced both in committee reports and in the speeches of individual members;[1] that the choice is permissible was early indicated by the Supreme Court.[2]

A statute of 1920 gives the Federal Power Commission discretionary control over water-power development within the public parks and monuments of the United States. In 1921 this control is resumed by Congress.[3] In the conventions for the safety of life and property at sea, the administrative branch of the government, in collaboration with foreign states, works out the rules of the way and Congress adopts them by law, while, at the same time, additional regulations may be adopted by the Department of Commerce touching rules of the high seas and complete regulations for certain navigable waters of the United States.[4] Congress

on this statement see H. W. Bickle, "Jurisdiction of Certain Cases Arising under the Interstate Commerce Act," 60 *University of Penn. Law Rev.* 1.

[1] E. g., see *Senate Report* No. 595, part 1, 67th Cong., 2nd Sess. (1922); Senator Underwood's remarks on the rural route system and the foreign mails system, *Cong. Rec.*, 66th Cong., 2nd Sess. (1920), pp. 7411-7412, and Senator Jones' remarks on the Merchant Marine Bill, 1920, *ibid.*, p. 7402.

[2] I. C. C. *v.* Cinn. etc., Ry. Co., 167 U. S. 479 (1897).

[3] 41 Stat. 1062 (1920) and 41 Stat. 1353 (1921).

[4] 26 Stat. 320; 28 Stat. 645; Rev. Stat. Secs. 4489, 4488, 4412, 4405,

at times names the value of foreign coins in terms of United States money, while at other times this power is delegated to the Secretary of the Treasury.[1] Although for nearly a quarter-century the Secretary of Agriculture exercised within the terms of law the power to establish standards of agricultural products, such standards now are set up in detail by statute.[2] In fact, while the prevailing tendency at the present time is to delegate more and more powers that involve scientific questions, there has been a counter tendency, especially where political considerations are important, toward the resumption of such powers by Congress.[3] This counter tendency has met a check, however, whenever the bases for applying the general purpose of the legislature are unstable.

4233. Further illustrations of ante-natal and post-natal adoptions by Congress of administrative regulations almost identical in content are found in *Military Laws of the United States*, vol. ii, p. 1430 (1922).

[1] 2 Stat. 411 (1806); 4 Stat. 700 (1834); 28 Stat. 552 (1894); 42 Stat. 858 (1922).

[2] 32 Stat. 1158 (1903); 42 Stat. 1500 (1923). The latter statute contains almost the identical standard previously set up by the Secretary. If Congress had had knowledge of a particular scientific standard when the earlier statute was under consideration, it would not have been necessary to delegate the power. See *Circular* 136, p. 5, Dept. of Agric., June, 1919. It is possible that direct and all-embracing legislation will be found to follow administrative regulations where the Executive as a result of experience can name reasonably scientific standards.

[3] E. g., H. R. 2697, S. 862 and S. 2327, 68th Cong., 1st Sess. (1925). All these bills are attempts to reduce the power of the I. C. C. by substitution of more direct legislation.

CHAPTER III

The History of Administrative Legislation

It is an erroneous supposition that the great mass of administrative legislation now playing such an important part in the government of this nation sprang full-grown out of the complex conditions of modern life. If, for purposes of convenience, one divides the history of national law making roughly into four periods, viz., 1789-1824, 1825-1860, 1861-1890, and 1891-1926, he will find that Congress has departed all along the way from its general rule of issuing laws complete in themselves and effectual without the interposition of some other will than its own. The development of the detailed class of delegated legislation is followed in this chapter only through the first three periods. Chapters VII and VIII are depended upon to give a sufficient view of this class during the fourth period.[1] The line of develop-

[1] The following statutes are considered, or referred to, in chaps. vii and viii:

(a) Department of Agriculture: 34 Stat. 35 (national forests); 38 Stat. 693, 39 Stat. 476, 42 Stat. 1517 (cotton standards); 39 Stat. 482 (grain standards); 39 Stat. 486, 42 Stat. 1282 (warehousing); 26 Stat. 416 (animal regulations); 42 Stat. 1435 (naval stores); 37 Stat. 847, 40 Stat. 755 (bird life conservation); 42 Stat. 159 (packers and stock-yards).

(b) Department of the Interior: 41 Stat. 437 (mining); 30 Stat. 85, 39 Stat. 128 (Indian lands); 39 Stat. 535, 41 Stat. 731 (public lands and parks).

(c) Federal Power Commission: 41 Stat. 1063 (water power).

(d) Treasury Department: 28 Stat. 372, 26 Stat. 31, 31 Stat. 1086, 34 Stat. 226 (public health); 41 Stat. 305 (prohibition); 38 Stat. 784 (habit forming drugs); 32 Stat. 194 (adulterated butter); 36 Stat. 97 (customs); 39 Stat. 756, 40 Stat. 300, 40 Stat. 1057 (internal revenue).

ment of the contingent class of executive legislation, however, is followed through the four periods. It is done partly for the reason that there is less opportunity for getting a view of its history during the last period from chapters VII and VIII, and partly for the reason that this class represents, per delegation, more striking examples of executive legislative discretion.

I

It is believed that the following review of administrative legislation, together with chapters VII and VIII, will show that the legislature was inclined to share the burden of legislation with the Executive often during the first period; that this practice was continued to some extent during the second; that Congress was liberal in delegating discretion during the third period; and that during the fourth period the practice was generally established. Furthermore, the review will reveal that, although the President received a major portion of all delegated legislation during the first three periods, a division of labor was appearing in the administrative branch of the government and the basis for practically all legislative powers exercised at the present time by the major departments was being laid. The Secretary of the Treasury and the Commissioner of Internal Revenue, the War and Navy Secretaries, the Postmaster-General, the Secretary of the Interior, the Land Office Commissioner, and the Commissioner of Agriculture (Secretary, 1889) were beginning to exercise the supplementary rule-making power. The activities of the State Department were in the hands of the President, as well as the control of aliens—a control which developed the need for the establishment of the Commerce and Labor Department. The Secretary of the Treasury was performing the law-making activities of the future Department of Commerce.

The first session of Congress was initiated by the passing of a statute delegating general legislative power to the heads of the newly-created departments.[1] The chief of each department was authorized to " prescribe rules and regulations, not inconsistent with law, for the government of his Department, the conduct of its officers, the distribution of its business, the custody, use, and preservation of the records, papers, and property appertaining thereto ". Although it is not known whether Congress realized the extent of the power thus given to administrative officers, it is a fact that this very provision has served as a basis for a great deal of legislation framed in the absence of specific delegations.

A further survey of the statutes of this early period presents a rather imposing sphere of executive discretion built up from congressional acts. By law the President is empowered to carry out the details in regard to the establishment of a lighthouse near the entrance of Chesapeake Bay.[2] He is authorized, although he must remain within the limits of a lump sum named in the law, to fix the salaries of all officers engaged in the foreign service of the United States.[3] Military pensions are to be paid for the period of one year under such regulations as the Chief Executive may prescribe.[4] Superintendents, in granting licenses to Indian traders, " shall be governed in all things touching the said trade and intercourse by such rules and regulations as the President shall prescribe ".[5] Commissioners, appointed for the various states to receive subscriptions to the national domestic debt, are to " observe and perform such direction and regulations as shall be prescribed to them by the Secretary of the Treasury ".[6] The President is authorized to specify and to carry out measures to protect the national revenue, provided

[1] 1 Stat. 28 (1789).
[2] *Ibid.*, 54.
[3] *Ibid.*, 128.
[4] *Ibid.*, 129.
[5] *Ibid.*, 137.
[6] *Ibid.*, 139.

he remains within the maximum amount appropriated therefor.[1] The President is to regulate the issuing of letters patent, granting title to bounty lands.[2] "A mint shall be established under such regulations as shall be directed by law." The President is given full power to do the directing.[3] "Every printer of newspapers may send one paper to each and every other printer of newspapers within the United States, free of postage, under such regulations as the Postmaster-General shall prescribe."[4]

The Secretary of the Treasury shall have discretion to "regulate . . . the marks to be set upon casks [of distilled spirits] and the forms of the certificates which are to accompany the same".[5] It is made the duty of the "Secretary of War to provide at public expense, under such regulations as shall be directed by the President, the necessary books . . . for the use of the army corps".[6] The Chief Executive may specify the salaries that are to be paid in certain ship-building activities, the only limitation being a maximum lump sum.[7] Trade with the Indians shall be carried on only under such rules and regulations as the President may prescribe.[8] The President is authorized and empowered, within maximum limits, to equip and fit out a Navy.[9] To him also is delegated the power to establish regulations governing the armed merchant vessels of the United States.[10] Citizens of potential enemy countries are to be controlled by regulations of the President. This delegation gives as much freedom of action as is found under any law of the recent Great War or

[1] 1 Stat. 28 (1789). See also, *ibid.*, 462.

[2] *Ibid.*, 183.

[3] *Ibid.*, 225.

[4] *Ibid.*, 238, 738.

[5] *Ibid.*, 269.

[6] *Ibid.*, 366.

[7] *Ibid.*, 399. Same principle in *ibid.*, 429, 432, 450.

[8] *Ibid.*, 452.

[9] *Ibid.*, 552. See also 2 Stat. 451.

[10] *Ibid.*, 573.

under any law that is now on the statute books.[1] It shall be lawful for the President to cause to be established " fit and proper regulations for estimating duties on goods, wares, and merchandise imported into the United States, in respect to which the original cost shall be exhibited in depreciated currency, issued and circulated under authority of any foreign government ".[2] The Postmaster-General may make regulations governing partial payments that must be made in advance for the posting of newspapers.[3]

The Secretary of the Treasury is given the power to supplement the statutory regulations governing the book-keeping and accounting relative to the sale of public lands.[4] The Commissioners of the Navy Pension Fund are " authorized to make such regulations as may appear to them expedient " for the admission of persons on the roll of the Navy, and for the payment of pensioners.[5] Foreign armed vessels, on entering the ports of the United States, " must conform to such regulations concerning health, repairs, supplies, stay, intercourse, and departure " as the collector, under the authority of the President, may prescribe.[6] Under a statute preventing permanent settlement on lands ceded to the United States, the Secretary of the Treasury is delegated the authority to issue permits with rules governing the locations of tenants-at-will.[7] The statutory embargo of 1809 is to be enforced according to such rules and regulations as the President may formulate.[8] The Secretary of the Navy is empowered to prepare the necessary rules and regulations for the government of the Marine Hospital. All regula-

[1] 1 Stat. 28 (1789).

[2] *Ibid.*, 673.

[3] *Ibid.*, 740.

[4] 2 Stat. 77 (1800).

[5] *Ibid.*, 294.

[6] *Ibid.*, 341.

[7] *Ibid.*, 445.

[8] *Ibid.*, 509.

tions, however, are to be reported to Congress at the subsequent session.[1] The general regulations of the War Department are to be prepared by the Secretary of War and are to be submitted to Congress at the subsequent session. Presumably, such regulations are to be effective as administrative law until Congress shall see fit to act thereon.[2]

The Secretary of the Treasury is to establish regulations suitable and necessary for carrying into effect the provisions of a certain tax law.[3] Collectors of customs are ordered to enforce the terms of an embargo act in accordance with such rules as the President may prescribe for that purpose. The collectors, however, are permitted to offer the regulations as a perfect defense against any party suing for damages caused by the enforcement of the President's regulations.[4] The Secretary of the Treasury is given the power to make rules and regulations for effectuating the terms of a federal land tax law.[5] The Chief Executive is to set up rules for the guidance of inferior officers in making restitution for losses sustained during the War of 1812.[6] The Secretary of War is required to adopt such forms of evidence relative to pension applications of soldiers and their families as the President by regulation may prescribe.[7] The Chief Executive is authorized to prescribe the rules which ship commanders are to follow in protecting American merchant vessels from piratical depredations.[8] The President is empowered to issue rules and regulations that will reasonably insure the welfare of the Indian tribes.[9]

[1] 2 Stat. 77 (1800).
[2] *Ibid.*, 819.
[3] 3 Stat. 26 (1813).
[4] *Ibid.*, 91.
[5] *Ibid.*, 166.
[6] *Ibid.*, 286.
[7] *Ibid.*, 286.
[8] *Ibid.*, 510.
[9] *Ibid.*, 516.

In 1820, Congress made its first general delegation to the Secretary of the Treasury to issue regulations under all laws having to do with the collection of taxes.[1] This general provision appeared in substance in tax statutes passed in 1846, 1856 and 1870, and is now Section 251 of the Revised Statutes. The breadth of supplementary legislation that falls to the Secretary from this delegation can best be judged by reading the words of the original provision:

> The Secretary of the Treasury shall make and issue from time to time such instructions and regulations to the several collectors, receivers, depositories, officers . . . as he shall deem best calculated to promote the public convenience or security, and to protect the United States, as well as individuals, from fraud and loss; he shall prescribe forms of entries, oaths, bonds, and other papers, and rules and regulations, not inconsistent with law, to be used under and in execution and enforcement of the various provisions of internal-revenue laws, or in carrying out the provisions of laws relating to raising revenue from imports or to duties on imports, or to warehousing; he shall give such directions to collectors and prescribe such rules and forms to be observed by them as may be necessary for proper execution of the law. . . .

II

A close examination of the national legislative output for the second period, 1825-1860, reveals a general tendency on the part of Congress to have the Executive play the rôle of subordinate lawmaker. By law the Secretary of the Treasury, provided he has the approval of his chief, is given the authority to prescribe the hydrometer that is best calculated to measure the proof of liquors. After the choice has been made all duties imposed upon distilled spirits shall be levied, collected, and paid according to the proof ascertained by this

[1] 2 Stat. 77 (1800).

hydrometer.[1] The same officer, with the President's approval, shall from time to time establish regulations, not inconsistent with law, which will "secure a just, faithful, and impartial appraisal of goods, wares, and merchandise imported into the United States".[2]

The President is given the power to accept volunteers and to equip and organize them under such regulations as the service may demand.[3] The Commissioner of Indian Affairs is to control all matters relating to the Indians under such regulations as the President may from time to time prescribe.[4] The Secretary of the Treasury, with the approval of the President, shall make the necessary rules and regulations for securing "a just, faithful, and impartial appraisal of merchandise and a just and proper entry thereof".[5] The breaking of a regulation made under this statute was held by the Supreme Court to be a violation of the law of the United States.[6] The head of the Treasury is empowered to make "such rules and modes of proceeding to ascertain the facts upon which an application for remission of a fine . . . is founded as he deems proper".[7] The Commissioner of Pensions shall enforce the pension laws under such regulations as the President may prescribe.[8] The President is given almost full discretion to make rules and regulations for the disciplining of the marine corps.[9] He is given full discretion to put into effect by rules and regulations the various laws pertaining to the Indians.[10]

[1] 4 Stat. 79 (1825).

[2] *Ibid.*, 274.

[3] *Ibid.*, 533.

[4] *Ibid.*, 564.

[5] *Ibid.*, 583.

[6] Aldredge *v.* Williams, 3 How. 1.

[7] 4 Stat. 597.

[8] *Ibid.*, 622.

[9] *Ibid.*, 713.

[10] *Ibid.*, 738.

All purchases of supplies for the Navy are to be made "under such directions and regulations as the Executive may make"; but all rules and regulations made for such purposes must be laid before Congress.[1] Affidavits concerning public land entries are to be filed under such rules and regulations as the Secretary of the Treasury may prescribe.[2] The Commissioner-General of the Land Office is empowered to decide concerning all cases of suspended land entries, in accordance with general rules and regulations prescribed by the Secretary of the Treasury, the Attorney-General and himself, as well as principles of justice and equity.[3] The Secretary of the Treasury is authorized to make from time to time such regulations, not inconsistent with law, as may be necessary to give full effect to the provisions of a certain tax law.[4] He shall issue regulations to enforce a prompt presentation of drafts for certain public securities, in order that such drafts may not be used as a medium of exchange.[5] He shall also prescribe all regulations necessary to protect the United States from fraud in the granting of drawback allowances.[6]

For unnecessary and unreasonable delay of the mails the Postmaster-General is permitted to name the fines which are to be imposed upon contractors carrying the mails to and from foreign countries, "provided the fine for one default shall not exceed one-half of the contract price paid for one trip".[7] The Secretary of War, with the approval of the President, shall grant all pensions under such rules, regulations, restrictions and limitations as he may prescribe.[8] The

[1] 5 Stat. 536 (1842).

[2] 9 Stat. 9 (1846).

[3] *Ibid.*, 51.

[4] *Ibid.*, 55.

[5] *Ibid.*, 77.

[6] *Ibid.*, 77.

[7] *Ibid.*, 241.

[8] *Ibid.*, 250.

Secretary of the Treasury, with the approbation of the President, is authorized, under such regulations as he may prescribe to protect the revenue from fraud, to permit vessels laden with products from Canada to load and unload at any port or place in the United States which he may designate.[1] The Postmaster-General is given authority, with the consent of the President, to reduce or enlarge, from time to time, the rates of postage upon all letters or other mailable matter conveyed between the United States and any foreign country.[2]

The Secretary of the Treasury may prescribe regulations governing bonds for transporting goods from one warehouse of one collection district in the United States to another, and for naming the times when such transfers shall be made.[3] He may also permit owners to change the names of their ships under such regulations as he may prescribe.[4] This delegation, since Congress withdrew it in 1859 and has been more or less jealously retaining it to the present day, seems to have been a very important one. The President may prescribe the fees to be charged for all official services, but he must report to Congress annually thereon.[5] He may also prescribe the manner of conducting all government business of the foreign service.[6]

III

During the first half of the third period the general delegation to the Executive of supplementary legislation was doubtless increased as a result of the tightening up of law enforcement during the Civil War and the years of recon-

[1] 9 Stat. 9 (1846).

[2] *Ibid.*, 587.

[3] 10 Stat. 270 (1854).

[4] 11 Stat. 1 (1855).

[5] *Ibid.*, 57.

[6] *Ibid.*, 60.

struction that followed. The latter part of this third period was one of transition from the stress of war and its aftermath to that of more or less normal progress. Under such conditions one would naturally look for a continuation and a development of the practice of using the Executive for effectuating the purposes of general laws. The following list of representative examples, gleaned from the statutes passed during the years 1861-1890, shows this expansion of the Executive's delegated legislative power.

The Secretary of the Interior may make rules to prevent the government from being imposed upon in the execution of the law relative to the re-issuing of lost land warrants.[1] The Secretary of the Treasury, with the approval of the President, may make all necessary regulations for enforcing the provisions of the tariff law which pertain to the assessment and collection of duties on shipboard.[2] The same official may prescribe rules and regulations for the disposal of unclaimed warehouse goods.[3] The Commissioner of Internal Revenue is empowered to make all additional regulations and to require all additional securities necessary for the proper protection of the revenue on distilled spirits and for carrying out the spirit and intent of the revenue law.[4] The Secretary of the Navy, with the approval of the President, is authorized to set up regulations for the control of the Navy.[5] This power was upheld in the case of *Ex parte* Reed.[6] The amount of the drawbacks on imports shall be ascertained in accordance with the rules and regulations of the Treasury, and in no other way.[7] The same official is authorized and

[1] 12 Stat. 91.

[2] *Ibid.*, 256.

[3] *Ibid.*, 294.

[4] *Ibid.*, 449.

[5] *Ibid.*, 565.

[6] 100 U. S. 13 (1879).

[7] 12 Stat. 742. *Cf.* 13 Stat. 15, 16, 17.

required to make all necessary regulations, and, in order to prevent smuggling, to change them from time to time.[1] The Secretary is empowered to give effect to the act providing for the disposal of coal lands on the public domain, under such regulations as he may prescribe.[2] He may also make regulations for the surveying of city sites and for regulating the fees to be charged the public by the General Land Office.[3]

The Secretary of the Treasury is to issue a full set of regulations for putting into effect the statutory embargo upon the importation of all cattle.[4] He is required to admit duty-free certain articles under such regulations as are necessary to protect the interests of the government,[5] and to refund taxes illegally collected on cotton in accordance with rules laid down by himself.[6] The Commissioner of Internal Revenue, subject to the approval of his superior, shall establish such regulations, not inconsistent with law, as may be necessary to make prompt collection of all revenues due and accruing to the government.[7] The Commissioner is further authorized to make regulations for securing a uniform and correct system of inspecting, weighing, marking, and gauging spirits;[8] for withdrawing distilled spirits from bonded warehouses to be exported without the payment of the stamp taxes;[9] and for the inspection of tobacco and the collection of taxes thereon.[10] The head of the Treasury shall frame the regulations necessary to protect the govern-

[1] 13 Stat. 197 (1864).
[2] *Ibid.*, 343.
[3] *Ibid.*, 344.
[4] 14 Stat. 1 (1866).
[5] *Ibid.*, 48.
[6] *Ibid.*, 100.
[7] *Ibid.*, 472.
[8] 15 Stat. 125 (1867).
[9] *Ibid.*, 148.
[10] *Ibid.*, 160.

ment from fraud in cases where machinery is imported duty-free for the purpose of having repairs made.[1]

The President shall adopt regulations governing the entrance to the civil service.[2] The Secretary of the Interior is authorized to set up regulations under which certain Indians are to be declared qualified to receive individual land allotments.[3] The Secretary of the Treasury is empowered to make regulations relative to sugar and wool samples used as a basis for collecting duties,[4] and for establishing proof of the identity of articles admitted free of duty.[5] The same official is to see that dangerous articles are carried on passenger vessels under regulations that will make for the safety of the passengers and crews.[6] To the Secretary of the Interior is delegated the power of regulating all trading within Indian territories and of making the necessary rules to prevent recalcitrant traders from having commercial intercourse with the Indians.[7] The Secretary is empowered to issue regulations for enforcing the law which permits steam machinery to enter duty-free;[8] which allows salt to be imported in bond for the curing of fish;[9] which provides for drawbacks on imported spirits which are to be exported;[10] and which permits the withdrawing of tobacco from warehouses for exportation without the payment of stamp taxes.[11] He is also permitted to establish regulations under which the recovery of illegally-collected taxes may be made.[12] The regulations which issued from this provision of the law

[1] 14 Stat. 1 (1866).

[2] 16 Stat. 514 (1871).

[3] *Ibid.*, 557.

[4] *Ibid.*, 262, 263.

[5] *Ibid.*, 266.

[6] *Ibid.*, 441.

[7] 17 Stat. 457 (1873).

[8] *Ibid.*, 237.

[9] *Ibid.*, 237.

[10] *Ibid.*, 241.

[11] *Ibid.*, 254.

[12] 19 Stat. 248 (1877).

were held valid in the case of Rock Island Railroad Company *v.* United States.[1] The Secretary of the Interior is given the power to make regulations for the cutting of timber on the public lands of the United States.[2] The Commissioner of Internal Revenue is authorized to establish, alter, and change the revenue stamps used for the collection of taxes.[3]

The Secretary of the Treasury is authorized to establish regulations according to which articles intended for the international exposition may be entered free of duty,[4] and for the purpose of admitting articles duty-free which are to be used by the negroes of the United States.[5] To the Commissioner of Agriculture is delegated the authority of preparing regulations which may be necessary for the speedy and effectual eradication of existing cattle diseases.[6] The regulations that were issued under this law were held valid in the case of United States *v.* Slater.[7] The Commissioner of Internal Revenue is authorized to prescribe the stamps and brands for the identification of packages of oleomargarine sold by retailers.[8] The Commissioner's regulations were held to be good law in the case of In *re* Kollock.[9] The same officer is required to make rules which are to guide manufacturers of oleomargarine and renovated butter in making their bonds, inventories, and records.[10] The Secretary of War is empowered to make the necessary rules and regulations for protecting the improvements being made on the

[1] 245 U. S. 141 (1920).

[2] 20 Stat. 88 (1878).

[3] *Ibid.*, 351.

[4] 21 Stat. 62 (1880).

[5] *Ibid.*, 66.

[6] 23 Stat. 31 (1884).

[7] 123 Fed. 115 (1903).

[8] 24 Stat. 209 (1886).

[9] 165 U. S. 526 (1896).

[10] 24 Stat. 210, 212.

South Pass of the Mississippi River.[1] This delegation was upheld by the court in the case of United States *v.* Breen.[2] The Secretary of the Treasury is authorized to make all necessary regulations to prevent the spread of certain diseases beyond state boundary lines.[3]

IV

Contingent legislation seems, from the very beginning, to have been a preferred method of handling policies that had to do with foreign affairs.[4] So extensively was it applied in matters of this nature, one could well believe that the practice of continental European states was taken over without change. International relations were put upon an uncertain basis by the endeavor of the United States to place herself properly within the society of nations. A theretofore practically unknown kind of neutral status was demanded in order to protect her citizens and property on the high seas, to win, if not to compel, the respect of other nations, and incidentally to secure revenue. There were threats of war, there was commercial war, and finally actual war. These conditions were reflected in the statute law and in the power given the Executive during the years 1789-1824. The contingent laws were based for the most part

[1] 25 Stat. 424 (1888).

[2] 40 Fed. 402 (1889).

[3] 26 Stat. 31 (1890).

[4] Matters of domestic, or of semi-domestic, concern did not seem to be handled so much through contingent legislation. The following examples illustrate this use: 1 Stat. 300; *ibid.*, 353; *ibid.*, 420; *ibid.*, 440; *ibid.*, 571; *ibid.*, 627; 4 Stat. 623; *ibid.*, 57. A series of public land statutes, such as 4 Stat. 421 and 5 Stat. 456, seemed to fall under this form of legislation. Almost all of such legislation, however, was apparently too much mixed up with the ordinance power of the President for even Congress to clarify by any other method than that of sanctioning what had gone before and delegating for the future (36 Stat. 84).

upon the commerce and finance clauses of the Constitution, bolstered up by the "necessary and proper" clause.[1]

At first the statutes provided for the complete suspension of commercial intercourse with certain states, the legal duration of the embargo being dependent upon the existence of certain facts or conditions.[2] The assertion of the Court that the "obvious intention of the legislature of the United States, by the non-intercourse laws, was to prohibit American citizens and property from commerce with foreign nations"[3] is quite correct as a statement of the means of forcing recognition of the rights and claims of the newly-formed American state. To prohibit intercourse with a particular state in retaliation for its denial of very valuable commercial rights and privileges was one way of asserting independence and equality. But since Congress recognized that the embargo was merely a very disagreeable means of forcing the extensions of trade—a means to be got rid of as quickly as possible—the plan of leaving it to the President to determine when the embargo had accomplished the whole or part of its purpose was adopted. After foreign states as a result of the non-intercourse laws had begun to see that absolute prohibition was a poor means of building up a great commerce, trade began gradually to open up to the United States. It was accompanied, however, by harassing discriminations in duties on tonnage and goods, in preferences given to domestic ships, and in various other matters. Congress promptly met such discriminatory charges by passing retalia-

[1] Constitution, Art. I, Sec. 8, pars. 1, 3, 18. Other contingent legislation, to be sure, appears during this early period. It is found especially under military preparedness, e. g., 1 Stat. 223 (1791); 1 Stat. 243 (1792); 1 Stat. 424 (1795); 1 Stat. 569 (1798); 2 Stat. 553 (1802); 4 Stat. 652.

[2] E. g., 1 Stat. 615; 2 Stat. 7; 3 Stat. 740.

[3] The *Sally* and Cargo, 1 Gallis. C. C. R. 58, quoted in 2 Stat. 528, note (a).

tory measures of a similar nature.[1] Again, the President was empowered to lift or to impose burdens discriminating against the whole or a part of the commerce of a foreign state, contingent upon his finding certain facts or conditions.

Whether or not the statutes had reference to non-intercourse or to discriminations, the finding of the future fact or facts was at times comparatively easy and allowed of little or no discretion on the part of the President or his representatives. To quote one of the statutes: "On satisfactory evidence being given to the President of the United States that the ports in the islands of the West Indies . . . have been opened to vessels of the United States, the President shall be, and hereby is, authorized to issue his proclamation declaring that the ports of the United States shall thereafter be open to vessels of Great Britain." [2] The determination of such a simple fact of the future leaves no room for the exercise of discretion. It is practically an automatic action which can be performed by the lowliest clerk upon securing information from the British Embassy. In another Act all that the President has to ascertain before reviving an embargo law by proclamation is whether a particular statute of the British Parliament has been set aside or repealed, by Orders in Council or by the body responsible for it.[3]

In other cases this simple power was extended. One statute provides that "it shall be lawful for the President . . . , if he shall deem it expedient and consistent with the interest of the United States, by his order, to remit and dis-

[1] E. g., 3 Stat. 361, Ch. 39, Sec. 2; 3 Stat. 224, Ch. 77; 3 Stat. 740, Ch. 22, Sec. 3; 4 Stat. 2, 3, Ch. 4, Sec. 4.

[2] 3 Stat. 681, Sec. 1 (1822). Even this simple power is enlarged by the following clause: "such reciprocal rules and restrictions as the President . . . may, by such proclamation, make and publish, anything in the laws . . . to the contrary notwithstanding."

[3] 3 Stat. 740, Sec. 6. For proclamation see *Messages and Papers of the Presidents*, p. 941.

continue, for the time being," the embargo against France and her colonies "with which commercial intercourse may be safely renewed"; and that the orders may be revoked when "in his opinion the interests of the United States shall require".[1] Almost complete power appears in a statute of 1794: "The President . . . [shall] be, and hereby is, authorized and empowered, whenever, in his opinion, the public safety shall so require, to lay an embargo on all ships in the ports . . . , under such regulations as the circumstances of the case may require, and to continue or revoke the same, whenever he shall think proper".[2] There is little doubt that the President, under the last two statutes, has the power to play an important rôle in the formulation of the legislative will.

[1] 1 Stat. 615, Sec. 4; proclamation, 11 Stat. 758. The same is repeated in 2 Stat. 9, Sec. 6; proclamation thereunder, *Messages and Papers of the Presidents*, p. 292.

[2] 1 Stat. 372, Ch. 4. A similar power, based upon public interest, is found in the discretionary power of raising embargoes upon munitions of war (1 Stat. 44, Ch. 53). The policy of laying and lifting embargoes on war materials where the interests of the United States might be furthered has been continued in permanent laws and the execution has fallen upon the President. 30 Stat. 739 gives him unlimited power to prohibit all such export traffic except that which he may allow under regulations; 37 Stat. 630 limits the field to American states and to those suffering domestic violence; 42 Stat. 361 adds to the field "any country in which the United States exercises extra-territorial jurisdiction" and extends the rule limit by adding "which may be promoted by" to the phrase domestic violence "which are." Almost all of the proclamations issued have been absolute although President Wilson's proclamation of July 12, 1919, against Mexico delegated the power to make rules for exceptions to the Secretary of State (41 Stat. 1762). President Coolidge, by proclamation, invoked the power given in 42 Stat. 361 in regard to Mexico, January 7, 1924. By excepting certain importations, he went the whole length of the administrative power to aid President Obregon against the rebel, De la Huerta. It might be noted that heavy fines and prison sentences or both constitute the penalties for the violation of the proclamations. Either Congress or the President may revoke such proclamations.

Under the head of discriminatory legislation, laws are found during this period that give both narrow and wide legislative functions to the Executive. A certain article is permitted to be imported from states that do not allow United States vessels to carry it therefrom, provided any such foreign country having regulations against importing this article into the United States shall discontinue such regulations. The fact of the discontinuance is to be ascertained and announced by proclamation.[1] In this instance little leeway is given the Executive, save that of deferring the proclamation. Contingent legislation, however, frequently accompanies the carrying on of commercial wars with the maritime nations of Europe.[2] In a majority of cases the formula by which the President is endowed with broad discretionary powers in ascertaining some future condition or fact is set forth in the following clause: " . . . whenever the President shall be satisfied that the discriminating or countervailing duties of such foreign nations, so far as they operate to the disadvantage of the United States, have been abolished ".[3] Revival of discrimination is generally authorized by giving the Chief Executive power to revoke the order or proclamation which sets it aside. The objective elements that go to make up the determination of discrimination cover a very broad field. The task of the Executive is easy where the elements have been crystallized into law. Where such elements must be searched out among involved and subtle practices the burden is great, implying

[1] 3 Stat. 361, Ch. 39 (1817); proclamation, *Messages and Papers of the Presidents*, p. 605.

[2] Sec. 4228, Rev. Stat., continues permanently the Executive's power in this field. It was utilized by appropriate proclamations on January 15, 1913, for the benefit of both Austria and Hungary.

[3] E. g., 3 Stat. 224, Ch. 77 (1815) and proclamations, *Messages and Papers of the Presidents*, pp. 665, 666, 752; 3 Stat. 740, Ch. 22, Sec. 3 (1823); 4 Stat. 419 (1830).

considerable discretion within the field named in the statute. But the freedom of the embargo acts is not approached. A boundary line there certainly is. Evidently Congress was under the impression that it was setting up a future condition which could be determined with comparative ease.

The second decade of the nineteenth century was well started before the question as to the constitutionality of such contingent legislation reached the Supreme Court. The *Brig Aurora* Case[1] tested a statute of this kind and the proclamation thereunder.[2] The revived statute provided for a complete embargo against Great Britain and France, with the proviso that the embargo would not apply should the President proclaim that certain edicts had been so modified as "not to violate the neutral commerce of the United States". The Act expired but was revived by Section 4 of the Act of May 1, 1810, which stipulated that if the President should find that either Great Britain or France had so modified the edicts complained of that they no longer violated American neutral commerce, proclamation thereof would relieve that state from the penalty. If, however, one failed, the pertinent sections of the previous Act of March, 1809, would be in full force and effect against it. Great Britain failed to qualify after the proclamation of November 2, 1810. The Court in a brief opinion said: "We can see no sufficient reason, why the legislature should not exercise its discretion in reviving the Act of March 1, 1809, either expressly or conditionally, as their judgment should direct." To say the least, a few of the insufficient reasons might have been recorded to set off the drabness of this conclusion. The purpose of the law, in the first place, was to rid Amer-

[1] 7 Cranch 382 (1813).

[2] 3 Stat. 605, reviving 2 Stat. 528; President Madison's Proclamation thereunder, No. 2, 1810.

ican commerce of foreign discriminations. It smacks somewhat of treaty-making by statute, with the President as the authority to carry on negotiations or to close them. The case is certainly not one upon which to build a rational argument for contingent legislation.

It has been said, in connection with the *Brig Aurora* Case,[1] that retaliatory contingent legislation had never before been questioned in the courts. This does not mean that there had never before been a challenge. From 1789 to 1807 it might be said that the loosest kind of legislation was passed without much discussion. The Embargo Act of June 4, 1794,[2] and successive acts[3] of like nature illustrate the almost extravagant power delegated to the President. The period was a trying one and the difficulty of convening Congress made it almost necessary to sub-let the will-making power.

The Embargo Act of April 22, 1808,[4] however, was apparently the first legislation of its kind to provoke a vigorous discussion as to the constitutionality of delegated legislation. Although the speeches in the Senate were not reported, the bill seems to have been stoutly resisted on constitutional grounds.[5] The debate in the House of Representatives was reported at some length. Although John Randolph of Virginia led the opposition the legal argument was supplied by Philip B. Key of Maryland.[3] The latter's argument was

[1] 7 Cranch 382 (1813).

[2] 1 Stat. 372 (1792). See also *Ann. of Cong.*, Apr. 19, 1808, p. 2230.

[3] 1 Stat. 613, 615, Sec. 4 (1799); 2 Stat. 7, 9, Sec. 6 (1800). See *Ann. of Cong.*, Apr. 14, 1808, p. 2144; 2 Stat. 351, 352, Sec. 5 (1806); 2 Stat. 411, Sec. 3 (1806); *Ann. of Cong.*, Dec. 21, 1808, p. 295 and Apr. 19, 1808, p. 2216.

[4] 2 Stat. 490, Ch. 52 (1808).

[5] *Ann. of Cong.*, Dec. 21, 1808, p. 259; Jan. 7, 1808, p. 315.

[6] *Ibid.*, Apr. 13, 1808, pp. 2124-25; Apr. 18, 1808, p. 2212.

to the effect that the President might lift the embargo by proclamation, provided the law should definitely specify the conditions under which the Executive was to act. If this officer, argued Mr. Key, were permitted to determine for himself the conditions justifying the removal of the embargo, he would be exercising legislative power. To delegate such legislative power to another branch of the government was not only unconstitutional but was contrary to the principles of republicanism. Josiah Quincey of Massachusetts and others argued that the question was not one of constitutionality but merely one of expediency.[1] Mr. Campbell of Tennessee, who was directing the course of the bill, took a middle ground. But in so doing, he claimed a rather wide range of discretion for the President.[2] There is evidence here of some sort of alignment on the separation-of-powers theory set forth in the Constitution.

V

Although the embargo bill in due course of time became a law, the debate had its effect upon the then-usual power of the President "by order to remit and discontinue [the embargo] whenever he shall deem it expedient, and for the interest of the United States". Mr. Key's idea of definitely named conditions appeared in one provision of the Act. The President was empowered to withdraw the embargo "in the event of peace or suspension of hostilities between the belligerent powers". There was inserted, however, an additional clause giving the President power to suspend the embargo when in his judgment the belligerent powers had so changed their regulations governing neutral commerce as to render the commerce of the United States "sufficiently

[1] *Ann. of Cong.*, Apr. 14, 1808, pp. 2129-30; April. 19, 1808, pp. 2200-02.

[2] *Ibid.*, Apr. 13, 1808, pp. 2141-44; see, also, Whitney, "The Reciprocity Acts of 1890," 31 *Amer. Law Reg.* 186 *et seq.*

safe ". This Act, and the subsequent challenge of the power to delegate legislation made in the case of the *Brig Aurora,* indicate a tendency to recede from the previous practice of almost free delegation. By 1825 the restraint on the Executive's contingent legislative power was evident. Indeed, it might be said that the third period witnessed a minimum of such practice. This was due in large part, however, to the absence of any great need therefor.[1] The Act of March 5, 1845,[2] provided for the suspension of discriminatory laws " upon satisfactory evidence " of equality of duties on tonnage and cargo; the Act of August 5, 1854,[3] provided for the suspension of such duties " on satisfactory evidence " that Great Britain had actually executed certain treaty terms.

VI

Although the third period contains a number of delegations of contingent legislative power, practically all of them fall within the years covered by the Civil War. With these the present discussion does not deal, however much they may furnish good precedents for future war delegations. There were a few, however, that could be considered normal. A statute of 1866[4] prohibited the importation of foreign cattle into the United States because of the prevalence of certain diseases in the countries whence such cattle came. The

[1] In the case of Martin *v.* Mott, 12 Wheat. 19, decided during this intermediate period a more or less permanent statute (1 Stat. 420) was unsuccessfully attacked. The President was given power, in case of war with the Indians or with foreign nations, or in case there was more or less danger of war, to call forth any number of militia he thought necessary. A militiaman refused to serve and a heavy fine was imposed. The Court said that the power was great, but that since Congress had felt the need of placing such a great discretion in the Executive the delegation was good.

[2] 5 Stat. 748 and proclamation, 9 Stat. 1001.

[3] 10 Stat. 587 and proclamation, 10 Stat. 1179.

[4] 14 Stat. 1.

President was given the power to set aside this law whenever he should come to the conclusion that no further danger from the disease existed. A similar law [1] of the same year prohibited the entry of neat cattle and provided that the Chief Executive might set aside its terms whenever he should find that there was no further danger from the spread of disease among cattle in America. The Act of June 26, 1884,[2] authorized the President to collect such an amount of duty levied by the Act as might not be in excess of the duty placed upon American goods. These laws show that there was an attempt to set up sufficiently definite conditions upon which the President could act, even though in practice the discretion might not be small.

VII

The intermediate ground which Congress had been holding in regard to contingent legislation during the second and third periods was suddenly given up. By 1887, reversion to the eighteenth-century practice of delegating freer, looser power was in evidence. It appeared first in the Canadian Fisheries Retaliation Act, best set forth in the following quotation: [3]

> Whenever the President . . . shall be satisfied that American fishing vessels or American fishermen, visiting or being in the waters or at any port or places of the British Dominions . . . , are or then lately have been denied or abridged in the enjoyment of any rights secured to them by treaty or law, or are or late

[1] 14 Stat. 3.

[2] 23 Stat. 57.

[3] 24 Stat. 475. Although this law was enacted in 1887 it is placed, since in spirit it really so belongs, in the fourth period. It is still on the statute books in spite of the fact that no proclamations have been found to issue thereunder.

have [been] unjustly vexed or harassed in the enjoyment of such rights, or subjected to unreasonable restrictions, regulations, or requirements in respect of such rights; or otherwise unjustly vexed or harassed in said waters . . . ; or whenever the President . . . shall be satisfied that any such fishing vessels or fishermen, having a permit under the laws of the United States to touch and trade at any port . . . in the British Dominions . . . are or then lately have been denied the privilege of entering such port . . . , and under the same regulations as may exist therein applicable to trading vessels of the most favored nation or shall be unjustly harassed in respect thereof, or otherwise be unjustly harassed or vexed therein . . . , then, and in either or all of such cases, it shall be lawful and it shall be the duty of the President . . . , in his discretion, by proclamation to that effect, to deny vessels, their masters and crew . . . any entrance into the waters, ports . . . within the United States; and . . . to deny entry . . . of fresh or salt fish or any other product coming from said Dominions.

Power is given to apply this law generally or locally, to modify, revoke, or reissue proclamations. Any violation of a proclamation is declared illegal and both goods and vessels are made subject to forfeiture, while the persons responsible are threatened with dire punishment.

This measure was non-partisan. Its purpose was to retrieve national honor, which many believed lost because of the harsh, peremptory, and confiscatory measures put into effect by Canada against the United States fishing interests. As Senator Morgan explained, the Foreign Relations Committee "have not thought it best to advise the Government to come to a positive determination of law, in advance, that there should be no intercourse, and allow the President to suspend as to certain articles or as to any importation of their goods, based upon satisfactory evidence brought to his attention that the Government have treated our men of commerce and our fishermen also with injustice ".[1] Senator Hale considered the bill a happy bit of diplomacy by legislation, and Senator Evarts argued at length for its passage.[2] The constitutionality of the bill was never questioned. The only difference in attitude between the House and the Senate lay in the fact that the former thought the latter had not gone far enough in extending the President's powers. No one mentioned the lack of definiteness in " unjust treatment and harassment " or even of the treaty rights which had been in dispute ever since 1818. Attention was called to the purposely vague language and to the apparent contradiction in the closely related phrases " duty to " and " in his discretion ". Senator Morgan summarily stated the case thus: " So it is, whipping back and forth, that this power in the hands of the President is a necessary power to preserve the balance of commercial differences between nations." [3] A *casus belli* had been committed and the Executive, backed by the express power of Congress, was given full discretion to adjust the situation with a weapon falling far short of war.[4]

VIII

The Food Act of August 30, 1890,[5] illustrates further the large discretion, coupled with a broad sweep of power, in regard to foreign trade. Among other things this Act provides, " . . . whenever the President shall be satisfied that unjust discriminations are made " by a foreign state against American products, " . . . he may direct that such products

[1] *Cong. Rec.*, 49th Cong., 2nd Sess., p. 938 (1887).

[2] *Ibid.*, pp. 941, 942.

[3] *Ibid.*, p. 937.

[4] *Ibid.*, pp. 1821, 2127, 2166, 2282, 2387, 2452-54, 2583, for a discussion in full.

[5] 26 Stat. 414, Ch. 839, Sec. 5.

of such foreign state, as he may deem proper, shall be excluded from the United States", and he may " . . . revoke, modify, terminate, or renew any such direction as in his opinion the public may require". There is no attempt to embody the theory proposed by Mr. Key in 1808 [1] that the legislature should name specific facts, or a state of things easily recognizable, which, when found by the President to exist, would put the policy of the statute automatically into operation. Not only is the term "unjust discriminations" broad enough for the exercise of law-making discretion but —a further and important delegation—the President may choose the products that he will exclude.

IX

The famous reciprocity legislation of the Fifty-first Congress would not be complete without reproducing in part Section 3 of the Tariff Act of October 1, 1890,[2] which was being worked out along with the Food Act of the same year. The President, "whenever . . . he shall be satisfied that the government of any country producing and exporting [certain named products] of the United States, which, in view of the free introduction of such [articles] into the United States, he may deem to be reciprocally unequal and unreasonable, shall have the power, and it shall be his duty to suspend, by proclamation to that effect, the provisions of this act relating to the free introduction of such [articles], for such time as he shall deem just, and in such case and during such suspension duties shall be levied, collected, and paid upon" such articles in accordance with a specifically named tariff rate for each article. Senator Evarts of New York, who in 1887 spoke at length in behalf of the President's blanket legislative power in the matter of the Canadian

[1] *Supra*, p. 71.

[2] 26 Stat. 567, 612.

fisheries, promptly took exception to this delegation. In the course of the debate he offered an amendment to the effect that when the President had found what he deemed a reciprocally unequal and unreasonable burden or other exaction, he should communicate to Congress the facts ascertained, to the end that Congress might impose its own duties upon the above-mentioned articles, until then exempted from duty by this Act.[1]

The constitutionality of such broad contingent legislation is here once more attacked. The Senator goes back to the argument of 1808, viz., that there must be little or no discretion in the ascertainment of contingent facts but that the act itself must define such facts. The amendment does not attempt to describe the conditions but cuts through the heart of the matter by casting the determination back upon Congress, which, after viewing the facts presented, must take action. In giving the President this power, he asserted, there is the "insurmountable difficulty of deputing to the executive authority an ascertainment that he will put a duty on articles imported from certain countries, if he thinks that imposition is justified by inequalities of treatment by foreign countries on the whole range of our revenue". This he held to be nothing more than a delegation to the President of the power to make a treaty and to raise and remit taxes without the consent of the legally constituted authorities.[2] If this is a mere expression of the will of Congress, it is the will to abdicate the revenue and the treaty-making scheme, leaving it for the time being to the President.

But the law and the practice were against Senator Evarts and were the chief stay of the sponsors of the reciprocity section of the Tariff Act of 1890. The legislative function of the Chief Executive had a century of congressional ap-

[1] *Cong. Rec.*, 51st Cong., 2nd Sess., p. 9882.

[2] *Ibid.*, pp. 9882-83.

proval behind it and a long-standing blanket sanction by the Judiciary.[1] Again the so-called loose constructionists had their way, although it was not an undisputed way.

X

A proclamation of the President, in accordance with Section 3 of the Tariff Act of 1890, precipitated litigation before the Supreme Court in 1892.[2] The constitutionality of this provision was questioned, *inter alia,* on the ground that it delegated legislative functions to the executive branch of the government contrary to the separation-of-powers rule.[3] "That Congress cannot delegate legislative power to the President is a principle universally recognized as vital to the maintenance of the system of government ordained by the Constitution", was a postulate set forth in the brief of Solicitor-General W. H. Taft.[4] According to the words of the opinion the tariff law does not vest the President with legislative functions in any real sense; the duties invoked by the proclamation are specified; there is nothing involving expediency or just operation; "may deem" contains no marked discretion; suspension is required upon ascertainment of the contingent fact; discretion appears only in determining the duration of the suspension of the law. Although the Court accepted the *Brig Aurora* case it said that if the decision in that case "had never been rendered, the practical construction of the Constitution, as given by so many acts of Congress and embracing almost the entire period of our national existence, should not be overruled unless upon conviction that such legislation was clearly incompatible with the supreme law of the land".[5] The Court apparently was convinced[6]

[1] *Brig Aurora,* 7 Cranch 382 (1813).

[2] Field *v.* Clark, 143 U. S. 649 (1892).

[3] Question was raised only collaterally.

[4] Field *v.* Clark, 143 U. S. 649, 692.

[5] *Ibid.*, p. 691.

[6] *Ibid.*, pp. 691-93.

of the practical necessity of wide discretion on the part of the Executive in protecting the country's interest against the self-interest of foreign states. The very laws that best exhibited delegated law-making were past history and their results could be evaluated. Provided the more or less simple social-economic life of the past had justified them, certainly the more complex international conditions of 1892 and of the future would accentuate their value.

Although the "no-delegation" rule is adhered to in this case it is not as the strict constructionist understood it; his position is overthrown. There is no definitely-named and readily-ascertained contingent fact which determines the lifting of the advantages of Section 3. On the contrary, there is interposed between the will of Congress and the consummation of the act of imposing a duty a will that is not the legislature's but that of the President. If there had been a rule laid down in the Act sufficiently definite to guide the Executive in arriving at reciprocal inequality or unreasonableness, then the strict and loose constructionists might have approached nearer each other. When, however, the President, always with the American free-entry in mind, must determine whether duties or other exactions imposed upon the whole or a sufficiently large part of imported American products is equivalent to inequality and unreasonableness, he has a field where guesses are permissible and politics possible. Into the determination of this field the Court could not or would not enter.[1] The dicta in the case indi-

[1] Mr. Marion De Vries, one time Judge of the Court of Customs Appeals, in a brief supporting the tariff bill of 1922, attempts to reduce the general formula to a workable rule: "The delegation of authority here upheld is 'that the facts, conditions of trade, or state of things,' by comparison of which the President was to determine 'reciprocal equality and reasonableness,' were the effects upon our trade of the tariff laws, not only of the United States but of foreign countries. ..Congress made both the dutiable rates levied and the free-entry pro-

cate that where experience has shown the necessity and wisdom of contingent legislation on the part of the executive branch of government, the judicial rule of "no-delegation" will be tempered, especially in international matters.[1]

XI

The Field *v.* Clark decision was made some five months before the Act of July 26, 1892,[2] known as the Saint Marys Falls Canal Toll Act, was passed. The purpose of this Act seems to have been that of forcing from Canada certain reciprocal advantages. Under its terms whenever the President "shall be satisfied" that any United States commerce passing through the Canadian-controlled parts of the Great-Lakes-to-the-sea system "is prohibited or is made difficult or burdensome by the imposition of tolls or otherwise, which, in view of free passage through the Saint Marys Falls Canal, now permitted [the commerce of all nations],

visions therein provided effective, subject to a finding and proclamation by the President as to the competitive conditions in trade to be by him ascertained and proclaimed, not only in the markets of the United States but also in the markets of foreign countries." *Cong. Rec.*, vol. 62, 67th Cong., 2nd Sess., pp. 12198-99.

[1] Dissenting opinion of Mr. Justice Lamar, concurred in by Mr. Chief Justice Fuller, 143 U. S. at page 697: "Sec. 3 deputes to the President the power to suspend another section in the same Act whenever 'he may deem the action of any foreign nation . . . to be reciprocally unequal and unreasonable'; it further deputes to him the power to continue that suspension and to impose revenue duties on the articles named 'for such time as he may deem just'. This certainly extends to the Executive the exercise of those discretionary powers which the Constitution has vested in the law-making department."

[2] 27 Stat. 267, Ch. 248, Sec. 1. Had the Conservative party got control of the Canadian government (1925) and put an embargo on pulpwood, as was suggested by the *New York Times*, July 26, 1925, Sec. 1, p. 1, what power would have been placed in the hands of the Executive with reference to U. S. coal or other essential products from this side of the boundary line? The 1887 and 1892 idea would be likely to have been put into effect.

he shall deem to be reciprocally unjust and unreasonable, he shall have power, and it shall be his duty, to suspend, by proclamation to that effect, for such time and to such extent [even to prohibition] as he shall deem just, the right of free passage to" Canadian commerce. The maximum rate per ton and per person is named in the law; but the President has the rate-making power within that maximum. Again, Congress did not choose to prohibit or suspend outright the passage of a foreign state's commerce through navigable waters of the United States. The usual plan is employed of putting a club in the Chief Executive's hand for bringing about satisfactory terms. The ascertainment of any fact or condition that might amount to prohibition or to a burden upon American commerce, measured in the light of proffered free passage, would by law immediately shut off free passage. The rather narrow field of traffic limits the extent of the executive discretion in comparison with that granted in the terms of the Tariff Act of 1890; but, within the limits of the grant, the rule is broad enough to allow any necessary play before the mandatory words of the statute take effect. This law further strengthens the arm of the President in that he is given supplementary rule-making power of determining the amount of retaliation. A levy of one-tenth of the maximum rate allowed [1] succeeded in bringing Canada to terms within a short time.[2] If rate-making within the maximum is considered the same as an absolute rate there is no difference between the penalty that falls as a result of executive discretion and the additional and specified tariff applied to certain goods, the legality of which was dealt with in Field *v.* Clark. But the power to make a rate within a rate, on the same principle as the naming of a reasonable rate, is supplementary legislation.

[1] 27 Stat. 1032.

[2] 27 Stat. 1065.

XII

Support was again sought in the Field *v.* Clark decision when the Republican Party took upon itself the task of revising the tariff in 1897. High protection and a slight lowering thereof for the sake of reciprocal foreign trade made necessary the incorporation of a great deal of contingent legislation. The aggressiveness of the new Administration in extending the country's foreign commerce called for a further consideration of the scheme used in Section 3 of the Tariff Act of 1890. While the Tariff Act of 1897 [1] was going through the initial legislative process, its sponsors stated that although the 1890 section had been restored in almost every detail, an additional provision had been incorporated for its enlargement. Senator Aldrich insisted that even greater power should be given the President in carrying out the principle of reciprocity.[2] Section 3 of the 1897 Act [3] contained the old provision which was inserted by the House, the constitutionality of which could not be successfully questioned. The House also included in Section 3 the following variation: for the "purpose of equalizing the trade of the United States with foreign countries . . . producing and exporting" certain specifically-named articles, the President is authorized at once to begin negotiations with such governments "with a view to the arrangement of commercial agreements in which reciprocal and equivalent concessions may be secured" in favor of United States goods, and when he has made what he judges to be such agreements, he is "empowered to suspend" during their life the duties named in the Act and to put into effect a specifically named lower

[1] 30 Stat. 151, Ch. 11.

[2] *Cong. Rec.*, 55th Cong., 1st Sess., pp. 123, 133, 1233. Mr. Dingley's and Mr. Hopkins' statements are found here also.

[3] Put into effect by the Chief Executive as evidenced by proclamations; e. g., 31 Stat. 1974, 1979; 34 Stat. 3231; 35 Stat. 2140, 2178, part 2.

rate. Instead of the President's deciding that, in view of this or that highly complicated condition, a nation has no right to import duty-free, he is authorized to go out among the commercial nations of the world deliberately to make the terms of a trade contract by using his discretionary power as to whether or not he has properly "butted advantages" with the rival nation. In the alternate duty schedules lies his power of bargaining.

The Senate amended the House extension of the old 1890 Section 3 by striking out the content and substituting therefor what finally became Section 4. The discussion of this Section is of value here only in getting the viewpoints of the Senate in debate. It provided that the President, by and with the advice and consent of the Senate within a period of two years, shall enter into commercial treaties with foreign states concerning the importation of American goods into such states, deemed by him to be advantageous, in consideration of a reduction for a maximum of five years of the duties imposed by the Act up to 20 per cent thereof upon specified articles, or the transfer of such goods from the dutiable to the free list, or the retention on the free list for a period not exceeding five years. When a treaty thus negotiated has been ratified by the Senate and approved by Congress, and proclamation has been made thereof,[1] its terms are to become operative. Senator Vest challenged the first draft of this Section for the reason that it delegated the entire treaty-making power to the President. Senator Allison admitted that the original draft had not included the "by and with the advice and consent of the Senate" phrase but informed the challenger that it had later been inserted.[2] After the further question had been raised as to whether the treaty-making agents could, under terms of the Constitution,

[1] 30 Stat. 1774; 33 Stat. 2136.

[2] *Cong. Rec.*, 55th Cong., 1st Session., p. 2227.

legislate on matters financial, Senator Hoar promptly denied that the President and the Senate in so acting were legislating. He asked, " Is not this simply an enactment by the national legislature that whenever a certain treaty shall have been made, a certain law shall take effect and be in force? " [1] This, of course, is simply another twist given to the use of the principle of delegated legislation. Senator Morgan, a strict constructionist, made the following observation:

> If the President, acting alone, could lawfully pass upon the conditious of foreign commerce, as he was authorized to do under the act of 1890, and could form a judgment thereupon, whereupon the act of taxing the various articles could be suspended absolutely, and if in so doing that he did not repeal that statute, if in doing that he did not legislate at all, I cannot understand why the President and the Senate, in the exercise of the treaty-making power, may not put this upon the same footing by an agreement between two countries, and why the act of Congress, if now passed, would not operate in advance to ratify and confirm a treaty and make it fully applicable to the subject. . . . The Senate serves as an extra guard.[2]

Despite this reliance upon the Field *v.* Clark decision, the " no-delegation " adherents replied that it would be legal to say, " When sugar reaches a certain price per pound, there shall be a duty of one cent or two cents per pound, but that is a contingency which the law provides for and anticipates and determines what shall be done when it is reached ". The submission of a contingent fact or status to the executive mind, revised by the senatorial mind, cannot be done because the law-making authority knows nothing about what will be the executive mind or the senatorial mind.[3] Senator

[1] *Cong. Rec.*, 55th Cong., 1st Session, p. 2228.

[2] *Ibid.*, pp. 2231-32.

[3] *Ibid.*, p. 2235.

Morgan dropped out of the discussion with the statement that laws with broad legislative functions delegated to the Executive are common, that the Judiciary has pronounced them good, and that it is the Executive's duty to exhaust his resources under them in promoting the welfare of the people of the United States. Partly as a result of the incisive remarks against the extent to which the subrogation of legislative functions had been carried, and partly as a result of the jealousy of the House, not only were the three plans retained in the final conference report but a complete check was added to Section 4, that of giving Congress the final word upon all treaties made.

XIII

President Taft, in his Second Annual Message, December 6, 1910,[1] praised highly the Payne-Aldrich Tariff of 1909[2] for its adjustability, especially the provisions found in Section 2. A minimum schedule of dutiable articles was given in Section 1. Section 2 added 25 per cent *ad valorem* to the minimum schedule, beginning April 1, 1910, thereby setting up a maximum rate. There was a proviso to the effect that "whenever, after March 31, 1910, and so long thereafter as the President shall be satisfied, in view of concessions granted by the minimum rate", that no other state imposes any "terms or restrictions, either in the way of tariff rates . . . trade or other regulations, charges, exactions, or in any other manner, directly or indirectly upon importation into or the sale in such foreign country" of any United States goods, "which unduly discriminate against the United States or the products thereof, and that such foreign country pays no export bounty or imposes no export or prohibition upon the exportation of any article to the United States which

[1] Richardson, *Messages and Papers of the Presidents*, pp. 7492, 7501.

[2] 36 Stat. 11, Ch. 6, part 1.

unduly discriminates against the United States or the products thereof, and that such foreign country accords to the goods of the United States "treatment which is reciprocal and equivalent", the President is authorized to proclaim such facts, thereby putting the minimum tariff into effect as regards that particular country or law-making subdivision thereof. In summarizing this provision Mr. Rainey of Illinois said that the President is authorized to employ as many persons as might be required to secure information to be used by him in "determining whether after March 31, 1910, the average tariff imposed against any one country or against all countries shall be 45.87 per cent *ad valorem* or 70.87 per cent *ad valorem*".[1]

No claim was made that the Executive could, under the Constitution, create the original Act. The evidence in this case, however, shows that under the Act no change in the tariff schedule can be made without the President's going through the same process that Congress itself would go through in reducing the duty on imports from a foreign country, i. e., he must accumulate as many or as few facts as he cares to[2] and decide whether, in view of the general com-

[1] *Cong. Rec.*, 61st Cong., 1st Sess., Appendix, p. 133.

[2] By the Act of March 4, 1911 (36 Stat. 1363, Ch. 285), an ill-defined Tariff Board was created, a part of the duties of which was to ascertain the facts necessary to aid the President in acting under Sec. 2. By the Act of Sept. 8, 1916 (39 Stat. 795, Ch. 463, title VII), a well organized Tariff Commission was created. The board idea which had been introduced more than once before this period, resulted in a temporary fact-finding Tariff Commission in 1882 created to aid in supplying information for the making of the Tariff of 1883 (22 Stat. 64, Ch. 145). During the discussion of the 1909 tariff bill, Senator Newlands (see *Cong. Rec.*, 61st Cong., 1st Sess., p. 4842) went so far to suggest that such an agency should regulate the tariff in a scientific manner, using as a guide in this instance the Republican rule of "equalization of costs of production at home and abroad, plus a reasonable profit". President Taft, in a letter to the Committee on Ways and Means of the House, 1909,

mercial policy of the United States, it would be best to apply the minimum rate in the case of a particular country. This is nothing more or less than the deciding upon, and putting into effect of, a particular part of that general policy which Congress does not feel competent to lay down in the law. The statute does not prescribe that if a certain foreign government's tariff on an American article is not 1 per cent higher than that upon a similar article from another state, or that if no specifically named trade or other regulation or no denominated charge, exaction, or other hindrance is imposed upon such an article that is greater by a definite measure than that imposed upon a similar article of another state, the President shall apply the minimum rate. The prescription is that the Chief Executive, in his discretion, may compare and admeasure with the minimum rate of the United States the named and unnamed impositions and determine therefrom whether the treatment is reciprocally equivalent. If he finds it to be so, he may bring the reduced schedule into operation. The formula by which the contingent fact is to be calculated varies so widely from the mathematical that it amounts to nothing more than " whatever the President thinks ". Since Congress cannot anticipate the mental conclusion of a person or of a group of persons it is unable to make such an unknown thing a definite contingent fact upon which an alternative provision of a law shall go into effect. To attempt to do so is to delegate the legislative function.

said he " would be the last to advocate a commission with any power to fix rates, if that were constitutional, *as it would not be*, or with any function other than that of furnishing evidence" (Quoted from a speech by O. G. Foelker, *Cong. Rec.*, 61st Cong., 1st Sess., Appendix, p. 27). Why permit the President to exercise a similar power? Is it a matter of degree? See T. W. Page, *Making the Tariff in the United States*, Chs. ii and iii (1924), for criticisms by a man who has been chairman of the Tariff Commission.

Although the debates and " speeches by leave " give little evidence of doubt as to the constitutionality of Section 2 of the 1909 tariff, all members of Congress seemed to sense the great power placed in the hands of the Chief Executive. Mr. McGuire, in comparing this section with the similar one in the Dingley Tariff Act, said, " The universal rule in every revenue and taxation system, whether through statutes or constitutions, is that the principle should be maximum instead of minimum in the limitations on administrative power to levy taxes ".[1] Mr. Lowden became dissatisfied with certain amendments to the original bill on the ground that their adoption would " make the maximum and minimum provisions absolutely automatic, so as to dispense with the intervention of the executive department in any way ". His hope was that the Committee on Ways and Means would realize the impossibility of having such an automatic arrangement in place of negotiation by the Executive. He preferred that some way be found for authorizing the President to put any or all of the maximum duties into effect, unless equivalent concessions should be granted to the United States by countries enjoying the minimum rates of the Act. But in weighing the comments of authorities, he was not persuaded that the Field *v.* Clark case, the chief basis for hope, would permit such an arrangement.[2] Mr. Rainey thought the Act opened up an interesting legal question which would " in all probability be tested in the courts soon after March 31, 1910 ", because some of the protected interests would bring up the question as to the President's right to reduce the tariff 25 per cent.[3] Senator Daniel, quoting from an article in the *Washington Herald* of July 31, 1909, said that such power given to the President was further evidence that this country

[1] *Cong. Rec.*, 61st Cong., 1st Sess., p. 1049.

[2] *Ibid.*, p. 1285.

[3] *Ibid.*, Appendix, p. 133.

had the most centralized government in the world; that the United States had arrived at that stage in its evolution where the executive department expected to make the laws, thereby usurping the functions of the legislature; and that the Constitution has now become a book, laid away on the table, about which the directors of the government gather now and then.[1] For the most part, the criticism of Section 2 was not legal but political. There was sufficient criticism from both parties, however, to show that strict construction was still holding out against liberal construction in matters pertaining to the " no-delegation " rule of law—although the latter still had the advantage.[2]

XIV

Reciprocity clauses found in Section 3 of the Tariff Act of 1890, Sections 3 and 4 in the Tariff Act of 1897, and Section 2 of the Tariff Act of 1909, were succeeded in the Tariff Act of 1913[3] by Section 4, Paragraph A. The competitive tariff of the Democrats was one under which domestic and foreign producers could compete in such a way that both could get a reasonable profit.[4] It would supposedly have a larger duty-free list and a lower dutiable schedule than a Republican tariff calling for equality of production and a reasonable profit to the domestic producers. Constant watch and instant action were, perhaps, not necessary under

[1] *Cong. Rec.*, 61st Cong., 1st Sess., p. 4782.

[2] Vol. 36, pt. 2, *Stat. at L.*, gives 150 or more proclamations applying the minimum schedule under Sec. 2, while those found on pp. 2524 and 2600 serve as specific examples. President Taft's Second Annual Message, *Messages and Papers of the Presidents*, p. 7492, discusses such proclamations. Departmental Order (Treas. Dec. 30484) announces that the President has given the minimum tariff universal application, stating that any territory not covered by proclamation by inadvertance will be so covered.

[3] 38 Stat. 114, Ch. 16.

[4] Taussig, *Tariff History of the United States*, 7th ed., p. 419.

the former rule. At any rate, Section 4, Paragraph A, did not embody the rapidity of action that was called for under the preceding laws. It appears, although anything approaching a national emergency might prove otherwise, to have had a greater respect for the doctrine of the separation of powers. To adjust present duties and to encourage foreign commerce, the President was authorized to negotiate trade agreements looking toward freer trade relations and further reciprocal expansion of commerce, provided that such "trade agreements before becoming operative shall be submitted to Congress for ratification or rejection". The national legislature temporarily resumed important legislative functions previously delegated to the Executive and adopted in its most extreme form the theory put forth by Mr. Key and elaborated upon by Senator Evarts.[1]

XV

Before three years had passed, the leaders of the Democratic Party had apparently forgotten all about the necessity of referring all executive acts of a legislative character to Congress for its formal approval.[2] The Revenue Act of 1916 provided " . . . whenever during the existence of war in which the United States is not engaged, the President shall be satisfied that there is reasonable ground to believe that any state or sub-division thereof is preventing or re-

[1] See division viii, *supra*; also, Tariff Act of 1913, par. 631, as to the changing of tin from the free to the dutiable list.

[2] Even in the Tariff of 1913, Sec. 4, par. E., the bounty provisions of Sec. 5 of the Tariff of 1897 and of Sec. 6 of the Tariff of 1909 are reproduced, giving the Secretary of the Treasury power to search out any form of bounty given by foreign states upon dutiable articles exported to the United States and to add the amount of such bounty to the established duty, thereby increasing the duty according to a measure more or less difficult to ascertain but which can usually be found somewhere in law. This power was approved in Nichols and Co. *v.* U. S., 7 Ct. Cust. Appls. 97, 106 (1916).

stricting the importation of United States products contrary to the law and practice of nations, " he is authorized to prohibit or restrict the importation into the United States of " . . . similar or other products of such country as in his opinion the public interest may require ".[1] After proclamation has been issued naming the article or articles prohibited or restricted, any attempt to import goods contrary thereto was to be heavily punished. The President might change, modify, or revoke such proclamation " in his discretion ". The United States was once more a neutral in a world of conflict, with a decided drift toward belligerency. The revival of such complete discretionary power of the Chief Executive corresponds to the facts of American history, viz., where there is a crisis or near crisis, where there is a strong demand for instant action, the executive department immediately is thrust to the forefront equipped not only with its own constitutional powers but also with a sufficiency of delegated legislative power. Evidently the fear of an American executive, regardless of his " double dose of original sin ", is not so impelling as the fear of foreign governments.

This provision was not discussed as to its constitutionality, everyone apparently taking it for granted that the power conferred had ample authority in law and practice. Senator Simmons accepted the provision in the Finance Committee and Senator Underwood remarked that he would support it for the reason that it would be of " great value in protecting shipments of tobacco into neutral countries against the discriminations now being made against it by the warring countries of Europe ". In other words, the delegation was supported by all parties in Congress on its merits.[2] All this, however, does not alter the fact that the

[1] 39 Stat. 799, title viii, Sec. 805.

[2] *Cong. Rec.*, 64th Cong., 1st Sess., pp. 13485-86.

President was given practically complete discretionary control over a large volume of commerce.

XVI

The anti-dumping provision of the Emergency Tariff Act of 1921 [1] illustrates the trend of commercial legislation after the World War. It reads as follows: Whenever the Secretary of the Treasury, " after such investigations as he deems necessary, finds that an industry in the United States is being or is likely to be injured, or is prevented from being established ", by reason of the sale of imported goods below fair value, he shall then make such information public to the extent that he thinks necessary, together with a description of such goods for guidance of the appraising officers. Section 202 levied an additional duty equal to the difference between the purchase price and the greater export value, as determined by the appraisers. In 1922 the Secretary of the Treasury announced nine such decisions against Canadian goods, six against English goods, three against imports from Czechoslovakia, two against Italian merchandise, and one each against Swiss and German articles.[2] The Secretary had here sufficient discretion as to investigations, publicity and range and condition of industries to aid, injure or destroy industries born and unborn. To the appraisers was delegated the actual rate finding; yet the whole process was dependent upon the discretion of their chief. Although this officer was entrusted with conditional tariff legislation earlier in history,[3] by this Act duties comparable to those of the President were temporarily thrust upon him.[4]

[1] 42 Stat. 11, Ch. 14, Secs. 201 and 202.

[2] E. g., Treas. Dec. 39177, Treas. Dec. 39360, Treas. Dec. 39294, Treas. Dec. 39208, Treas. Dec. 39025.

[3] 4 Stat. 578, Ch. 207 (1832).

[4] Jacob Viner, *Dumping: A Problem in International Trade* (1923), pp. 258 *et seq.*, emphasizes this aspect of administrative power in the 1922 Act.

XVII

The stimulation given by the World War to the hope of the United States becoming the commercial center of the world, the desire to retain the receding advantages gained during the decade preceding 1922 and the domestic ills consequent upon the instability of post-war economics—all seemed to call on the new Administration for a hardy tariff as a panacea and a guarantee of national ambition. In such a tariff the nation as a whole or in sections—at times regardless of party lines—placed its confidence. The Underwood Tariff of 1913, partially scrapped before September, 1922,[1] was almost completely set aside by the Fordney-McCumber Tariff of 1922.[2] Certain it is that the hobbled section of the 1913 Act requiring the approval of Congress for all commercial agreements made by the President was relegated to the Democratic hope chest, and the pertinent portions of the protective laws of 1890, 1897 and 1909 were restored in superlative degree. Senator McCumber, who was aware of the extent of the power conferred upon the Executive, voiced both fear and confidence in the wisdom of going so far, when he remarked: " . . . the exigencies of the chaotic condition that now confronts us in the commercial world are thorough justification for the added power that is given the President, and I want it taken away just as soon as those exigencies no longer exist." [3]

In reading the Tariff Act of 1922 one recognizes that Sections 315, 316, 317 and perhaps to a less extent Section 303 make up the very core of the policy of Congress and the President. Each has its own historical background. Countervailing duties on imports of bounty-fed commodi-

[1] Emergency Tariff Act, May 27, 1921, 42 Stat. 11.

[2] 42 Stat. 858, Ch. 356.

[3] *Cong. Rec.*, 67th Cong., 2nd Sess., p. 11155.

ties, unfair methods of competition and unfair acts in importation, foreign discriminations against American commerce, the principle of the equalization of the cost of production at home and abroad are all represented in these provisions Constituting the so-called Harding flexible tariff they are thus referred to in one of his letters:

In a time when wide differences in producing costs and a well-nigh universal tendency to erect barriers against international trade were menacing our commerce and industry, we have passed tariff legislation which first protects our own producers, and second, *through its provisions for administrative adjustment of duties to changing conditions,* makes it possible, to adapt them to shifting economic relations and enables us to encourage foreign trade.[2]

The United States Tariff Commission, in its report to Congress December 4, 1918, presented an analysis of the experience of this country with reciprocity treaties and with such bargaining features as were found in previous tariff laws. In addition to the recommendation that a commercial policy should be adopted, based upon the principle of equality of treatment, it was urged that the successful accomplishment of such a policy could, in the light of past experience, be brought about best "by leaving the actual imposition of additional duties to the discretion of the President, who

[1] Quoted from W. McClure, *A New American Commercial Policy,* pp 59-60 (italics are the author's). President Harding, in the Address by the President of the United States to Congress, Dec. 6, 1921, p. 7, foreshadows administrative control in these words: "I know of no manner in which to effect this flexibility other than (sic) the extension of the powers of the Tariff Commission..." The Senate Report (No. 595, 67th Cong., 2nd Sess.) on the tariff bill refers (p. 3) specifically to the President's speech as the suggestion that influenced the Finance Committee greatly in inserting the elastic provisions. He was encouraged in this attitude by the Tariff Commission, especially by Vice Chairman Culbertson, as shown by *Sixth Annual Report of the Tariff Commission* (1922), and W. McClure, *op. cit.,* pp. 53.

[should] act always in conformity with a stated general principle and subject to general limitations defined by statute ".[1]

XVIII

Section 316 of the Tariff Act of 1922 incorporated the above recommendation. All unfair methods of competition and unfair acts in the importation of articles into this country or their sale by the owner, importer, consignee, or agent of one of them are declared unlawful if their effect or tendency is to destroy or to injure seriously an efficiently operated industry, to prevent the setting up of such an industry, or to restrain or monopolize United States trade and commerce. It is plainly an attempt " to inject into international relations the principles upon which the Federal Trade Commission works for fairness and decency in domestic business ".[2] Instruction is given to the Tariff Commission to investigate any alleged violation of this provision. If supported by evidence the findings are final although appeal may be made to the Court of Customs Appeals on questions of law, the decisions of such Court to go to the Supreme Court for review only upon *certiorari*.[3] The findings of the Commission, with the full record of proceedings, are to be sent to the President. If he himself is satisfied that unfair methods or acts have been employed, he is directed to levy upon the imported articles in question additional duties sufficient to offset the effect of the unfair

[1] *Sixth Annual Report of the Tariff Commission* (1922), pp. 4, 5.

[2] McClure, *A New American Commercial Policy*, p. 57.

[3] The facts in the case involving the simulation of Smith and Wesson revolvers has been interpreted as involving " unfair methods " and no appeal has been passed over. Hence, the Commission and the President determine what is an unfair method although only an *ad interim* order of exclusion has been issued to date (April, 1926). See letter of Secretary of Tariff Commission to the writer, dated March 25, 1926.

practice—not less, however, than ten, nor more than fifty, per cent of their value as determined for the purpose of assessing ordinary duties. Where, in his opinion, extreme cases of unfair acts have been established by the investigation, he shall direct that such articles as he considers the interests of the country require shall be excluded from entry into the United States.

The great measure of discretion allowed the President, contingent upon the formation of a judgment concerning a huge mass of facts as to the penalties to be imposed, naturally raises the constitutional question as to whether or not Congress can delegate so much power. The penalty itself is the levying of a tax, within established maximum-minimum limits—an act purely legislative in character. What mathematical rule has the Tariff Commission discovered for ascertaining the exact tax which would offset any unfair method or act? What still more perfect formula has the President available for arriving at the balancing duty? What is an unfair act? Furthermore, what are the extreme cases in which the Executive may prohibit absolutely the importation of the commodities in question? This one Section might well bring about the exclusion of articles with which industrious protectionists would not care to compete under any conditions.[1]

Dr. W. S. Culbertson, then Vice Chairman of the Tariff Commission, made the following interesting remark relative to this provision:

> Under this section additional duties may be imposed upon importations by any individual engaging in unfair price cutting,

[1] For a discussion of this provision and the comment of Senator Walsh of Montana, see Jacob Viner, *Dumping: A Problem in International Trade* (1923), pp. 246-254, and note 1, p. 250. See also Senate debates on its constitutionality, *Cong. Rec.*, Vol. 62, 67th Cong., 2nd Sess., pp. 5874 and 6493 *et seq.*

full-line forcing, commercial bribery, or any other type of unfair competition, and if the unfair competition is of an aggravated character, the offending person may be prohibited from importing goods into the United States. *This is admittedly a difficult field, but it must be evident that in some such flexible provision as this lies the only hope of an effective portection of American industry against the variety and subtlety of the attacks which may be included under the term unfair competition.*[1]

XIX

Section 303 of the Fordney-McCumber Tariff Act, imposing countervailing duties on imports of bounty-fed commodities, goes further than the clause of previous tariff laws dealing with the same subject.[2] By the insertion of a dozen words the old clause makes the penalties apply not only to those persons who import goods from countries which grant export bounties thereon but also to those who import goods from countries wherein production or export bounties are granted by any " person, partnership, association, cartel, or corporation ". The effect of these additions is to give the Secretary of the Treasury power to add countervailing duties to commodities fed unofficially by

[1] Address made before the American Manufacturers Export Association, delivered Oct. 26, 1922, and taken from McClure, *A New American Commercial Policy*, pp. 53-54 (italics are the author's). Since the passage of the Act of 1922, the Commission has reported to the President the following:

(a) Revolvers simulating revolvers of the manufacture of Smith and Wesson.

(b) Sanitary Napkins simulating Sanitary napkins manufactured and sold under the name " Kotex ".

Although the President has taken no action, a temporary order of the Treasury is now excluding revolvers under (a) and will hold them until the President acts (letter to writer from Executive Secretary of the U. S. Tariff Commission, dated March 25, 1926).

[2] See Viner, *op. cit.*, pp. 268-272.

bounties regardless of whether the exporter has absorbed such bounties or whether there results from them an injury to the domestic industry of the United States. Section 303 dovetails with Section 316 in such a way that a double penalty might be imposed upon the importer for dumping goods upon which he has received an official or unofficial export bounty—one penalty because the goods have been sold to American purchasers at a price lower than the foreign home price and another because the importer has received a bounty on such goods.[1]

While the language of Section 303 is couched in different form the power of the Secretary of the Treasury is exercised under the contingency of finding certain conditions to exist, viz., whether or not an official or unofficial bounty has been given. The former type, to be sure, involves less discretion than the latter. The extension of the Secretary's power, it seems, lies in the unofficial bounty. The departmental decisions, as well as those of the Judiciary, have consistently held that countervailing duties are applicable to " imports of goods from countries in which bounties are granted that kind or class of goods, whether or not the particular shipment has received such a bounty ".[2] Unless the Court of Customs Appeals plays a prominent rôle, the Treasury will have a difficult task in determining the appropriate penal duty in unofficial bounty cases. It has been suggested that there might be, for example, ten producers of the same class or kind of imported goods in the exporting country, nine of whom grant bounties varying in amount from producer to producer, the tenth granting no export bounties at all. How will the Secretary apply the rule as stated above? Suppose the tenth producer to be the only offending party? How will the department arrive at the total of " a cumulative

[1] See Viner, *op. cit.*, p. 270.

[2] *Ibid.*

bounty increasing at every stage of the productive process, and subject to complex and frequently revised adjustments at each stage"? There is nothing in the Act which prescribes that the bounty paid on exports to this country shall be taken as the basis for assessment of the countervailing duty.[1]

XX

Section 317 of the present tariff law (the Act of 1922) delegates to the Chief Executive ample power for meeting discriminations of foreign states, or subdivisions thereof, against the commerce of the United States. It follows, in a general way, the scheme set forth in the maximum-minimum provision of the Tariff Act of 1909 (Section 2) which had as its purpose the securing of equality of treatment for American foreign commerce. The Tariff Com-

[1] Quotations from Viner, *op. cit.*, pp. 271-272. Thus far, the Treasury has had no serious difficulty in administering Section 303. Official documents of the offending state seem to have been furnished to the Department of State by the Treasury which also gives the proper order to the customs officials. The following is a statement from a letter of the Assistant Director of Customs to the writer, dated April 3, 1926, giving all actions taken since 1922:

> I enclose herewith... copies of Treasury Decisions 39541, 39789, 39812 and 40001, relative to countervailing duties on certain articles [sugar content of certain articles and fencing wire, traction engines, wire netting, etc.] from Australia. The Collectors of Customs have also been instructed to suspend the liquidation of entries covering coal exported from Spain, slaughtered cattle and beef exported from the Union of South Africa, and live stock exported from the mandate territory of Southwest Africa. No importations of such merchandise from Spain or Africa have, however, been brought to the attention of the Department and no countervailing duty has been assessed thereon.

Mention of the Treasury's order tentatively putting into effect this Section against Tata Iron and Steel Company, Bombay, India, April, 1926, is made in the *New York Times*, May 21, 1926; a copy of the Treasury's order against the Raw Steel Syndicate of Dusseldorf, Germany, is also found in the same issue of the *New York Times*.

mission considered the new provision more flexible and adaptable to changing conditions than that of 1909.[1] The President, bound only by the general legislative policy that the country's foreign trade must have equality of treatment, has the task of removing or warding off anything that tends toward unequal commercial treatment. Discriminations of practically all varieties are anticipated in a directive manner. Unreasonable burdens, not suffered by all nations alike, upon United States products in the process of disposition in, transportation through, or re-exportation from the territory of the offending state are to be penalized; discriminations through law, administration or practice in import, export or other duties, regulations or restrictions are to be fought if they place the United States at a disadvantage commercially as compared with other foreign countries. Subdivision (e) of this Section gives the Executive similar power over products of a third country, provided it can be shown that such country has benefited from discriminating acts practiced by any country against the United States.

Whenever the President finds burdens actually being imposed upon American products, he shall, when he believes " the public interests will be served thereby ", issue a proclamation effective within thirty days, levying such new or additional rate or rates of duty " as he shall determine will offset such burdens, not to exceed 50 per centum *ad valorem* or its equivalent ". The additional levy applies also to countries profiting from such discriminations. If this process is not effectual, the President is " authorized, if he deems it consistent with the interests of the United States ", to proclaim absolute prohibitions against any or all articles of the offending state. The penalty for violating such a prohibitive order is the same as that which is used in smuggling, i. e., the confiscation of the goods brought in. Any procla-

[1] *Sixth Annual Report of the Tariff Commission*, pp. 5, 6.

mation issued by the President may, if he " deems public interests require ", be suspended, supplemented, amended, or revoked. To be sure the Chief Executive cannot administer the details of this Section. Subdivision 9 makes it the duty of the Tariff Commission " to ascertain and at all times to be informed whether any of the discriminations against the United States are practiced by any country ". If any such acts are disclosed the Commission must " bring the matter to the attention of the President, together with recommendations ".

The scope of executive discretion is limited only by such general terms in Section 317 as when " public interest " will be served, when " any unreasonable limitation " shall be made, when new or additional rates of duty are to be levied " which will offset such burdens ", when the additional rates or exclusion orders are limited as to products affected by the " article enumerated in such proclamation ". When generalities like these abound in a law the administration thereof is entirely within the discretion of the Executive. The President has the final authority to name the act that discriminates against this country's commerce. Those who are familiar with the intricacies of international higgling in the market through maximum-minimum tariff-rate systems, through special treaties that are exceptions to general rate schemes, through rates levied on the process of manufacture, through general laws that really hit specifically an important product of one country and through many other indirect methods can see no end to executive discretion as to what will be considered a discrimination. Surely this means that there is actually little limitation to his authority under this law.[1] Furthermore, there is no limitation as to the number

[1] See W. McClure, *op. cit.*, pp. 30-42, for the possibilities; see also Senator Smoot's speech, *Cong. Rec.*, Vol. 62, 67th Cong., 2nd Sess., p. 5879. The Executive Secretary of the U. S. Tariff Commission, in a

and kinds of articles that may be penalized by additional duties, if the President is once satisfied that there has been discrimination as to one article. This power, of course, extends to both free and dutiable articles. A 50 per cent additional duty on a high-tariff commodity would be likely to result in the prohibition of many products from an offending country or from a third state that had profited by such offense against the United States. Defensive tariffs so levied are likely to arouse vengeance rather than to beget obedience. This would bring the prohibition power into play. The refrain that runs throughout the Section and lulls the believer therein to peaceful slumber is " the public interest will be subserved, whatever action the President takes ". Indeed, it is discretionary with him whether or not he will apply a penalty after a discrimination has been proved. It is, moreover, doubtful whether the President's advisory commission is other than a partisan body.[1]

XXI

Section 315 of the Tariff Act of 1922 provides, in brief, that when the President shall ascertain by investigation that any duty named in the Act does not equalize the difference between foreign and domestic costs of producing the article on which it is levied, it is his duty to see that this equalization be brought about. After the difference has been found

letter to the writer dated March 25, 1926, makes this statement: "Reports by the Tariff Commission to the President under provisions of Section 317 have been submitted in confidence and have not been made public."

[1] See progress of Senate Investigation of Tariff Commission by a special committee, in the *New York Times*, March 24, 25, 26, and April 1, 1926. For the Senate debate on the constitutionality of this section, see *Cong. Rec.*, Vol. 62, 67th Cong., 2nd Sess., pp. 5874 and 6493 *et seq.* Senator McCumber willingly said he thought that in Section 317 Congress was "pressing closer to the 'twilight zone' of uncertainty as to the constitutionality of the provision" than in any other section of the Act. McClure, *op. cit.*, p. 81.

the adjustment can be made by the Executive in one of three ways: the classification of the article may be changed so as to make it dutiable under a different rate; the rate named in the law may be changed; or the basis of assessing the rate of duty may be changed from the foreign value to that in the American market. In the first and second cases the change is limited to a maximum increase or decrease of 50 per cent of the rate specified in the Act. The third possibility is brought into play when it is impossible to make the adjustment by the other methods. The change from the foreign to the domestic selling-price value is presumed to cover sufficiently the increase necessary although a decrease of 50 per cent of the specified rate may be made.[1]

Subdivision (c) of this Section purports to give directions to the President in ascertaining differences in costs of production at home and abroad. He shall, "in so far as he finds it practicable", take into consideration differences in conditions of production and in wholesale selling prices in American markets, advantages granted the producer by his government or by private authorities, and "any other advantages or disadvantages in competition". So general are these directions that the Tariff Commission considers them as merely supplementary to any inquiry into the differences in costs of production, since the "statutory issue remains the same, viz., the differences between foreign and domestic production costs".[2] In a later report[3] the Commission said, "Only by the accumulated precedents of cases can the exact effect of subdivision (c) . . . upon the interpretation of the laws be determined." The same body, since its members could not agree upon the congressional intent,[4] in its

[1] American selling price is defined in Sec. 402, subdivision (f).

[2] *Seventh Annual Report of the Tariff Commission* (1923), pp. 32, 33.

[3] *Eighth Annual Report of the Tariff Commission* (1924), p. 8.

[4] *Ninth Annual Report of the Tariff Commission* (1925), p. 17.

1925 report, appealed to Congress to direct more specifically what course was to be adopted in executing the various provisions of subdivision (c). The Executive cannot make any proclamation of change until the Tariff Commission has made an investigation and reported its findings. Changes in classification and specific rates are effective after thirty days' notice; changes resulting from switching to the domestic valuation become enforceable fifteen days after proclamation.

In 1922 there was great dissatisfaction with the methods of tariff-making in this country. The United States Chamber of Commerce insisted that Congress should determine the general tariff policy and that an independent administrative agency should fix the tariff rates within the limits of such policy.[1] Under such a flexible scheme it would be possible, they asserted, " to maintain a consistent tariff policy under changing economic conditions ". Coupled with this idea of a " scientific tariff " was the party principle of " equalizing the cost of production at home and abroad ".[2] While the House of Representatives insisted upon the American valuation method, the Senate held to the familiar foreign valuation plan. Out of this hodgepodge of principle and method came the provisions of Section 315.[3] All parties obtained something upon which they had insisted. The tariff schedules were based upon what appeared to be the equalization of costs theory; the Chief Executive had a lee-

[1] Chamber of Commerce Referendum No. 8, pp. 3, 7, 8; *Change in Our Tariff Methods*: Publications of U. S. Chamber of Commerce, March 22, 1922, p. 8. Both are quoted from Page, *Making the Tariff in the United States*, pp. 41-47. Dr. Culbertson wishes to see the Tariff Commission a final adjuster of a scientific tariff. See *New York Times*, May 25, 1926, p. 6.

[2] Page, *op. cit.*, p. 61.

[3] See Taussig, *The Tariff History of the United States* (1925), pp. 478-480.

way of 50 per cent above and 50 per cent below specified rates; the same official could change from the Senate's foreign valuation basis [1] to the House's cherished American valuation basis, thereby transcending all of the rate limits. The Tariff Commission was to be the scientific, and therefore non-partisan, administrative agency to advise the final authority. In brief, the President was given the power, on the Commission's report, to accomplish that which Congress as a whole could not or would not effect through specific legislation.

Both the policy and the constitutionality of the delegation feature of Section 315 were the points round which discussion raged. One might infer that the attempt to create doubt regarding the power of Congress to give away any of its authority over customs duties was chiefly a method of defeating the delegation policy. The Administration leaders frankly acknowledged that the great emergency was the only excuse for entrusting the Executive with such power.[2] Despite the uneasiness of the proponents as to the legality of such a derogation, the Senate Finance Committee, citing Field *v.* Clark (143 U. S. 649), stated that the "elastic provisions [were] regarded . . . undoubtedly constitutional".[3] The Committee, however, took pains to have an elaborate brief, prepared by Mr. De Vries, formerly of the Court of Customs Appeals, read into the record supporting the elastic provisions. This brief attempted to meet at every point the cogent argument of Senator Walsh of Montana. Apparently no law, no judicial opinion and no practice was over-

[1] All standard *ad valorem* rates are based upon foreign value, Senate Report No. 595, 67th Cong., 2nd Sess., pp. 4, 5, 8.

[2] *Cf.* Senator McCumber's statement, *Cong. Rec.*, 67th Cong., 2nd Sess., p. 11155, and his committee's report, Senate Report No. 595, pt. 1, p. 3, 67th Cong., 2nd Sess.

[3] Senate Report No. 595, 67th Cong., 2nd Sess., p. 3.

looked in this document. The thesis of the brief was, in substance, that Congress had clearly set forth the policy, rule, or purpose, i. e., to equalize the costs of production at home and abroad, and had indicated what the President might do to accomplish that purpose.[1] The opponents could only insist that all rules of a directory nature were so general and the purpose so impossible of accomplishment that the administrative authority could not conceivably arrive at congressional intention or follow the methods laid down.[2]

Is it the consensus of opinion that the elastic provisions of Section 315 have accomplished the purpose for which they were established? Has experience shown the practicability of ascertaining, in a scientific way, the relative costs of production at home and abroad? Mr. W. S. Culbertson, formerly Vice Chairman of the Tariff Commission, felt in 1922 that an affirmative answer could readily be given to the first question.[3] Professor F. W. Taussig emphatically denied that any system of administration could accomplish the end in view.[4] Thomas W. Page, a member of the Tariff Commission from 1918 to 1923, is on record as saying that the use, in a general tariff act, of a thing " so fleeting, evasive, and shadowy " as the ascertainment of comparative costs of production for measuring duties is neither constitutional nor possible.[5] The pressure upon Congress for an investigation

[1] *Cong. Rec.*, Vol. 62, pt. 2, pp. 11162-11179, 67th Cong., 2nd Sess.

[2] For the constitutional debate in the Senate, see the speeches of Senators Smoot and Walsh of Montana, *Cong. Rec.*, Vol. 62, pt. 6, 67th Cong., 2nd Sess., pp. 5874 and 6493 *et seq.* It is noticeable that the minority report of the Senate Finance Committee attacked policy and did not mention constitutionality. See Senate Report No. 595, pt. 2, 67th Cong., 2nd Sess.

[3] Address before American Manufacturers Export Association, Oct. 26, 1922. Quoted from McClure, *op. cit.*, p. 58, note 2.

[4] *Tariff History of the United States* (1925), pp. 480-481.

[5] *Making of the Tariff in the United States*, p. 42, Mr. Page cites these

of the administration of Section 315 became so strong that a special Senate Committee was chosen to make inquiry.[1] Chairman Marvin testified that it was administratively impossible to ascertain the costs of production for any of the more important schedules such as steel, cotton, wool and aluminum. Hence their time was devoted to the less important schedules. He seemed, on the whole, to be dissatisfied with the results of its administration.[2]

The Commission's now famous report on sugar made in July, 1924, and the reply of the President, June, 1925, illustrate the great difficulty of carrying out the " equalization of costs " principle under the flexible provisions of Section 315. In the first place, while a majority of the members of the Commission recommended a lowering of the duty, the minority was in favor of an increase. In fact, had not one member been disqualified to sit, there would have been an equal division of the six members. Although the President, in his refusal to accept the majority recommendation, spent much effort upon party and economic justification of his action, he did strike at the vital weakness in the administration of Section 315. He stated that the divergent conclusions of the members of the Commission were " the result of different interpretations of the same basic data, approached with equal conscientiousness on both sides ". He pictured himself as the final authority for deciding what

figures on cost of producing sugar, in Cuba and Louisiana, as the estimate of the Commission:

1919-20.	6.588	cents more per lb. in La.
1920-21.	6.269	" " " " " "
1921-22.	1.806	" " " " " "
1922-23.	1.246	" " " " " "

[1] See *New York Times*, March 22, 1926, pp. 6-7. The personnel of the Committee is Wadsworth (N. Y.), Reed (Penn.), La Follette (Wis.), Robinson (Ark.), Bruce (Md.).

[2] *New York Times*, March 31, 1926.

action should be taken in the face of the opposing opinions of two groups of assistants, both of whom had so acted as to show the difficulties of decision and the doubts involved in the consideration of the question at hand. He even admitted that "a wide variety of conclusions . . . [could] readily be obtained . . . by alternative methods of interpretation of the same basic data". Time and additional information from other sources resolved the situation in favor of the *status quo*.[1]

The main point is that if it is impossible to ascertain the differences between costs of production at home and abroad—and testimony points that way—then administrative authorities, instead of accomplishing the purpose which Congress intended, must be floundering around in confusion. Any change or no change in tariff duties appears to be a sort of subjective and irresponsible fixing of them. It is no wonder that Chairman Marvin, in his testimony, to which reference has just been made, came to the conclusion that the flexible provision is of doubtful constitutionality and that all recommendations of the Commission, in order that the legislative branch of the government might "resume its intended function of fixing tariff duties", should be made to Congress instead of to the President.

Importers of goods actually affected by the flexible provisions of Section 315, are openly asserting the doubt of constitutionality which was back of the testimony of Chairman Marvin. Protests are accumulating before the Board of General Appraisers against the assessment of additional duties by presidential proclamation. This is the beginning

[1] *Ninth Annual Report of the Tariff Commission*, pp. 116-118, Appendix 3; *Pol. Sci. Quart.*, XLI, p. 68. Perhaps the most forceful, concrete criticism of the flexible provisions of the 1922 Tariff Act, as well as of the administrative customs laws in general written from a practical attorney's viewpoint, is Benjamin Arthur Levetts' *Through the Customs Maze* (1923).

of a process that will lead eventually to final judicial determination. Protests are on file against the raising of the duty on sodium nitrite on the ground that Section 315 is "unconstitutional and void by reason of the fact that therein and thereby the Congress of the United States had endeavored to delegate to the President . . . the constitutional power to lay and collect a tax, contrary to the terms and provisions of Article VIII, Section 1, Subdivision 1, of the Constitution . . . "; against the raising of the duty on wheat for the reasons that the Section is contrary to Article I, Sections 1 and 7 of the Constitution and that "the rate of the increased duties is not provided in a valid revenue bill originating in the House of Representatives; against the increasing of duties on wheat flour, barium dioxide and oxalic acid on the grounds that no laws of Congress have levied such duties, that the executive department can not legislate, and that property of citizens cannot be taken without due process of law.[1]

[1] See *Ninth Annual Report of the Tariff Commission*, pp. 20-22 (and note (1), p. 111). Over against these doubts and protests is the opinion of the Attorney General of Oct., 1923: "The power of Congress to delegate to the President powers of the character of those included in Section 315 of the Act is no longer open to question and the exercise of this discretion in that respect can not be questioned even by the courts (Clark *v.* Field, 143 U. S. 649, 690)." This quotation is found in *Seventh Annual Report*, p. 84.

Since the above discussion on the constitutionality of Section 315 was written, the U. S. Board of General Appraisers rendered a decision in favor of the power of Congress to delegate the power to raise or lower the Tariff on barium dioxide in the case of J. W. Hampton and Co. *v.* United States. The court split two to one. Judges Charles P. McClellan and J. B. Sullivan denied that the President's proclamation raising the duty from 4 cents to 6 cents per pound was bad because it violated Article I, Sections 1 and 7, par. 1, and Section 8, par. 1, of the Constitution. The President, said the majority, was but carrying out the expressed will of Congress and such action was in no sense usurpation of the constitutional privileges of that body. This follows the contention made in the debtates in the Senate in favor of the constitutionality of the

Furthermore, the congressional committee of inquiry has received testimony tending to show that, since 1922, the the Chief Executive has known in advance the tariff bias of each appointee [2] before making appointments to the Tariff Commission. If this is so—and there is evidence pointing that way—the President now has a high tariff body, for the most part, and knows in advance that recommendations will be made upon a partisan basis rather than upon that contemplated in the law, viz., the scientific ascertainment of the costs of production at home and abroad. This would tend further to deflect the administration of the flexible provision from the purpose to be attained and from any directive rules

provision, viz., that Congress has set down clearly the purpose to be attained and the rule to be followed by the President in applying the facts.

Judge George S. Brown dissented vigorously. He denied that the law set down a sufficiently clear rule for the President to follow, thereby distinguishing the Field *v.* Clark Case, 43 U. S. 649. He said that nothing could be certain which inherently involved uncertainty; that the rule based upon supposed differences in costs of production at home and abroad was of too indefinite and conjectural a nature to furnish the basis for a finding of fact upon which the operation of a legislative act could be made to take effect or depend; and that the so-called finding of such alleged cost differences under the provision necessarily involved so much descretion, choice, and judgment that there is a delegation of legislative power to the Executive.

[1] See testimony of Professor Taussig and Thos. W. Page, former members of the Commission, and Commissioner Dennis (*New York Times*, March 24, 25 and April 1, 2, 1926, reporting the investigation made by the Senate Special Committee). It was charged that even the staff of the Commission was dictated by the President (Harding) against the will of some of the commissioners. The *New York Times*, Jan. 24, 1926, reports Senator Norris as saying in the Senate that President Coolidge threatened former Vice Chairman Culbertson with prosecution for alleged illegal acts if he should aid in sending in the sugar report during the campaign year (1924). Mr. Culbertson accepted the appointment as Minister to Roumania in 1925, according to rumor, after five other diplomatic posts had been offered him. *Pol. Sci. Quart.*, Vol. XI, p. 68. But see Dr. Culbertson's testimony before the Committee, May 18, 1926, *New York Times*, May 19, 1926, pp. 1 and 5.

laid down for attaining that purpose. Even though the Commission does attempt to balance the costs of production, the President has the final word. Out of the 225 requests made for relief from the statutory tariff duties since 1922, 125 have been for relief through the increase of rates, and 100 for relief through rate decreases. Of the ten recommendations made by the Commission and acted upon by the President, only one complete request for decreased duty has been granted. It has been indicated, too, that partisanship has ruled in the selection of schedules to be investigated and in pushing to completion cases indicating increases at the expense of those indicating decreases.[1] But what has caused the most trouble, apparently, has been the practice of keeping all reports to the President secret unless he sees fit to make a proclamation thereon. The blame here evidently lies with

[1] Senate Special Committee testimony, *New York Times*, March 25 and April 1 and 2, 1926. The total of 225 cases referred to were evidently the estimated number ordered investigated, since the total number of applications for investigation, according to the *Ninth Annual Report of the Tariff Commission*, p. 76, Table I, is about 360. The same Report, pp. 84-85, Table II, Appendices 4 and 5, gives the following data on the action taken by the President on reports of the commission:

(*See table on page 112.*)

the President and hints of his fear of publicity. Chairman Marvin wanted even the sugar report published![1]

Commodity	Date Ordered	Date Reported	Date Proclaimed	Changes Made
Oxalic Acid	3/27/23	12/19/24	12/29/24	Increase, 4c to 6c per lb.
Barbital	3/27/23	11/ 6/24	11/14/24	Assessment basis changed from foreign to American selling price.
Barium Dioxide	3/27/23	5/ 4/24	5/19/24	Increase, 4c to 6c per lb.
Potassium Chlorate	3/27/23	4/ 3/25	4/11/25	Increase, 1½c to 2¼c per lb.
Sodium Nitrite	3/27/23	4/26/23	5/ 6/24	Increase, 3c to 4½c per lb.
Wheat and Wheat Products	11/ 4/23	3/ 4/24	3/ 7/24	(a) Wheat increase, 30c to 42c per bu. (b) Flour increase, 78c to $1.04 per 100 lbs. (c) By-prod. decrease 15c *ad valorem* to 7½c *ad valorem*.
Live Bobwhite Quail	5/19/25	9/28/25	10/ 3/25	Decrease, 50c ea. to 20c ea.
Cotton Warp Knit Fabric	3/27/23	....	....	President refuses unknown recommendation.
Cotton Gloves of Warp-knit Fabric	3/27/23	....	....	In letter of Oct. 3, 1925, President refuses point blank recommendation of increase from 60% to 112%.
Wall Pockets	3/27/23	10/ 1/25	10/ 3/25	No change recommended and no change made.
Taximeters	5/ 4/23	....	....	Rate changed from $3.00 each plus 45% *ad valorem* on the foreign value to $3.00 each plus 27.1% American selling price.

The facts are supplemented by a letter from the Secretary to the Commission to the writer, dated March 25, 1926.

[1] The Senate special committee subpoenaed the reports to the President on sugar, butter, halibut, print rolls, and linseed oil. See *New York Times*, March 31, 1926.

CHAPTER IV

THE CONSTITUTIONAL ASPECTS OF DELEGATED LEGISLATION

I

THE actual existence of a great mass of delegated legislation, because of the nature of the United States constitutional system, has resulted in certain legal complications. In a matter of this nature all that need concern the majority of European states is the question of policy or expediency. The American national government, to be sure, must also bother itself with the policy and expediency of such legislation. But the legal phase takes precedence; all delegation must be worked out under the confines of the Constitution. Mr. De Vries, formerly of the Court of Customs Appeals, in his brief in behalf of delegated legislation under the proposed Tariff Act of 1922, said: [1]

> Perhaps no question of greater magnitude or of more far-reaching consequence in our system of government has been presented to our Supreme Court than the principle supporting such legislation. Only upon the extended development of our national enterprises did the importance of the issue become apparent and the question of whether or not our Constitution was adequate to our national development become dominant.

This statement makes up the introduction to an elaborate argument designed to convince wavering members of the Senate of the validity of the proposed legislation. But

[1] *Cong. Rec.*, 67th Cong., 2nd Sess., p. 12197.

neither he nor any of the doubting Senators could find sufficiently definite authority in the terms of the Constitution. The reason, of course, is perfectly obvious. The fundamental law, stripped of its customs and of judicial interpretations, states that Congress shall have the making of all substantive and adjective law [1] and that the President shall enjoy the executive function.[2] The Fifth Amendment seems to have as its object that of holding the two departments within their respective limits. The reader of the Constitution may reasonably wonder whence comes the power of the Executive to exercise delegated legislative power.

II

Any person with a bent for resolving the apparent contradiction between the word and the deed might well hunt for principles that would aid him in reconciling the seeming contradiction. "We the people . . . do ordain and establish this Constitution" are words which indicate that the sovereign people have endowed the several departments with certain powers which must be exercised, if at all, by those departments. The principle *delegata potestas non potest delegari,* applicable to public law as well as to private law,[3] offers little aid in the solving of the problem. This conclusion is strongly supported by the older commentators on the Constitution. Judge Cooley in the following words gives the most extreme view of the principle: [4]

> One of the settled maxims in constitutional law is that the power conferred upon the legislature to make laws cannot be

[1] Art. I, Secs. 1 and 8, par. 18; but see *ibid.*, Sec. 7, pars. 2 and 3.

[2] Art. II, Sec. I, par. 1.

[3] Hart, *op. cit.*, p. 128.

[4] *Constitutional Limitations*, 7th ed., p. 163, quoted in *Willoughby on the Constitution*, Sec. 773.

delegated by that department to any other authority. When the sovereign power of the state has located the authority, there it must remain, and by that constitutional agency alone the laws must be made until the Constitution itself is changed. The power to whose judgment, wisdom, and patriotism this high prerogative has been entrusted cannot relieve itself of the responsibility by choosing other agencies upon which the power shall be devolved, nor can it substitute the judgment, wisdom, and patriotism of any other body.

This exceedingly broad doctrine has had its peculiar adaptation to the American Constitution. Appearing under the name of the separation-of-powers theory it gets its American twist in part from the words of the fundamental law referred to in the beginning of this chapter. According to Professor Goodnow it was the courts that took up a "somewhat nebulous theory of political science" and transformed it into "an unworkable and inapplicable rule" of constitutional law.[1] In its absolute application the rule would have precluded any exercise of delegated legislative power by the Executive. Under such conditions an operation for its removal from the body of the Constitution by the formal surgery of Article Five might have been altogether imperative. Fortunately such drastic action has not been necessary. Possible harmful results to the progress of the national life have been minimized by congressional prescriptions, approved always by the highest judicial consultants.

Regardless of the fact that the Supreme Court has never declared a specific delegation of legislative power by Congress unconstitutional,[2] it has enunciated again and again

[1] *Politics and Administration*, p. 21.

[2] For corroboration, see Professor Thomas I. Parkinson, *Amer. Bar Assoc. Journal*, March, 1923, pp. 177-178; also 35 *Harvard Law Rev.* 956, note 26, and Hart, *op. cit.*, p. 131. On the other hand, the Supreme Court

the rule that Congress cannot delegate its functions to administrative officials for the simple reason that such derogation would violate the separation-of-powers theory of the Constitution.[1] The Judiciary, by persistently holding to this guiding rule and at the same time sanctioning actions apparently contrary thereto, has brought no little criticism against itself. One writer asserts that the Judiciary has attempted to solve the problem of how to prevent the delegation of power from becoming in fact a delegation in law, thereby saving, through camouflage, the theory of separation of powers.[2] Another writer goes so far as to state that the courts have side-stepped the separation of powers in their attempts to meet the demands of expediency, at the same time insisting that they are applying the old legal principle.[3]

On the other hand there are those who are not satisfied to say that the courts are merely circumventing the Constitution in their endeavor to harmonize the fundamental law with the needs of the time. They attempt rather to resolve the apparent contradiction by a rational construction of the general terms of the Constitution. Such a position necessarily calls for a more liberal interpretation, based upon the spirit of the framers as opposed to the more conservative

has reversed decisions of the lower federal courts negativing the power of legislative delegation because of the theory of sparation of powers. See Selective Draft Cases, 245 U. S. 366, 389 (1918); McKinley *v.* U. S., 249 U. S. 397 (1919); U. S. *v.* Grimaud, 220 U. S. 506 (1911). For other cases, see 35 *Harvard Law Rev.* 95, note 6.

[1] For example, see Field *v.* Clark, 143 U. S. 649, 692 (1892); Buttfield *v.* Stranahan, 192 U. S. 470 (1904); Union Bridge Company *v.* U. S., 204 U. S. 364 (1907); U. S. *v.* Grimaud, 220 U. S. 506 (1911). In each of these cases, the specific delegation was allowed.

[2] James D. Barnett, "The Delegation of Legislative Power by Congress to the States," 2 *Amer. Pol. Sci. Rev.* 347-377.

[3] Andrew A. Bruce, 62 *Central Law Journal*, 199-205. See also R. P. Reeder, "Rate Regulation and the Distribution of Powers in Constitutions," *Univ. of Penn. Law Rev.*, vol. 57, 1908 (reprint).

interpretation which calls for the literal acceptance of the terms of the fundamental document as drawn up in 1787 and interpreted by the non-delegation dicta of the courts. The liberal solution does not involve the denial of the reality of the theory of separation of powers; but it does involve a distinction between the essentials of the legislative process that may not be delegated and the non-essential parts of the process that may be delegated. One writer puts it as follows:

> The rule then, if there is one, against the delegation of legislative powers, is not a prohibition against the delegation of legislative functions or of the duty to do acts legislative in their nature after Congress has laid down the broad rule; but it is the prohibition of the attempted sub-delegation of the very power itself, the duty of meeting in annual session and declaring the national will in some form of enactment in the general laws.[1]

III

The question might well be asked whether the proponents of the liberal interpretation of the general terms of the Constitution are merely rationalizing in their attempt to find a legal basis for the action of the Judiciary by excepting from the no-delegation rule the practice of law making by administrative officers. A mere rationalization of a practice that has been found good, regardless of whether or not it has a real basis in the terms of the Constitution, will not excuse

[1] John B. Cheadle, "Delegation of Legislative Functions," 27 *Yale Law Journal* 892. See also Bondy, *Separation of Governmental Powers*, pp. 79-80; R. P. Reader, "Rate Regulation and the Distribution of Powers in the Constitutions," reprint from the *Pennsylvania Law Review*, Vol. 57 (1908-1909); Cardozo, *The Nature of the Judicial Process*; Woodrow Wilson, *Constitutional Government in the United States*, p. 159; Roscoe Pound, "An Introduction to the Philosophy of Law and Justice and Science in the Law," 31 *Harvard Law Rev.* 1047; Hart, *op. cit.*, Chs. v and vi; Newton D. Baker, *Progress and the Constitution*.

the Judiciary from a charge of having actually effected a legal revolution. A far more scientific support of the legality of delegated legislation is necessary. It has been attempted with some success.[1]

Mr. Hart checks up rather critically the " bits of contemporaneous and historical evidence " in support of the legality of executive legislation. After searching the records of the Constitutional Convention of 1787 he finds but one reference to this question and that is non-conclusive. Mr. Madison on June 1, 1787, attempted to have a clause added which provided that the Executive should be empowered " to execute such other powers not legislative or judicial in their nature as from time to time may be delegated by the national legislature ". This suggestion was not adopted because Mr. Pinckney insisted that the additive power of seeing to it that the national laws be executed was included in that already given, and later adopted.[2] Although Mr. Madison's motion seemed to preclude the delegation of legislative power to the Executive, since the added clause meant something it is reasonable to infer that it meant the delegation of quasi-legislative or delegated legislative powers, as well as of quasi-judicial powers. Mr. Madison did not seriously object to the defeat of his amendment, perhaps for the reason that his conception of the " power to carry into effect the national laws " covered the executive activities which are now included in the term delegated legislation.

But Mr. Hart does not depend solely upon this rather inconclusive argument. He presents the contemporary evidence found in legislative, executive and judicial construction of the Constitution during the period immediately following

[1] James Hart, *op. cit.*, ch. vi, makes the best attempt; A. H. Snow, *The Administration of Dependencies*, especially p. 448 *et seq.*, notes the value of scientific support for the legality of delegated legislation.

[2] Hart, *op. cit.*, pp. 135-137; also, Snow, *op. cit.*, p. 448. The original statement is found in Farrand, *Records of the Convention*, vol. i, pp. 66-67.

its adoption. It was a time when many of the members of the Convention and of the state conventions which were called together to ratify the Constitution occupied positions of trust in the three branches of the government.[1] That delegations of legislative power were actually made by Congress and carried out by executive officials can readily be seen from the examples given in a previous chapter.[2] This very practice, although not so extensively employed as it is now, is good evidence that the men who framed the Constitution and who made it the legal ground-work of the nation considered its terms did not prohibit Congress from delegating certain steps in the process of legislation to the Executive if at any time there was sufficient need.

It is contended that the Supreme Court, in at least three of its early decisions, gave additional support to the contention that the powers of the Executive include quasi-legislation. The *Brig Aurora* Case,[3] already reviewed in connection with the history of delegated legislation, denied that the President was exercising discretion of a legislative character in reviving the law placing an embargo against French and British commerce. When this decision was made in 1813 it did not occur to the members of the Court that there was even a necessity to set out the reasons for allowing the Executive to exercise such discretion. It was necessary only to make the general statement that no sufficient cause could be seen "why the legislature should not exercise its discretion in reviving the Act of March 1, 1809, either expressly or conditionally, as their judgment might direct". As all the members of the Court were in a position to know the views of the Fathers of the Constitution relative to the powers of the President it is reasonable to assume they were,

[1] Hart, *op. cit.*, pp. 137-145.

[2] See chap. iii.

[3] 7 Cranch 382 (1913); see chap. iii, p. 69.

or thought they were, validating a specific act that was in perfect harmony with the duties involved in the "execution clause". Of course such complacency in the attitude of the Court was not entirely due to its ignorance of the question in the case instant. There was a difference of opinion as to what the fundamental law really meant, else the contest would not have come about. It must be admitted, too, that individual members of Congress had expressed themselves rather vigorously against such delegation.[1] In 1825 the Supreme Court, through Chief Justice Marshall, conceded that there were exceptions to the no-delegation principle of the Constitution.[2] The same Court also actually upheld a very broad delegation of contingent legislative power to the President.[3]

To the inferences drawn from the Convention debates and the early judicial decisions is added the judicial respect for legislative construction. In a number of cases it is shown that a statute passed by Congress has, for the courts, every presumption in its favor. Particularly is it so when legislative interpretation has been cumulative from early times and when doubt exists as to its constitutionality.[4] It was upon this long-standing construction of the Constitution by Congress that the Supreme Court relied chiefly for its favorable decision in Field *v.* Clark. In this case the Court said that had the *Brig Aurora* decision never been rendered the practical construction of the Constitution, as given by so

[1] See chap. iii, p. 71. John Randolph of Virginia and Philip Key of Maryland considered such delegation contrary to the Constitution when they were discussing the bill in the House which later became 2 Stat. 490, 1808.

[2] Wayman *v.* Southard, 10 Wheat. 1.

[3] Martin *v.* Mott, 12 Wheat. 19.

[4] U. S. *v.* Gettysburg Electric Railway Co., 160 U. S. 668; Willoughby, *Constitutional Law of the United States*, vol. i, p. 25; Fairbanks *v.* U. S., 181 U. S. 283; Hart, *op. cit.*, pp. 140-145.

many acts of Congress and embracing almost the entire period of the national existence, would not have been overruled unless "upon conviction that such legislation was clearly incompatible with the supreme law of the land".[1] Whenever such legislation is being weighed the Court, if there is doubt as to its constitutionality, seems to let the question of its effectiveness in accomplishing the undoubted powers of Congress weigh heavily. Thus, in the leading case of Field *v.* Clark, the words of the well-known Pennsylvania case are quoted with approval: [2]

> The legislature cannot delegate its power to make a law; but it can make a law to delegate a power to determine some fact or state of things upon which the law makes, or intends to make, its own action depend. To deny this would stop the wheels of government. There are many things upon which wise and useful legislation must depend which cannot be known to the law making power, and must, therefore, be a subject of inquiry outside of the halls of legislation.

In a previous chapter [3] it has been shown that, whatever one may think as to the constitutional bases for judicial action, the Supreme Court has given its sanction to the delegation of legislative powers to the Executive. The main fact to keep in mind is that administrative legislation, whether exercised by the President, the Cabinet, or the independent establishments, has been practiced from the beginning of the Union and has had the approval of the supreme judicial tribunal. This conclusion is clear in the *Brig Aurora*,[4] Field *v.* Clark,[5] Buttfield *v.* Stranahan,[6] Union

[1] 142 U. S. 649, 691; see chap. iii, p. 78 *et seq.* for details.

[2] Locke's *Appeal*, 72 Penn. 491. This idea is stressed in Buttfield *v.* Stranahan, 192 U. S. 470, and in Mutual Film Co. *v.* Industrial Commission, 236 U. S. 230.

[3] Chap. iii.

[4] 7 Cranch 382 (1813).

[5] 143 U. S. 649 (1892).

[6] 192 U. S. 470 (1904).

Bridge Co. *v.* U. S.,[1] St. Louis I. M. and S. R. Co. *v.* Taylor,[2] Interstate Commerce Commission *v.* Goodrich Transit Co,[3] Intermountain Rate Cases,[4] First National Bank *v.* Fellows,[5] Brushaber *v.* Union Pacific R. Co.,[6] U. S. *v.* Grimaud,[7] and the Selective Draft Cases.[8]

IV

The demission of the will-making power, then, is no longer a question for the courts to decide. The answer to any contention to the contrary is now being met by *stare decisis* affirmations.[9] There is still, however, an important legal question bound up with the limits to which the Executive may go in exercising delegated legislative power. One searches the books in vain to find a clear-cut Supreme Court decision which negates the scope of discretion in any particular case. It is only by reading what the courts would apply in accordance with dicta or by studying the actual limitations which have been approved, that some idea of the attitude of the Judiciary can be obtained.[10]

In 1825 the Supreme Court began to feel its way toward the solution of this question. At the same time it acknowledged that there was a field of legislation which Congress

[1] 204 U. S. 364 (1907).

[2] 210 U. S. 281 (1908).

[3] 224 U. S. 194 (1912).

[4] 234 U. S. 476 (1914).

[5] 244 U. S. 416 (1917).

[6] 240 U. S. 1 (1916).

[7] 220 U. S. 506 (1911).

[8] 245 U. S. 366 (1918).

[9] Maryland Casualty Co. *v.* U. S., 251 U. S. 342, 349 (1920); First National Bank *v.* Union Trust Co., 244 U. S. 416, 427 (1917).

[10] Note I. C. C. *v.* Ill. C. R. R. Co., 215 U. S. 452, 470 (1910); Philadelphia Co. *v.* Stimson, 223 U. S. 605 (1912); U. S. *v.* Atchison, etc., Co., 234 U. S. 486 (1913); Utah, etc., Co. *v.* U. S., 234 U S. 389 (1916).

might delegate to another coordinate branch of the government. Chief Justice Marshall, in accepting all the law-making power that Congress cared to bestow upon the Judiciary, said:[1]

It is not contended that Congress can delegate to the courts or to any other tribunals, powers which are strictly and exclusively legislative. But Congress may certainly delegate to others powers which the legislature may rightfully exercise itself. . . . The line has not been exactly drawn which separates these important subjects, which must be entirely regulated by the legislature itself, from those of less interest, in which a general provision may be made, and the power given to those who are to act under such general provisions, to fill up the details. To determine the character of power given to the courts by the Process Act, we must inquire into the extent. . . . It is, undoubtedly, proper for the legislature to prescribe the manner in which these ministerial offices shall be performed, and this duty will never be devolved on any other department without urgent reasons. . . . The difference between the departments undoubtedly is, that the legislature makes, the executive executes, and the judiciary construes the law; but the maker of the law may commit something to the discretion of the other departments and the precise boundaries of this power is a subject of delicate and difficult inquiry, into which a court will not enter unnecessarily.

This opinion points out the direction which all the federal courts have taken in their endeavor to set up more or less general limitations within which subordinate legislation must be carried on. In its attempt to "put over", by means of symbols, the general characteristic of that legislation which may not be delegated, as well as that which may, the

[1] Wayman *v.* Southard, 10 Wheat. 1, 311, 325. A far better, if less authoritative, statement of the case for delegated legislation is found in U. S. *v.* Webster, 28 Fed. Cases 509, 515 (1840).

Judiciary since 1825 has failed to make very great progress in setting limitations. Only in the steady accumulation of examples has there been a contribution. In Wayman *v.* Southard,[1] Chief Justice Marshall used the terms "general principles", "great outlines", "important outlines" to express that part of legislation which, in his opinion, could not be delegated. Later the terms "purpose",[2] "criterion",[3] "general provisions",[4] "general rules",[5] "terms of the statute",[6] "predicate",[7] "theory of the Act",[8] "congressional intention",[9] "purely legislative power",[10] "legal principles that control",[11] "policy of the law",[12] "objects of the law",[13] "vital provisions",[14] "general scheme",[15] "primary standard",[16] merely variations of the original

[1] 10 Wheat. 1, 311, 315; *cf. Ex. parte* Milligan, 4 Wall. 139: "The power to make necessary laws is in Congress and the power to execute is in the President. The extent of powers must be determined by their nature and by the principles of American institutions. [Each power] includes all authority essential to its due exercise."

[2] Buttfield *v.* Stranahan, 192 U. S. 470 (1904); U. S. *v.* Anti-Kamnia, 231 U. S. 654, 667 (1914).

[3] Railroad Co. *v.* Smith, 9 Wall. 95, 99 (1869); French *v.* Fynan, 93 U. S. 169, 176 (1876).

[4] Thacher's Distilled Spirits, 103 U. S. 679 (1881).

[5] Louisville, etc., Co. *v.* I. C. C., 184 Fed. 118, 122 (1910).

[6] Morrill *v.* Jones, 106 U. S. 466, 467 (1882).

[7] U. S. *v.* Grimaud, 220 U. S. 506 (1911).

[8] U. S. *v.* Foster, 223 U. S. 515 (1914).

[9] Utah, etc., Co. *v.* U. S., 243 U. S. 389 (1917).

[10] I. C. C. *v.* Goodrich, etc., Co., 224 U. S. 194, 214 (1912).

[11] Mutual Film Corporation *v.* Ohio Industrial Commission, 236 U. S. 230, 245 (1915).

[12] *Ibid.*

[13] U. S. *v.* Dastervignes, 118 Fed. 199 (1902).

[14] Cook *v.* Bumquist, 242 Fed. 321, 329 (1917).

[15] U. S. *v.* Gurley, 279 Fed. 874, 875 (1922).

[16] Buttfield *v.* Stranahan, 192 U. S. 470 (1904).

expressions have been used to express the same idea. Whatever, by these general expressions, may be concealed or brought to light concerning how far the legislature itself must go in the legislative process, it is the duty of that body to perform the function required thereby.

If, of course, the understanding were perfectly clear as to just what the legislature must do, then it would be an easy matter to determine the scope of discretion to be conferred upon the Executive. Perhaps the Court in Wayman *v.* Southard thought the expressions used in indicating what legislation could be delegated would give more definite content to the essential duties of the law-making body, thereby suggesting the limitations upon delegation. At all events, " subjects of less interest ", " filling up the details ", " minor regulations " were expressions used to define legislative delegation.[1] Consciously or not, later attempts on the part of the courts failed to find better language with which to express the same idea. " Administration ",[2] " mere details ",[3] " supplementary rules ",[4] " mere administrative rules ",[5] " power to apply general rules ",[6] " rules fulfilling the objects of the statute ",[7] " subordinate and supplemental details ",[8] " aids or adjuncts ",[9] " the determination of some fact or state of things ",[10] are some of the terms later used.

[1] Wayman *v.* Southard, 10 Wheat. 1, 311, 325 (1825).

[2] Mutual Film Co. *v.* Ohio Industrial Commission, 236 U. S. 230, 245 (1915).

[3] Union Bridge Co. *v.* U. S., 204 U. S. 304 (1907).

[4] U. S. *v.* Manion, 44 Fed. 800, 801 (1890).

[5] U. S. *v.* Matthews, 146 Fed. 306, 319 (1906).

[6] I. C. C. *v.* Goodrich Transit Co., 224 U. S. 194 (1912).

[7] U. S. *v.* Penn. Co., 235 Fed. 961, 964 (1916).

[8] Lewis Pub. Co. *v.* Wyman, 182 Fed. 13 (1910).

[9] I. C. C. *v.* Ill. Cent. R. R., 215 U. S. 452 (1910).

[10] Field *v.* Clark, 143 U. S. 649 (1892); Mutual Film Co. *v.* Ohio Industrial Commission, 236 U. S. 230.

V

What conclusions can be drawn from the generalities of these judicial pronouncements as to the degree of discretion delegable to the Executive by Congress? In other words, what fraction of the law-making process will the due-process clause of the Fifth Amendment allow Congress, in the exercise of its constitutional powers, to confer upon administrative officers? The attempt to summarize general statements can be of little value other than to harmonize the terms used by the Judiciary. It will be undertaken, after which the emphasis will be shifted to a series of examples with the hope that the nature of such powers may be "best recognizable in illustrations".[1]

The general answer to the preceding question seems to be that once Congress, in legislating on a particular question, has indicated an intent sufficiently clear for the courts and administrative officials to comprehend it, the Executive may be delegated the requisite amount of discretion for making the intent effective.[2] This statement, of course, can be made

[1] The words of the Court in its endeavor to give the nature and scope of executive discretionary power, Mutual Film Company *v.* Ohio Industrial Commission, 236 U. S. 230 (1916).

[2] Doubt exists in the minds of some writers as to the constitutionality of the delegation of discretion to name penalties for criminal offenses. If it is illegal, the English practice of allowing administrative officials the power to prescribe a penalty, within a fixed maximum, would not be permissible. If it could not be done, certainly the delegation of power to prescribe a "reasonable penalty" could not be given. See 1 *Amer. Bar Assoc. Jl.* 332, Appendix B (1915), and Hart, *op. cit.*, pp. 151, 152. It seems that to date such power has not been delegated by Congress. When that body feels that necessity demands such delegation, it is possible that due process will permit it, just as it approved the naming of what actually constituted a crime in the case of U. S. *v.* Grimaud, 220 U. S. 506 (1911). It may well be, however, that the courts have already made due process "give until it hurts" and will be unwilling to bring

to cover the maximum, as well as the minimum, degree of discretion that may be conferred at the will of Congress. The embargo policy, determined upon by the national legislature to meet the restrictions upon neutral trade during the Napoleonic Wars, gave to the President the power to place or to remove embargoes "whenever in his opinion" the public safety should require [1] or "if he [should] deem it expedient or consistent with the interests of the United States".[2] These contingent delegations represent, perhaps, the maximum share of legislative discretion that could be given. The Judiciary, however, although it did not pass judgment directly thereon, years later referred with approval to these "practices of the past".[3] No small portion of discretion was conferred upon the Secretary of the Treasury under a statute of 1897,[4] wherein Congress declared that its purpose was to prevent the importation of teas that were impure, unwholesome or unfit for consumption, and wherein the Treasury was left the freedom of setting up objective standards for carrying out this purpose.[5] Again, in the Forest Reservation Law of 1897,[6] a department head was given wide rule-making discretion in effectuating the objects

further pressure. *Cf.* U. S. *v.* Hudson, 7 Cr. 32 (1812) and U. S. *v.* Coolidge, 1 Wheat. 415 (1816).

A court will get at the purpose by reading the act from "its four corners"; the legislative policy does not have to be expressly written into the statute, *Willoughby on the Constitution*, vol. ii, p. 1318.

[1] 1 Stat. 372 (1794).

[2] 1 Stat. 613 (1799).

[3] As in Field *v.* Clark, 143 U. S. 649 (1892).

[4] 29 Stat. 604.

[5] Buttfield *v.* Stranahan, 192 U. S. 470 (1904). This seems to be the rule whether the standard is set for sugar, grain, cotton, naval supplies, fruit containers, or the like. Congress apparently takes it for granted that the trade has some standards which the administrative officers will takes as a guide. This seems also to be the Court's attitude.

[6] 30 Stat. 35.

of the reservations provided for, viz., "to regulate their occupancy and use and to preserve the forests from destruction". Very stringent regulations have been upheld by the Court in connection with this law.[1]

Further summary of court decisions follows. There is a federal statute the main purpose of which is to settle all unpaid claims of army officers legally due. In the absence of any specified legislative authority the Secretary of the Treasury made a regulation expressly authorizing any state justice of the peace to administer oath as to such claims. It was held that when the end is required, i. e., the paying of all *bona fide* claims, the means can be formulated into law without specific authorization by the administrative authority.

Under the power to prescribe regulations to secure uniform and correct inspection, weighing, marking and gauging of spirits, the Commissioner of Internal Revenue issued a rule governing the identification of spirits emptied for purposes of rectifying and purifying. The regulation was fraudulently executed. The Court held that the intent of the law was to tax distilled spirits and the regulation was the carrying out or the administering of this main purpose. The violator was punished for breaking faith.[2] Another case: the law penalizes anyone who buys an article, knowing it has been taken from a letter stolen from an authorized mail-box. The Postmaster-General designated as a mail-box any receptacle for the depositing of mail on any mail route. The Court, taking as the main part of the law the protection of United States property, held that Section 161 of the Revised Statutes (which bestows general regulatory power upon the head of each governmental department as well as specific regulatory power over departmental prop-

[1] U. S. *v.* Grimaud, 220 U. S. 506 (1911).

[2] Thacher's Distilled Spirits, 103 U. S. 679 (1881).

erty) is sufficient authority for declaring what a mail-box is within the meaning of the law. It so decided because it is only in this way that the law can be enforced.[1]

Legal authority for fixing minimum just and reasonable rates for interstate commerce was held to amount to nothing more than the application—in an administrative capacity and in the proper situation—of rates in accordance with what is reasonable and just—the general rule set up by Congress.[2] With a law, the purpose of which was to secure purity of food and drugs and to inform purchasers of what they are buying, the Court allowed an inter-departmental commission, in order to fulfil the purpose of the law, to demand the giving of the name not only of a derivative of a drug, which the law specifically required, but to require the naming of the substance whence the drug is derived or of what it is a preparation.[3] The Secretary of Agriculture, under power granted by the Plant Quarantine Act (the essence of which is to preserve domestic plants from diseases by preventing the importation of plants or of plant products likely to have carriers of such diseases) established a quarantine against potatoes from Canada. It was held that a violation of such quarantine and the regulations thereunder subject a person to the penalty of a fine or imprisonment and the forfeiture of his property.[4] Upon the legal basis that the dumping of refuse into harbors is injurious to navigation and commerce, the regulatory power of the Secretary of War, exercised in naming the limits within which such dumping might be made, was held to be nothing more than properly effecting the general policy of Congress.[5]

[1] Pakas *v.* U. S., 240 Fed. 350 (1917). *Cf.* Lewis Pub. Co. *v.* Wyman, 182 Fed. 13 (1910).

[2] Louisville, etc., Co. *v.* I. C. C., 184 Fed. 118 (1910).

[3] U. S. *v.* Anti-Kamnia, 231 U. S. 554, 666 (1914).

[4] Daigle *v.* U. S., 237 Fed. 159 (1916), and 37 Stat. 315.

[5] Philadelphia *v.* Stimson, 223 U. S. 605 (1912); U. S. *v.* Romard, 89 Fed. 156 (1896).

One of the purposes of the Tariff Act of 1890 was to secure reciprocity in certain articles of commerce. The President was empowered to change such articles from the free to the dutiable list, contingent upon his finding that untoward conditions exist in a particular country. The court gave its approval, holding that the Executive acts merely as an administrator in carrying out the intent of Congress.[1] Under the Oleomargarine Act, the Commissioner of Internal Revenue was given rule-making power. He promulgated certain regulations requiring book-keeping and a monthly return from all wholesalers who deal in such food stuff. A penalty was named in the law for failure to comply with its provisions. The Court held the regulations to be valid on the ground that the main congressional intention was to tax adulterated butter and that the regulations were well adapted to accomplish the intention.[2] The Tariff Act of 1913 provided that all materials imported for making foods to be exported might be free from duty under certain conditions and under the rules and regulations of the Treasury. It was held here that the duty-free privilege can not legally be claimed by one who does not comply with the regulations, since the purpose of the Act was to exempt *bona fide* imports and since the regulations of the Treasury merely effected that purpose by guaranteeing in advance that no fraud should work against the government.[3] Under regulations of the Treasury claims for illegally-assessed taxes must first go to the Commissioner of Internal Revenue. By failure to comply with a form of application for a refund, a party was refused the benefits of a law, the object of which was to relieve the tax payer of unjust burdens of taxation.

[1] Field *v.* Clark, 143 U. S. 649 (1892).

[2] U. S. *v.* Lamson, 173 Fed. 673 (1909); In *re* Kallock, 165 U. S. 526 (1896).

[3] Agency Canadian Car Co. *v.* U. S., 10 Ct. Cust. Appls. 172, 176 (1920); U. S. *v.* Dominici, 78 Fed. 334, 338 (1897).

The regulation was held to be merely a necessary bit of procedure which the law exacts before the benefits are to be secured.[1] The Internal Revenue Act of 1916 requires accurate returns under oath to be made in such form as the Commissioner of Internal Revenue shall prescribe, and authorizes general regulatory power to require all data necessary for collecting the tax imposed. By a regulation neglect in filling out an item in one of the prescribed forms subjects the citizen to a heavy administrative fine. The Court held that since the Act was designed to search out all income for taxation the regulation was necessary in effecting the terms of the law.[2]

VI

Whatever may be the exact limits of the scope of delegable discretion, one derives from the reading of such decided cases and from a study of the practice under statutory law [3] the conclusion that the Executive has a rather large degree of freedom in carrying out the purposes of Congress.[4] Does

[1] Rock Island, etc., Co. *v.* U. S., 254 U. S. 141 (1920).

[2] Beam *v.* Hamilton, 289 Fed. 9 (1923). For the practice as evidenced in the law, see chap. iii.

[3] For examples, see chap. iii.

[4] Mr. De Vries, in defending the proposed Tariff Act of 1922 (*Cong. Rec.*, 67th Cong., 2nd Sess., p. 12204), suggests an extension of this discretionary power of the Executive. He says that the Courts have shown a tendency to permit administrative officers the exercise of more freedom in legislation that has to do with the substantive powers of Congress, when such powers are, by choice of Congress, considered a *means* of accomplishing a policy with respect to some other substantive power. Thus, if the power to tax is used as a means of regulating commerce (e. g. Russell *v.* Williams, 106 U. S. 623, and the "Cape Rule"); if the power to set the value of foreign coin is considered primarily as a means of properly enforcing the customs laws (e. g., Collector *v.* Richards, 90 U. S. 259; U. S. *v.* Klingenberg, 153 U. S. 93); if the borrowing power is employed as a means of carrying on war (e. g., U. S. *v.* Janowitz, 257 U. S. 42)—the Executive can legally, in as much as these substantive powers have been transformed into adjective

this freedom apply to all subjects over which the policy-forming branch has jurisdiction? Or is it limited to special subject matter and, therefore, to be considered exceptional? Without the aid of definite judicial pronouncements in resolving this question, the opinion is hazarded that the Executive may exercise delegated legislative power in regard to any subject matter over which the Constitution has given Congress the power to form policy, provided that that body chooses to make of this peculiar use of the administrative department a means by which the legislative purpose can reasonably be effectuated. There seems to be no reason why quasi-legislation, when it is used as a means of accomplishing congressional policy, does not fall within the principle laid down in McCulloch *v.* Maryland.[1]

VII

Two further legal aspects of this type of delegated power must be considered. In the first place, if this derogated power is to be counted within the terms of the statute under which it issues it must conform with no little degree of exactitude both in the process of being made and in the process of being applied to the procedure laid down in the law. If " men must turn square corners in dealing with government ", the government must turn square corners in dealing with men. The Supreme Court, speaking through Mr. Chief Justice Taft, once held that a state public utility rate was void even though it was not in itself unreasonable, because, in the procedure under which such rate was established, public hearings had not been held according to the terms of the statute. The Chief Justice said in part: [2]

or administrative powers, be given greater discretion. He accepts the broad interpretation of Chief Justice Marshall found in McCulloch *v.* Maryland, 4 Wheat. 316, as the basis of the power of Congress to establish legitimate means.

[1] 4 Wheat. 316 (1819).

[2] Wichita, etc., Co. *v.* Public Utility Commission, 260 U. S. 48 (1922).

In creating such an administrative agency the legislature, to prevent its being a pure delegation of legislative power, must enjoin upon it a certain course of procedure and certain rules of decision in the performance of its functions. It is a wholesome and necessary principle that such an agency must pursue the procedure and rules enjoined and show a substantial compliance therewith to give validity to its action. When, therefore, such an administrative agency is required, as a condition precedent, to make a finding of facts, the validity of the order must rest upon the needed finding. If it is lacking, the order is ineffective.

VIII

The second aspect involves the legal question as to whether or not subordinate legislation, made to carry a particular law into effect, is within the terms of the delegation. This question is, for practical purposes, one of paramount importance. It is upon this point that the courts have seen fit to kill such law making or let it live. It will be recalled that the terms of investment of rule-making power are not always so coupled with the law, or the subdivisions thereof, that the enforcing officer can readily see what his real power is. Thus, the general law of 1789, which gives to the heads of departments the power to prescribe rules and regulations not inconsistent with law, may or may not bestow upon the Secretary of the Treasury the authority to make rules and

See also Penn. Rd. Co. *v.* U. S., 288 Fed. 88, 90 (1925); I. C. C. *v.* Louisville, etc., Ry. Co., 227 U. S. 88 (1913).

Mr. Hart, *op. cit.*, pp. 174-176, suggests that the courts might justly make due process require notice and hearing in all administrative legislation dealing with industrial discretion, whether the statute, by its terms, requires it or not. He would, however, exempt political discretion from this absolute requirement. It will be shown in chaps. vii and viii that executive officers are tending more and more to give notice and hearing, even where there is not such a statutory requirement. This may be the result of a desire to arrive at the best method rather than to avoid legal difficulties.

regulations for carrying out the provisions of the current income-tax law. A similar power bestowed specifically upon the Secretary of the Navy may or may not enable him to issue binding regulations for enforcing a particular policy entrusted to his care. A blank delegation of such power for enforcing the Packers Act may not give the Secretary of Agriculture authority to promulgate rules for putting into effect specific provisions of that Act. It is possible for doubt to creep in as to whether or not the Secretary of Commerce has power to issue regulations relative to steamboat inspection when a single provision of law contains both the policy to be carried out and the investment of rule-making power. At times the source of authority may be found in several provisions. The officer must make the first guess and let the court determine whether such source is the correct one for effectuating the particular policy in question.[1]

If the courts find that the delegated power which is exercised to enforce a particular policy is the one which Congress intended should be used, it is, to this extent, within the terms of the law. But there is also another rule to be met: delegated legislation must bear a reasonable relation to the purpose of the law. It is difficult to ascertain just what the courts mean by this rule; it is another case of due process. Majority interpretations are numerous. When the Executive is given discretionary power to make "static principles dynamic", the measures adopted must accomplish or tend to accomplish that object.[2] Tests of reasonableness cannot be

[1] See chap. ii, p. 29 and notes, for additional exposition. This element of uncertainty affected the decisions in U. S. *v.* Eaton, 144 U. S. 677, and U. S. *v.* Bailey, 9 Pet. 238.

[2] Thacher's Distilled Spirits, 103 U. S. 679 (1880); in Lamette *v.* U. S., 254 U. S. 570 (1920), the court held certain regulations good because they were "consistent with the statute, appropriate to its execution, and reasonable in themselves"; U. S. *v.* Grimaud, 220 U. S. 506 (1911); U. S. *v.* Tsai, 9 Ct. Cust. Appls. 442, 44 (1919).

based upon a particular case but must take into consideration the possibilities and likelihoods that may arise or the difficulties of the statute's execution.[1] Of course it can be said with entire safety that illiberality, inequity, lack of wisdom, or features not conducive to the best results are not causes for throwing such legislation outside the meaning of "reasonable relation to the object".[2] But subsidiary legislation that effects results other than, or in addition to, those which the law intends to bring about is without this rule.[3] Negatively, a regulation which introduces conditions or limitations into a statute and operates to negate the rights and duties conferred therein, is, through unreasonableness, void. This is only another way of saying that that legislation which adds to, or goes contrary to, the policy of the statute ceases to be that of an agent and becomes that of an equal.

Few believe that such a rule is of any value in helping to reconcile administrative legislation to its authority, i. e., to the court. If neither objective nor subjective method can get at the factors that determine in advance whether or not

[1] U. S. *v.* Anti-Kamnia, 231 U. S. 654 (1914); U. S. *v.* Morehead, 243 U. S. 607 (1917); U. S. *v.* Gurley, 279 Fed. 874 (1922).

[2] Utah Power and Light Co. *v.* U. S., 243 U. S. 389 (1917); I. C. C. *v.* Ill. C. Ry. Co., 215 U. S. 452, 470 (1910).

[3] I. C. C. *v.* Chicago, etc., Ry., Co., 218 U. S. 88 (1910); Intermountain Rate Cases, 234 U. S. 486, 487 (1913); Williamson *v.* U. S., 207 U. S. 245, in which Chief Justice White said, "It remains only to consider the power of the Commissioner General of the Land Office to enact regulations by which an entryman would be compelled to do that at a final hearing which the act of Congress must be considered as having excluded, in order to deprive an entryman of a right which the act, by necessary implication, conferred upon him. To state the question is to answer it"; Morrill *v.* Jones, 106 U. S. 466 (1882); Merritt *v.* Welsh, 104 U. S. 694 (1881). La Bourgogne, 210 U. S. 95 (1908), sets aside a rule of the Steamboat Inspection Service, offered as a defense, because it failed to establish the life-boat capacity set up in the law, even though power had been given to go beyond the miminum.

a specific exercise of delegated legislative power will meet the unexplained rule, the administrator must rely on trial-and-error methods, trusting that the Court will apply the following rule of construction:[1]

We must apply the rule of decision which controls when an Act of Congress is assailed as not being within the power conferred by the Constitution; that is to say, a regulation adopted under Section 161 of the Revised Statutes should not be disregarded or annulled unless, in the judgment of the Court, it is plainly and palpably inconsistent with the law. Those who insist that such a regulation is invalid must make its invalidity so manifest that the Court has no choice except to hold that the Secretary has exceeded his authority and employed means that are not at all appropiate to the end specified in the Act of Congress.

[1] Boske *v.* Comingore, 177 U. S. 459 (1900); see also Cinn., etc., Ry. Co. *v.* I. C. C., 206 U. S. 142 (1906), and National Lead Co. *v.* U. S., 252 U. S. 140 (1920).

CHAPTER V

INTERPRETATIVE REGULATIONS: THEIR PLACE IN ADMINISTRATIVE LEGISLATION

I

As it has already been stated in a previous chapter, there are two general kinds of regulations, viz., administrative, or those which are accepted as law by the courts, and interpretative, or those which cannot be so accepted.[1] The former which are made pursuant to, in aid of and to carry out the purposes of a statute, although they are subject to change from time to time, have the force of law so long as they are operative. The latter purport to express the true meaning of a statute. Both are held by executive agencies to be necessary for the orderly enforcement of law. They are subject to modification or waiver as convenience may demand.[2] In many cases, since a large number of the so-called

[1] *Supra*, chap. ii.

[2] *Ibid.*; also letter from the Executive Secretary of the Fed. Power Comm. to the writer, dated Feb. 1, 1926; *Hearings of Senate Select Committee on Investigation of Bureau of Internal Revenue*, 68th Cong., 2nd Sess., p. 3618 (1924). This committee's work extended over a period of fifteen months. It published, as a partial report, Report No. 27, 69th Cong., 1st Sess. (1926). Since the hearings and report of this committee are frequently referred to in this chapter, it is but fair to state that partisan feeling displayed itself throughout its sessions. The Chairman, Senator Couzens, seemed to work with the two Democrats, Senators King and Jones (N. M.). Their aggressive action was opposed by the conservative Republican minority, Senators Ernst and Watson. This feeling is especially exemplified in the majority and minority reports. For the latter, made Feb. 6, 1926, see *New York Times*, Feb. 7, 1926, p. 16. Still one may reasonably accept the facts brought out by witnesses relative to Treasury practices and call attention to differences of opinion, based upon such facts, which the expert and the Congressman have upon the construction of indefinite provisions of the law.

regulations have material that is both explanatory and supplementary, it is almost impossible to separate the two classes of regulations.[1]

The power of the Executive to interpret the statutes may be compared with that of the courts to construe the various parts of the national law. Few persons who have studied the federal court decisions have failed to see that many of them are legislative in character. Likewise, the national administrative officers, acting in a quasi-judicial capacity, are always busy construing the numerous statutes which they are called upon to enforce, their views frequently prevailing over those of Congress. This is both a necessary function of the Executive and a condition precedent to the execution of the laws. Indeed, one might say that the officer has the advantage in that he gets the first chance at every statute which he is called upon to carry out and is sure to touch first every person who comes within the terms of the statute.

The general attitude of the Judiciary toward this particular field of official activity has been consistent in theory, if not in practice. It has insisted that interpretative regulations are valid if they properly construe the statutes to be enforced, and invalid if they do not.[2] In practice, great weight is nearly always given to administrative rulings—especially when such rulings have been applied over a long period of time,[3] have formed the basis of rights and interests,[4] and when Congress has given its implied consent to

[1] Testimony of the Executive Secretary of the Fed. Power Comm., cited *supra*; Regulations of the Comm. of Int. Rev., 1878-1924, especially series 2, 5, 6, 7, 8, 9, support this statement; Maryland Casualty Co. *v.* U. S., 251 U. S. 342 (1920), shows how confused the Supreme Court gets as to the real character of regulations; 26 Ops. Atty.-Gen. 517 (1908).

[2] Smith *v.* U. S., 170 U. S. 372 (1898); Lynch *v.* Tilden, 265 U. S. 315 1924); Smythe *v.* U. S., 23 Wall. 374.

[3] U. S. *v.* Falk, 204 U. S. 143; U. S. *v.* Hermanos, 209 U. S. 337 (1908); Amer. National Lead Co. *v.* U. S., 252 U. S. 140 (1920).

[4] U. S. *v.* Baruch, 223 U. S. 191 (1912).

them by inaction or by re-enacting the interpreted statutes without formally changing the rulings.[1] In other words, the courts must see very good reason for overthrowing the interpretations of men more skilled than the members of the judicial branch of the government in enforcing the will of Congress in a particular field.[2]

This chapter is an attempt to show the practical contribution of interpretative rules to the sum-total of executive legislation. Its development will take the following lines: the necessity of interpretative rulings; their classification; the attitude of the three branches of government as to the legislative character of such rulings; the presentation of cases selected from those of the Treasury in which both specific and general explanatory rulings have resulted, or may result, in legislation; and a brief discussion of some of the checks upon the Department that work for the protection of the taxpayer.

II

The necessity for the exercise of the explanatory function by the Executive has been recognized by all three branches of the government. As early as 1789 Congress gave the head of each department this general power.[3] Since that time specific authority had been found for the more important officers, each law usually including some reference to the agency that is to enforce it. For example, the Commissioner of Internal Revenue was given the continuing

[1] U. S. *v.* Falk, 204 U. S. 143; U. S. *v.* Hermanos, 209 U. S. 337; Amer. Sugar Refining Co. *v.* U. S., 211 U. S. 155 (1908).

[2] Logan *v.* Davis, 233 U. S. 613 (1914); U. S. *v.* Philbrick, 120 U. S. 52 (1887); U. S. *v.* Healey, 160 U. S. 136; U. S. *v.* Hill, 120 U. S. 169 (1886). See also Solicitor Gregg's comment, *Hearings of Senate Select Committee on Investigation of Bur. Int. Rev.*, 68th Cong., 2nd Sess., p. 3618 (1925); Holmes' *Federal Income and Profits Taxes*, Ch. 47 (1920).

[3] 1 Stat. 28.

power to " prepare and distribute all the instructions, regulations, directions . . . and other matters pertaining to the assessment and collection of internal revenue ".[1] The terms " charged with the law's execution ", and " to carry the law's provisions into effect " are usually found in the opinions of the courts.[2] Of late, however, the Judiciary has come out with the definite pronouncement that the authority to administer an act gives the Executive the implied authority to interpret it, since interpretation is necessary to the performance of its duty of administration.[3]

Administrative officers themselves have realized that one of their greatest tasks, as long as there are provisions of statutes that are not self-explanatory, must be that of interpretation. This, of course, means that their task is one which, under present conditions, will continue. The Senate Select Committee on the Investigation of the Bureau of Internal Revenue[4] was given a rather full statement of the administrator's viewpoint relative to this function. One of the officials of the Bureau said, in effect, that he did not see how it was possible for Congress to pass a law which would be sufficiently simple, plain, and clear on its face to relieve the administrative officials of the power to interpret its terms and to settle the thousands of questions that often come up in regard to one little item not specifically covered by the law. He asserted further that Congress in enacting a revenue law could not go into detail, which would anticipate and settle, beyond any question of controversy, the numerous questions that would eventually arise. Finally, he said that experience had shown the more Congress tried to cover specific cases,

[1] Rev. Stat., Sec. 321, as interpreted by 22 Ops. Atty.-Gen. 570 (1889).

[2] E. g., U. S. *v.* Hill, 120 U. S. 169; Robertson *v.* Downing, 127 U. S. 607.

[3] E. g., Hall *v.* Payne, 254 U. S. 343; Commercial Solvents Co. *v.* Mellon, 277 Fed. 548 (1922).

[4] *Hearings*, 68th Cong., 1st Sess., p. 232 (1924).

the greater the difficulty in performing the necessary function of interpretation.[1] This is only another way of saying that very few statutes can be made sufficiently explicit in their terms to warrant a perfect understanding by either the average government agent or the average citizen. The same forces that have made supplementary regulations necessary have added to the need for those that are merely interpretative. Indeed, the latter must precede, and often influence, the former.

III

The moment one asserts that this class of regulations has the force of law, legally-minded persons reply that not only is this not the case but could not be on account of the very nature of these regulations. They could have the force of law only on one or the other of two theories, viz., that they are made by the department in the exercise of a delegated, quasi-legislative power and are therefore in their very nature binding on the courts and administrative officers, or that they are made in the exercise of a quasi-judicial power to construe the law and are therefore not subject to review by the courts. If the former, there would be a pure delegation of both substantive and adjective law-making which is contrary to judicial pronouncements; and if the latter, the most zealously-guarded function of the judiciary would be seriously limited in scope, a situation not likely to be permitted. Their argument is in brief that regulations purporting to state accurately the meaning of a statute have no legal force *per se*—since the statute stands on its own base; a meaning once established by Congress is always established, until it has been changed by the specific action of that body.[2]

[1] For another government expert's opinion, see Fred T. Field, "The Legal Force and Effect of Treasury Interpretations," *Columbia Income Tax Lectures*, pp. 91-113.

[2] It was in connection with the viewpoints of the executive officials

But does this fit the facts? Administrative officers of the Treasury Department apparently do not always think so.[1] One Commissioner of Internal Revenue is reported to have remarked that many rulings are made which favor the government beyond the intent of the law and that if the Judiciary should have its turn at such interpretations, the rulings would very likely be set aside.[2] Mr. Mellon, Secretary of the Treasury, is quoted as saying that he and the Commissioner are forced to construe questions of law just about as important as those brought to the Supreme Court.[3] An engineer, member of the technical staff of the Bureau of Internal Revenue, upon being questioned as to whether the large number of rulings on Section 214 (a) of the Revenue Act of 1921 had materially changed the effect of that Section upon the taxpayers, answered in the affirmative.[4] An expert public accountant, formerly an employee of the Treasury Department and later an adviser in making the rulings that deal with amortization claims, stated before the Senate Committee that the Bureau had a progressive policy which it followed in interpreting the law, a policy of progressing from conservatism to liberalism. Regulations were harsh, he said, under the new law in order to discourage excessive claims for amortization, but later were amended to favor the taxpayer. He claimed that to interpret the law so as to favor

to the effect that rulings of the Executive have a legislative character that Mr. Taft said statutory construction was "practically the greatest of executive powers." *Our Chief Magistrate and His Powers*, pp. 78-79.

[1] Field, *op. cit.*,: Black, *Income Taxes*, 4th ed., p. 9; U. S. *v.* Standard Brewing Co., 251 U. S. 210; Goldfield Mining Co. *v.* Scott, 247 U. S. 126; Edwards *v.* Keith, 231 Fed. 110, 113.

[2] Montgomery, *Income Tax Procedure*, p. 492 (1918).

[3] *Hearings* of House Jud. Comm. on H. R. 6645, 68th Cong., 1st Sess., p. 10 (1924).

[4] *Hearings of the Senate Select Committee on Investigation of Bureau of Internal Revenue*, 68th Cong., 1st Sess., pp. 236-237 (1924).

the government and to permit a modification later if the taxpayers could prove that the original interpretation was incorrect was the proper course for tax officials to follow.[1] The taxpayer must then proceed to show the Bureau that its ruling was not the true interpretation of the intent of Congress, and eventually may ask the opinion of the Judiciary. One of the more experienced attorneys of the legal division of the Bureau was greatly pleased over the ability of his organization to exceed the collection estimates of the government actuary for 1920 by a third of a billion dollars, especially since the collections for 1919 had fallen short of the estimate for that year by over a million. He explained the 1920 excess chiefly on the basis of "harsh" interpretative regulations in favor of the government. He even went so far as to cite specific examples which the makers felt were actual substantive changes in the law, saying that these, if they should happen to be contested, would hardly prevail in the courts.[2]

There is recent evidence to indicate that members of Congress realize the legislative character of interpretative rulings —even though they may feel, more or less, the impotence of the national legislature to correct many of the abuses of the power exercised. Senator Couzens, Chairman of the Senate Select Committee on the Investigation of the Bureau of Internal Revenue, remarked that the investigation would be an effort to correct conditions and to find out how much the

[1] *Hearings of Senate Select Committee, op. cit.*, p. 257.

[2] A personal conversation with the writer, 1920; the rules cited were Regulations 45 (1919), Art. 1547, par. 2 (later altered by Treas. Dec. 3206 and Treas. Dec. 3238); Regulations 47 (1919), Arts. 22, 31, 33, 42; Regulations 53 (1919), Arts. 4-9. It is worth noting that Regulations 47 (1919), Art. 22, was upheld by a federal court, Malley *v.* Baker Co., 281 Fed. 41 (1922), but not until it had been very much amended in December, 1920.

government was losing through improper collections or " for allowing amortization and depletion charges and credits unwarranted by law or the rules ".[1] At this same investigation Senator King made the statement that he had read one of the Bureau's volumes containing nearly two thousand promulgated regulations; that some of the regulations therein obviously contained interpretations at variance with former interpretations; that some placed a construction which made them retroactive; and that, as a result, the decisions of the department tended to place the tax settlements of a large number of people upon an unstable basis.[2] If the type of questions asked and the comments recorded mean anything, one might say that the members of this Committee felt it unwise to leave such great freedom of interpretation to administrative officers unchecked.

IV

The rulings of all governmental agencies, whether they be of the General Land Office,[3] the Department of Agriculture,[4] the Interstate Commerce Commission,[5] the Bureau of

[1] *Hearings*, 68th Cong., 1st Sess., p. 507 (1924).

[2] *Ibid.*, p. 230.

[3] See *Land Decisions*. Apparently there is no attempt to separate the general from the particular rulings although a system for publishing all rulings has been in existence for years. E. g., see 28 Land. Decs. 439.

[4] E. g., see the *Federal Food and Drugs Acts and Decisions* (1914). Many of the regulations of the Department and all the Food Inspection decisions are the administrative views as to the meaning of the statutes dealing with these subjects. An attempt is made to publish all decisions made by the Department under the title "F. I. D." See F. I. D. 44 (1906) for the scope and purpose of such decisions. Although they interpret not only the law itself but the regulations issued thereunder, they are not binding upon those affected. If, however, parties do not observe the decisions and regulations of an explanatory character, they are subject to prosecution.

[5] See *Conference Rulings of I. C. C.*, Nos. 1-513 (1917). These seem

Internal Revenue,[1] the Customs Division or of any other branch of the Executive having the duty of enforcing laws, are usually classifiable under two main heads—general and particular. Space does not permit the consideration of all executive agencies in regard to this matter. For this reason, primarily, the rulings of the Bureau of Internal Revenue will be studied to the exclusion of all others, with the exception of one or two cases falling under the Customs Division. The clear-cut method of indicating the difference between, and the uses of, the two classes of rulings as found in the published reports of the Bureau, as well as the material that has been brought out by congressional investigation, relative to the actual practices of this agency, gives additional reason for selecting the Bureau for this study.

General interpretative regulations are rulings of general application having the stamp of the department as a guarantee that they are the official construction of the terms of the law to be enforced and are binding upon the officials until they are changed.[2] Appearing collectively under the name of regulations they are published in full at the time the law goes into effect. For example, Regulations 62 put into force the Revenue Act of 1921 and Regulations 65 appeared under the Revenue Act of 1924. Since the Treasury officials have, for the most part, the freedom to change their opinions as to what the law means, it is necessary to have some easy method that does not involve a complete revision for amend-

to interpret the law and the regulations. The rulings, general and specific, "express the views of the Commission on informal inquiries involving special facts or requiring an interpretation and construction of the law, and are to be regarded as precedents governing similar cases" (p. 3). Such rulings are announced from time to time through the press and are later edited and published. For examples, see Nos. 8, 110, 484, 513.

[1] See Fred T. Field, *op. cit.*

[2] All such regulations must be signed by the Commsr. of Int. Rev., by the Sec. of the Treasury or by both.

ing these regulations. Hence individual regulations of a general character are issued under the name of Treasury decisions.[1] These are published weekly without exception and are issued at the end of each fiscal year as part of the annual volumes of Treasury Decisions.[2]

The Treasury Department, in carrying out its duty of interpreting the broad terms of the laws which Congress formulates, has frequently been accused by interested parties of breaking or vaulting the fences which are supposed to delimit the bounds of its authority. Neither hobble nor yoke has yet been invented which is capable of holding this powerful agency. As fast as the legislature or the Judiciary mends one section of the barrier, another section is found in need of repair, in spite of cooperation between the Legislative Counsel of the House and Treasury Council in building the fence and "riding the line" every year.

During the seventies and eighties of the last century the Department was sorely tried by the universality of fraud connected with the importation of sugar. Although Congress was anxious to remedy the situation it was apparently blocked by indecision. The Committee of Ways and Means held a hearing December 17, 1878. Mr. Sherman, Secretary of the Treasury, upon being asked whether he could institute regulations that would prevent fraud, replied that the courts had decided he could not, by regulation, substitute anything which would affect the Dutch Standard provided for under the law [3]—a standard which made the evasion possible. This meant that the polariscope could not be used

[1] All Treasury decisions are not, however, general interpretative decisions.

[2] See Field, *op. cit.*; *Internal Revenue Bulletin Digest*, No. 13, pp. i-iv (1925); *Hearings of the Senate Select Committee on Investigation of Bureau of Internal Revenue*, 68th Cong., 2nd Sess., p. 3621 (1925).

[3] U. S. Rev. Stat., Title XXXIII, Sec. 2504.

to any advantage in testing for color. Nevertheless the Treasury, failing to get the help of Congress, took upon itself the curing of the evil by interpreting the law in such a way as to permit the use of the polariscopic method. A result was that the good, as well as the bad, elements of the trade were unfavorably affected. Consequently the Chamber of Commerce of the State of New York adopted a resolution condemning such action, asking the Secretary of the Treasury "to rescind his order of 2nd September, 1879, and to refund the excess duties collected under it above the lawful duties prescribed by the existing statute".[1] After suits covering more than a million dollars had been threatened, the government's attorney admitted that the claims should be paid without the necessity of going to court, and the Treasury agreed with him. Later, however, the same attorney refused absolutely to refund.

Until 1911 the Treasury, acting with the Chemistry Bureau of the Department of Agriculture, had given little thought to the question of adding to the usual tea standards the "no artificial coloring" clause. As a result of public agitation at that time the Tea Board suggested that no tea which had been artificially colored should be allowed entrance. This regulation was made after consulting the trade—although neither the Board nor the Secretary felt that the public health would be injured by the infinitesimal amount of coloring used. The exclusion was designed merely to be in harmony with the tendency to emphasize the natural quality of food products. An elaborate protest was made to the President by eastern tea importers. It was then that Secretary McVeagh wrote his famous letter to the President

[1] See the *Report of the Special Committee of the Chamber of Commerce of the State of New York to Investigate the Alleged Illegal Action of the Treasury Department in the Collection of Duties on Sugar* (pamphlet, 1881).

giving the story of the exclusion of colored teas and emphasizing the fact that the matter had nothing to do with public health but had come "wholly from sectional trade rivalries".[1] The embarrassing situation rose from the conflict between the absolutely prohibitive regulation and the standard set up by the Tea Board. Although this standard let in quantities of Chinese teas artificially colored, the Secretary stood by his policy of absolute exclusion! A chemical method, uniform in results, was then established for inspectors' use. Again, all Chinese teas were excluded at western ports, because the local authorities used a more accurate method for detecting coloring than the chemical test which the Department had instituted. Still the absolute exclusion was insisted upon, even though the universal test continued to wink at a certain amount of artificial coloring. It was not until six years later that the Supreme Court held that the Department had overstepped its authority in expanding the statutory standards "of purity, quality, and fitness for consumption of all kinds of teas imported" by an interpretative ruling.[2] "One extraneous substance", said the Court, "cannot be picked out of many and accorded supremacy in evil by an absolute rule, irrespective of any harm it may do." Just as a state may not pass a law discriminating between one citizen and another, so a department may not make a regulation discriminating against say Prussian blue at the same time allowing other impurities to run rampant among the leaves of tea. The point of importance here is that the regulation, although there was no authority for it, had been in force six years, greatly to the detriment of exporters and importers.

[1] Franklin McVeagh to Mr. President, Jan. 12, 1912.

[2] Waite *v.* Macy, 246 U. S. 606 (1918); the U. S. district court had supported the Tea Board and the Board of Appeals, but the Circuit Court of Appeals had reversed the decision.

The Treasury's long fight to win the sanction of the courts for its definition of adulterated butter under a statute of 1902,[1] backed up by the general administrative provisions of an earlier Act,[2] indicates further the power as well as the tenacity of the Executive in making its interpretative regulations law. Under the Act of 1902 adulterated butter is defined and a tax for the purpose of regulation imposed. The Treasury states in Regulation Number 9 (1907):

Adulterated butter is defined in the law, but the normal content of moisture permissible is not fixed by the Act. This being the case, it becomes necessary to adopt a standard for moisture in butter, which shall in effect represent the normal quantity. It is therefore held that butter having 16% or more of moisture contains an abnormal quantity and is classified as adulterated butter.

Under this general rule a federal court sustained a tax imposed by the Department, at the same time allowing a heavy penalty to be imposed for violation of certain requirements imposed by law as to packing.[3] In other jurisdictions[4] although the Treasury failed to have its ruling upheld, it continued to collect the tax wherever there was not a resort to the courts. Finally, in 1924, the Supreme Court held the interpretation to be contrary to the terms of the law.[5] This decision was made regardless of the fact that Congress had given its passive approval to the practice of the Department and had, in 1922, actually refused to take away the power of

[1] 32 Stat. 194.

[2] 24 Stat. 209 (1886).

[3] Coopersville Creamery Co. *v.* Lemon, 163 Fed. 145 (89 C. C. A. 595).

[4] See U. S. *v.* 1150 Pounds of Butter, 195 Fed. 607; Baldwin Creamery Assoc. *v.* Williams, 233 Fed. 607; Produce Co. *v.* Whaley, 238 Fed. 650; *Report of Commissioner of Internal Revenue*, p. 15 (1917).

[5] Lynch *v.* Tilden, 265 U. S. 315 (1924).

the Bureau of Internal Revenue to define the standard of maximum moisture that would save butter from being taxed as adulterated.[1]

In January, 1918, the Treasury made a regulation to the effect that where a gift was other than money, the basis for arriving at its value was the fair market value of the property at the time it was given.[2] Under this interpretative rule Senator Couzens of Michigan made a charitable gift of approximately $2,000,000 in securities. The regulation was apparently followed until February, 1920, when Treasury Decision 2966 was issued to the effect that the value of such gifts should be based upon the cost of the property, if acquired after February, 1913, or upon its market value as of March, 1913, if acquired prior thereto, less depreciation. The change was worked under the general terms of Section 214 (a) of the Act of 1918 which merely permitted the deduction, making no reference to the basis for it. The reason for the change apparently was to make the rules for charitable deductions conform to comparable rules for deductions from losses by fire, etc. A change of solicitors in the Bureau of Internal Revenue took place January, 1923. Three months later Law Opinion 1118 was submitted by the Solicitor's Office to the Commissioner reversing the existing rule of 1920 and holding that where a charitable contribution was other than in money, the basis for calculation of the amount of deduction allowed under the Act of 1918 should be the fair market value of the property at the time of the gift. The opinion was approved by the Commissioner on May 1, 1923;

[1] See House Report No. 1141, 67th Cong., 2nd Sess., 1922. Although butter standards were set up to govern pure food administrators, amendments providing similar standards for taxation were refused. The Treasury had asked for a statutory standard as early as 1916. See *Report of the Commissioner of Internal Revenue*, p. 22 (1916).

[2] Regulations 33 (revised), Art. 8, par. 92.

on June 16, 1923, Treasury Decisions 3490 and 3491 were amended to accord with this view and Senator Couzens had the opportunity of saving $1,000,000 in taxes.[1]

The amortization clause of the Revenue Act of 1921 [2] has been interpreted by the Treasury Department in its general meaning to apply to railroads. This has been done in the face of the contrary opinion of a Solicitor of Internal Revenue [3] and of a federal district court decision [4] to the effect that railroads are not producers but merely transporters of war materials, and that the specific inclusion of water-transportation facilities only tend the more to exclude railroads. The particular regulation to which reference has been made [5] permitted amortization upon railroad transportation facilities contributing to the prosecution of the War, even though the statute limits such amortization to facilities "acquired for production of articles contributing to the prosecution of the War". Amortization amounting to nearly $3,000,000 has been allowed to common carrier railroad corporations whose stock is owned by the United States Steel Corporation and its subsidiaries. Thus Treasury officials, in their endeavor to express the intent of Congress, have issued interpretative regulations that allow valuable deductions to railroads on the ground that their stock is

[1] *Hearings of Senate Select Committee on Investigation of Bureau of Internal Revenue*, 68th Cong., 1st Sess., 1924, pp. 228-231, 241. Although the Couzens case had not been settled at the conclusion of the hearings, a similar case, *re* Gray, had been decided on the basis of the new ruling—even though the gift had been made and tax returns filed before the new rule was promulgated. No objection to the correctness of the ruling was made by the counsel; its retroactive, not its prospective, effect was protested.

[2] Sec. 234, subdivision 8.

[3] Law Opinion 1074, *Cumulative Bulletin*, Dec., 1921, p. 159.

[4] Hampton, etc., Ry. Co. *v.* Noel, 300 Fed. 438 (1924).

[5] Regulations 62, Art. 183.

owned by a corporation owning the stock of another corporation which comes within the class entitled to such deductions. Only recently the Solicitor of Internal Revenue has ruled that this particular application of the regulation is illegal.[1] Nevertheless large allowances, aggregating $1,500,000, have been granted other railroad companies in similar conditions. The Senate Select Committee intimated that there were other allowances of smaller sums " as it was the policy of the engineering divisions to make [them], notwithstanding the rulings of the solicitor and the decisions of the courts, until this question was brought to the attention of the committee ".[2] It was also found that common carrier pipe lines and tank and refrigerator cars have realized for their owners huge sums by reason of their being owned by companies actually producing war necessities.[3]

V

According to Treasury documents particular rulings are those which express " the administrative application of the law, the regulations, and the Treasury decisions to the facts and principles under immediate examination ". These rulings are to be used, in so far as they are published, by both the departmental officers and the taxpayers as aids in studying the law and its formal construction. Ordinarily they do not commit the Department to any interpretation of the law which has not been approved and promulgated.[4] A certain small percentage, however, known as " novel " or " leading " cases, do, after very close consideration has been given them by the Rules and Regulations Division, the Solicitor, and the

[1] Senate Report No. 27, 69th Cong., 1st Sess., p. 142.

[2] *Ibid.*, p. 142.

[3] *Ibid.*, pp. 142-143.

[4] *Internal Revenue Bulletin IV*, No. 34, p. 8.

Commissioner of Internal Revenue, become precedents for the department.[1]

Rulings of particular application appear under various names such as solicitor's opinions, solicitor's memoranda, solicitor's recommendations, and recommendations of the old Committee on Appeals and Review. At present almost all such decisions are supposed to be published within three weeks after they are made. As a matter of policy, the Solicitor of the Bureau gives final approval to all decisions that are to be published. Once his approval has been received, the rulings are known as Income Tax Rulings (I. T's), appearing in the Income Tax Bulletin.[2]

Particular rulings, when they are published, point toward like rulings in similar cases in the future. Only a frank reversal of such rulings, if there be anything like consistency expected of experts administering a law, should prevent a precedent from becoming a rule in practice. It is not expected that *stare decisis* will control administrative officers to the extent that it does the Courts. It is easier for the former to change their minds. But a precedent should stand until it is overturned. This is what taxpayers expect. Whenever they can get the information they will be advised by particular decisions as to their liabilities. Hence there is reason for treating a particular decision, known to all, on practically the same basis as a general ruling whether it be one interpreting the statute itself or regulations and Treasury decisions thereunder.[3]

[1] *Hearings of Senate Select Committee on Investigation of Bureau of Internal Revenue*, p. 3622, cited *supra*.

[2] *Ibid.*, pp. 3621, 3647; *Internal Revenue Bulletin*, Digest No. 13, pp. 1-4 (1922-1924).

[3] A particular interpretative ruling which points the way to other taxpayers if upheld often enough becomes in effect a general rule binding upon all alike. *Report of the Commissioner of Internal Revenue*, p. 94 (1919).

Section 214, (a) and (b), of the Revenue Act of 1924, provides *inter alia* deductions from income for the depletion of "mines, oil and gas wells, other natural deposits, and timber". The discovery clause of this Section, however, refers only to "mines, oil and gas wells". By the terms of the law it seems that Congress has not intended the discovery clause should apply to "other natural deposits, and timber". The Committee on Appeals and Review of the Bureau of Internal Revenue made a decision allowing discovery value to be depleted on a gravel pit. From a technical viewpoint any natural deposit may constitute a mine, and any extraction of inorganic matter from or beneath the soil may be considered as mining. Yet, if the word "mine", as used in the discovery clause, is made to include deposits of gravel, sand, and the like, no force or effect can be given to the words "other natural deposits". The Committee's construction practically read these words out of the Act—despite the fact that the chief canon of statutory construction demands that force and effect must be given to every word of a statute, if it is at all possible to do so. Gravel pits and sand pits are not commonly referred to as mines, nor are laborers therein commonly designated as miners. To say the least, the Senate Committee certainly had some basis for criticizing this extension by specific interpretation of a well known word, with the immediate result of relieving a particular taxpayer of a large tax and with a future possibility of relieving taxpayers who find themselves in a similar position.[1]

The construction by Treasury officials of the indefinite language used in the discovery clause of this Section of the Revenue Act of 1924 brought further criticism from the

[1] Penn. Sand and Gravel Co., see *Hearings of Senate Select Committee on Investigation of Bureau of Internal Revenue*, p. 1399, 68th Cong., 1st Sess. (1924). This case is critically discussed in the Committee's Senate Report No. 27, 69th Cong., 1st Sess., p. 22 (1926).

Senate's investigators. The clause provides for the allowance of depletion, based upon discovery value, " in cases of mines, oil and gas wells, discovered by the taxpayer after February 28, 1913 ". The Commissioner of Internal Revenue has ruled that a " mine " or " well " means a developed mine or well which can be operated at a profit, and that there is no such discovery, within the meaning of the law, until it has been shown that a mine or an oil or gas well can be profitably operated. Under this ruling a number of taxpayers who discovered no oil or mineral deposits have been allowed discovery depletion on the ground that they discovered that " a previously known deposit could be profitably operated ". The conclusion of the Senate Select Committee was that the effect of such a construction defeated the purpose of the law, which was to stimulate prospecting.[1] The Committee showed further that an erroneous interpretation of these clauses necessarily leads to an erroneous construction of other clauses of the law that dovetail with the original provisions misinterpreted.[2]

In spite of precautions of publicity, the interpretation of the Treasury may be merged in an action which may have legal force irrespective of the correctness of the interpretation itself. Expressly stated or not, each action of the Treasury is an interpretation of a statute which has to do with assessment, collection, refund or any act incident thereto. To the extent that any one of these acts is binding, the construction of the statute involved is binding in that particular case. Assessment by the Commissioner of Internal Revenue, although based upon erroneous interpretation, is effective to the extent that it warrants the taking of

[1] Senate Report, pp. 23-28. Original ruling in The Penn. Sand and Gravel Co., The Texas Gulf Sulphur Co. and the Carson Hill Gold Mines, Inc. cases followed.

[2] *Ibid.*, pp. 29-34.

the taxpayer's property subject to an appeal upon liability to the courts within a given time; and very few appeals are made. Collection of a tax places the burden of showing that the levy is illegal or excessive upon the taxpayer and concludes him, unless he appeals within a given time to the Judiciary. Few taxpayers take action, even when they are convinced of the error of the administrative ruling.[1]

According to the statement of Mr. Field, particular rulings are not always published, and many are left to inference from the acts of the Treasury or are embodied in letters addressed to taxpayers interested therein.[2] To many of these unpublished decisions, he said, has been assigned the name of star-chamber or secret rulings. His statement is corroborated in part by testimony before the Senate Select Committee on the Investigation of the Bureau of Internal Revenue.[3] Solicitor Gregg testified here that previous to 1924 there were many unpublished rulings and that even since that time a number of decisions reaching the Solicitor through the Rules and Regulations Division have been held from the public, the reasons being that they could not be sufficiently separated from their personal element nor could ever serve as a precedent because of the peculiar facts upon which they were based. He had in mind some 30 per cent of all "novel" or "leading" cases and an unknown number of decisions upon questions certified to the higher officials from the different revenue units.[4] He said also that the chiefs of the auditing and engineering sections use their own

[1] Fred T. Field, "The Legal Force and Effect of Treasury Interpretation," *Columbia Income Tax Lectures*, pp. 9-113 (1921). Montgomery, *Income Tax Procedure* (1917), p. IV.

[2] *Columbia Income Tax Lectures*, pp. 91-113 (1921).

[3] *Hearings*, 68th Cong., 2nd Sess., pp. 3619-3647 (1925).

[4] Only about 15 per cent of total rulings relative to amortization and depletion charges were found by the Senate Select Comm. to be published. Senate Report No. 27, 69th Cong., 1st Sess., p. 7 (1926).

discretion as to whether or not they will ask for rulings on doubtful questions. In case they do not, no publicity is given to their decisions and they may continue to act upon their own rulings. Furthermore, according to Mr. Gregg, rulings based upon letters from taxpayers, since they are always covered by precedents, are never published. It is perfectly evident that there are still many specific rulings being kept from the public.

There is some evidence to show that these secret, unpublished rulings have resulted in relieving taxpayers from the specific terms of the law, from some authoritative regulation or Treasury decision, or from some published specific ruling that taxpayers might reasonably assume to point the way for future action under similar circumstances. This statement is not made to cast a shadow upon the motives of Treasury officials but to indicate the possible consequences of certain of their acts. This practice has been further increased by the use of the " settlement " which, in some cases, has amounted to nothing more than an extreme use of the secret ruling. The most recent evidence of the Treasury's activities of this nature are found in the Senate Select Committee's hearings and in its partial report summarizing its findings.[1] It is stated by this Committee that " many of the principles, practices, methods, and formulae applied in determining taxes have never been reduced to writing, and only about 15 per cent of the formal written rulings have ever been published ".[2]

In the Committee's partial report covering amortization of war facilities, depletion, valuation of natural resources for depletion and invested capital purposes, the following untoward results are enumerated: (a) gross discrimination in assessments due to insufficient information for the proper

[1] *Hearings*, 68th Cong., 2nd Sess., pp. 3619-47 (1925).

[2] Senate Report No. 27, 69th Cong., 1st Sess. (1926), pp. 229, 232 especially.

guidance of the employees of the Income Tax Unit; (b) the failure to claim allowances by many taxpayers that had been granted to others similarly situated; (c) the forcing of vigilant and aggressive taxpayers to pay huge sums to ex-employees of the unit for information which should be free to everybody, with attendant extraordinary labor turnover in the service; and (d) the failure to form a body of settled law and practice, with the elimination of personal bargaining.[1]

The law provides that allowances for the depletion of mines and other natural deposits shall be based upon the fair market value of the property. Nothing is said in the law as to whether the property, the value of which is to be the basis of depletion, is merely the tangible deposit of mineral which can be taken from the mine and sold or whether the depletable property is the taxpayer's business as a going concern. The analytic or present-value method of determining fair market value reflects every element which influences profits, while in the method of cost of replacement all elements of value, other than the value of the bare physical property or lease, are excluded from the value to be depleted. Regulations 65, Articles 206 and 207, provide that "analytic appraisal methods will not be used if the fair market value can reasonably be determined by another method [or] if profits arising from the exploitation of the mineral deposit are wholly or in great part due to the manufacturing or marketing ability of the taxpayer, or to extrinsic causes other than the possession of the mineral itself".[2] A certain taxpayer held three different leases for quarrying rock in a county in New Jersey in 1916. For one he paid 4 cents per ton for removal over a period of 5 years, for another, 3 cents for 8 years, and for the remaining one, 3 cents for 2 years. Records of leases made in the same county during

[1] Senate Report, *op. cit.*, pp. 7-8.

[2] *Ibid.*, p. 46.

1916, 1918, and 1920, calling for 5 cents for each ton of rock removed, were brought before the tax authorities. These showed that the market value in the leases in 1916 was due to the advantage of 2 cents per ton for two leases and 1 cent for one lease. On this basis the valuation engineers of the income tax unit fixed the value of the leases at $8,950.93. The taxpayer appealed to the Committee on Appeals and Review and, through that Committee's unpublished recommendation No. 1517, was allowed a value of $106,000, a figure based upon prospective profits or about 20 cents per ton instead of 1 or 2 cents. The evidence in the case shows that the Committee used the present value method under circumstances contrary to Regulations 65, Articles 206 and 207.

A memorandum by the chairman of the Committee on Appeals and Review, dated January 4, 1923, was sent to the chief of the Nonmetals, Valuation Section, in response to his protest at the decision on the grounds that it would be contrary to both the regulations and the many decisions already made. In this communication it was stated that conditions were special and as such " should not be treated as a general precedent ". As a matter of fact this inside ruling, according to the Senate Select Committee, did act as a precedent in three important cases as well as in many less important ones. Can the taxpayer, in general, assume that all rules laid down by the regulations promulgated by the Commissioner of Internal Revenue, approved by the Secretary of the Treasury and published for the guidance of all, will measure their rights and be enforced? [1]

The great number of oil valuations, upon which depletion in 1925 was to be allowed, were discovery valuations. The law provides that such determinations shall reflect the value

[1] Senate Report, *op. cit.*, pp. 52-55. A number of similar cases are reviewed, pp. 45-70.

on the date of discovery of a tract or lease of land or within thirty days thereafter.[1] Oil and Gas Regulations 45 and 62, Article 206 (A), provide: " where the fair market value of property at a specified date is the basis for depletion . . . such value must be determined . . . by the owner of the property in the light of conditions and circumstances known at that date ", regardless of later developments or improvements of method. This Article is practically identical with the law as to the date when the valuation shall be made. In the case of the Shumway Lease of the Gypsy Oil Company, the depletion unit of the Bureau disregarded both law and regulation by going beyond the " thirty-day period after discovery " in fixing prices of future production. In the words of the Senate Select Committee this case " is conclusive of the fact that subsequent developments were not only available for the purpose of pricing future production but were actually made retroactive by giving oil which had been produced during the thirty-day period at $1.75 a value of $1.90 ". This method was employed and the values allowed in all the property of the Gulf Oil Corporation and its subsidiaries, wherever the peak price for oil followed the thirty-day period.[2]

Oil and Gas Regulations 45, Article 223, permit a producer either to deduct development costs as current expenses incurred each year, or to capitalize such costs and deduct them through depletion. It is specifically stated that " an election once made under this option will control the taxpayer's returns for all subsequent years ". Rulings published in 1921 and 1923 are in conformity with the Regulations. The Standard Oil Company of California from 1918 to 1921 had elected to capitalize its capital costs. Its original re-

[1] Senate Report, *op. cit.*, p. 80. For terms, see Income Tax of 1918, 214 (a), (9).

[2] *Ibid.*, pp. 89-92.

turns conformed to this method and the tax computed thereon was paid. The Company, however, found that by converting development costs from capital into an expense item its taxes for the years 1918 to 1920 inclusive would be reduced $3,378,921. The chief of the Oil and Gas Valuation Section claimed that in 1922, as a condition of secretly waiving an unrecorded claim against the Treasury, the Company would be permitted to file amended returns for the three years preceding. A secret understanding was made with the Company in 1924 to the effect that amended returns would be permitted for 1918, 1919 and 1920, on the more advantageous basis in return for the waiver of some unknown claim against the Treasury. The chief of the Oil and Gas Valuation Section so informed the Company on September 1, 1922. On June 9, 1923, the taxpayer filed unsigned amended returns. The Rules and Regulations Section of the Income Tax Unit pronounced against the switch and was supported by the Solicitor. The head of the Oil and Gas Valuation Section, notwithstanding the regulations, the Solicitor's ruling and the many precedents, persuaded his superior to support him in accepting the amended returns. On September 29, 1923, the Deputy Commissioner of Internal Revenue ordered the case closed on the unsigned amended returns and so notified the taxpayer. This increase of assessment the Solicitor refused to sign, the Commissioner likewise—on the basis of "dangerous precedent" and "secret agreement". The case was to be decided by the Auditing Section at the last report. The Engineering Section has to date taken no steps to carry out the directions of the Commissioner of Internal Revenue. That such important matters cannot be settled even by the Commissioner, in opposition to his inferiors, seems to indicate a possible lack of central control over such subordinate men as are anxious to favor taxpayers.[1] This is the inference of the Committee.

The Income Tax laws of 1916 and 1917 contained no clauses allowing depletion to oil lessees; but such provision for them was made in the Income Tax Law of 1918. All published rulings on the matter of allowing depreciations for 1916 and 1917 under the 1918 law up to August 23, 1922, rejected the idea of retroaction. Nevertheless, on February 28, 1921, the Deputy Commissioner sent a letter closing up the Gulf Oil Company's tax reconsideration for 1916 and 1917, allowing depreciation for those two years. According to the records there was not even a law opinion on this ruling until December, 1921. It was not until August 22, 1922, that the ruling was published as Treasury Decision 3386. No internal revenue official could or would explain this special secret ruling; all that was done was to state that the Bureau had recently adopted the definite policy of giving to all affected by revised rulings the benefit thereof, although it could not be guaranteed that restitution would always be made. Professor Adams of Yale University, sitting as an expert adviser of the Senate Select Committee, made this remark about the secret rulings: " I personally am shocked beyond all expression to know that cases were passed upon and went out from the Treasury Department contrary to the printed regulations of the Department and I feel that I ought to express that opinion of it." [2]

[1] All these statements are taken from Senate Report No. 27, 69th Cong., 1st Sess. (1926), pp. 98-101; see also *Hearings of Senate Select Committee on Investigation of Bureau of Internal Revenue*, 68th Cong., 2nd Sess., pp. 2803-2832.

[2] *Hearings of Senate Select Committee on Investigation of Bureau of Internal Revenue*, 68th Cong., 1st Sess. (1924), pp. 279-523, especially p. 448.

VI

Since the power of interpreting carries with it the danger of misinterpreting the will of Congress in matters pertaining to revenues, there should, it would seem, be checks to minimize such danger. The actual lack of a complete centralization of responsibility for all decisions has been due to poor organization within the Bureau. The bad results issuing from this condition, however, are gradually being met by the placing of responsible reviewing authorities at the head of each unit or division; these officials in turn are supervised by still higher authorities such as the Rules and Regulations Section, which is under the direct control of the Solicitor. The latter important officer is responsible to the Commissioner, who is in turn responsible to the head of the Treasury Department.[1] The improved organization has, to a considerable extent, been the result of the recommendations of the Tax Simplification Board set up by Section 1327 (a) of the Revenue Act of 1921.[2]

The evils resulting from secret rulings, whatever their nature may be, are being remedied by the Bureau—but only gradually. Publicity of all rulings of a general nature has been the practice since 1924; and the particular decisions are beginning to appear in print, i. e., those which the Solicitor has had the opportunity of approving. Congress might well require the publication of all new rulings. From the facts brought out in the recent investigation of the Bureau, some doubt seems to exist as to the advisability of complete publicity. Solicitor Gregg, who appeared to be somewhat doubtful on this point, cited the English practice of keeping all decisions from the public. At any rate, the Treasury is

[1] See reports of the Secretary of the Treasury, 1918-1925; *Hearings of Senate Select Committee on Investigation of Bureau Internal Revenue*, cited *supra*, pp. 231, 543-545, 3618-3647.

[2] See report of this Board, Sen. Doc. No. 271, 67th Cong., 4th Sess. (1922).

beginning to respond to the opinion of taxpayers. It has gone far in publishing decisions that are based upon new facts or principles.[1]

Perhaps the most serious complaint against the Bureau lies in its apparent freedom in reversing its regulations and decisions.[2] The strict compliance with a ruling, while it may relieve a taxpayer from any charge of fraud or bad faith, will not relieve him of an additional liability as the result of a change of ruling brought about in accordance with the true meaning of the statute—provided, of course, that the statute of limitations has not run in favor of the taxpayer. The changed ruling may, in fact, if the taxpayer knew of the existence of the original and erroneous interpretation, have a retroactive effect as to taxes but not as to fraud.[3] But whatever the average citizen may think as to the good or bad results of a true ruling, it seems that such a ruling cannot, in a real sense, be retroactive. Since the ruling does not have the effect of law, " it is not legally active at all ". In practice, although the administrative official may or may not give a ruling retroactive effect, he is bound to enforce the law. His best judgment must be used in so doing and apparently his " last best judgment " is the law, as he sees it. Cases that have not been closed before the new ruling have usually been settled on the basis of the new decision. Criticism, of course, results. The practice of reopening closed cases on the basis of the new ruling, is somewhat more doubtful both from the standpoint of the duty of the administrator and from the standpoint of law. Arbitrariness,

[1] *Senate Select Committee on Investigation of Bureau Internal Revenue*, pp. 3621-3660.

[2] Of course, rulings reversed by the Supreme Court or any other court whose opinion is respected by the Department as binding are not considered here.

[3] A hint to this effect is given in Mayes *v.* Paul Jones and Co., 270 Fed. 121 and U. S. *v.* Baruch, 223 U. S. 191.

when this is done, is always charged, especially by the taxpayers who happen to be adversely affected.[1]

Congress did not see fit formally to sanction the power of the Treasury to change its rulings, or give them retroactive effect, in the Revenue Acts of 1909, 1913, 1916, 1917, and 1918.[2] In the Revenue Act of 1921, Section 1314, this power was recognized, discretion apparently being left to the Treasury to make a ruling law which, in the later judgment of the same authority, was not law. The provision seems to suggest to the administrative authority that, in most cases, "better judgments" should not govern—at least those cases already closed on the basis of a former and erroneous judgment. Leeway is, perhaps, given for discretion in aggravated cases. It is even contended that a taxpayer who overpays can force a retroactive application of the latest ruling.[3] It is the belief of the writer, however, that the Treasury will ponder a long time before the discretion given in the following paragraph will be exercised:

In case a regulation or a Treasury decision relating to the

[1] For this material, see Field, *op. cit.*, pp. 109-110. See also *Hearings of Senate Select Committee*, cited *supra*, pp. 300, 1067.

[2] Congress has, however, taken notice of Treasury decisions in the administration of customs. Section 2, 18 Stat. 469 (1875), reads as follows:

> No ruling or decision once made by the Secretary of the Treasury, giving construction to any law imposing customs duties, shall be reversed or modified adversely to the United States by the same or succeeding Secretary, except in concurrence with an opinion of the Attorney-General recommending the same, or a judicial decision of a circuit court or a district court of the United States conflicting with such ruling or decision, and from which the Attorney-General shall certify that no appeal or writ of error will be taken by the United States: Provided, that the Secretary of the Treasury may in his discretion decline to acquiesce in the judicial decision or ruling of an inferior court upon any question affecting the interests of the United States, when in his opinion such interests require final adjudication by a court of last resort.

[3] See Montgomery, *Income Tax Procedure*, p. 201 (1923).

internal-revenue laws, made by the Commissioner or the Secretary, or by the Commissioner with the approval of the Secretary, is reversed by a subsequent regulation or a Treasury decision, and such reversal is not immediately occasioned or required by a decision of a court of competent jurisdiction, such subsequent regulation or Treasury decision may, in the discretion of the Commissioner, with the approval of the Secretary of the Treasury, be applied with retroactive effect.

This provision was repeated in 1924, but with the following additional and definite, if limited, check upon the Treasury in giving new rulings retroactive effect: [1]

No tax shall be levied, assessed or collected under provisions of title VI of this Act on any article sold or leased by a manufacturer, producer or importer, if at the time of sale or lease, there was an existing ruling, regulation, or Treasury decision holding that the sale or lease of such article was not taxable, and the manufacturer, producer or importer parted with the possession or ownership of such article, relying upon the ruling, regulation or Treasury decision.

The following remark of the Supreme Court made nearly a century ago, still holds good in theory: [2]

The construction of the law is open to both parties, and each is presumed to know it. Any instructions from the Treasury Department could not change the law or affect the rights of the plaintiff. He was not bound to take or adopt that construction. He was at liberty to judge for himself and act accordingly.

Let it be granted that such is the case and that the taxpayer sees the law differently from the Commissioner of Internal Revenue, or one of his subordinates. Which has the advantage in enforcing his will? The obvious answer is, the

[1] 43 Stat. 339, Sec. 1001, (a), (b).

[2] Elliott *v.* Swartwout, 10 Pet. 137 (1836).

government's representative. If the taxpayer merely states that he is correct in his determination, he will have to pay his tax on the basis of the officer's opinion. If he decides to go to court, he may ultimately win back the amount of taxes which he claims are over and above the amount due under the law. Even if he does, the remedy is incomplete: it does not remove the hardship occasioned by an incorrect assessment.[1] Only the big taxpayer or the man who is fighting for the perpetuation of his business will undergo the expense and annoyance involved in a court procedure.[2] The conclusion is that the legal check upon the rulings of the Treasury does not protect directly the great majority of taxpayers.[3]

Various attempts have been made to create some sort of machinery of a judicial nature that will provide the average taxpayer with an easier and readier check upon revenue rulings. The Revenue Act of 1918 set up the so-called Advisory Board within the Bureau of Internal Revenue. Its control over interpretations, of course, was limited by the will of the Treasury. This Board was disestablished in 1919, even before its maximum existence had run its course. In its place the Treasury itself, in October, 1919, established the Committee on Appeals and Review. Its decision as to fact was made final in all questions; but the law was finally interpreted by the officials of the Bureau.[4] The Tax

[1] See comments on laws previous to 1924 in House Ways and Means Committee Report on the Revenue Act of 1924, quoted in Holmes and Brewster's *Procedure and Practice, Board of Tax Appeals*, p. 159; also a quotation from the Senate Finance Com. Report on same bill, p. 164.

[2] *Cf.* Montgomery, *Income Tax Procedure*, p. 203 (1923).

[3] A specific decision of a court invalidating a particular assessment does not guarantee that all assessments made on the basis of such decisions will be refunded. See *Hearings of Senate Select Committee on Investigation of Bureau of Internal Revenue*, pp. 3513-3514, *re* Geo. A. Joslyn.

[4] See Kitzmiller and Baar, *Consolidated U. S. Income Tax Laws*, p. 716 (1923).

Simplification Board, provided for in Section 1327 of the Revenue Act of 1921, recommended to Congress the establishment of a Board of Tax Appeals.[1]

In 1924, Congress, for the purpose of remedying the taxpayer's situation, did create such a Board of Tax Appeals, to function as a quasi-judicial body, independent of all other governmental revenue agencies.[2] The Senate Finance Committee thus summarized the position of the taxpayer before and after the passage of the 1924 statute:[3]

Under the existing law a taxpayer prior to the payment of his tax may appeal to the Commissioner, who has established the Committee on Appeals and Review, to determine these appeals for him. The objections that have been raised to this procedure are four: (1) The appeal is from the action of the Bureau of Internal Revenue but is taken to a committee in and part of the Bureau. It is urged that such an appeal does not involve a review by an impartial outside body, such as the taxpayer is entitled to prior to payment of the tax. (2) In the hearing on the appeal the person who is to decide the appeal acts both as advocate and judge, since he must both protect the interests of the Government and decide the question involved. Such conditions do not insure an impartial determination of the case. (3) If the decision on the appeal is in favor of the Government, the taxpayer has the right to test the correctness of the decision in the courts, but if the decision is in favor of the taxpayer, the action of the Bureau is final and the correctness of the decision can never be tested in the courts. It is contended that this condition results in the decision of most doubtful points in favor of the Government. (4) The taxpayer is usually forced to come to Washington for the hearing on his appeal, an expensive and burdensome procedure.

[1] See Report, Sen. Doc. No. 103, 68th Cong., 1st Sess. (1923).

[2] 43 Stat. 253, Sec. 900 (1924). *Cf.* Holmes and Brewster, *op. cit.*, p. v.

[3] Report, quoted in Holmes and Brewster, *op. cit.*, pp. 164-165; see *ibid.*, pp. 159-160, for quotation from the Report of the House Ways and Means Committee on this bill to same effect.

Under the provisions of the proposed bill creating a Board of Tax Appeals, the taxpayer may, prior to the payment of the additional assessment of income, war-profits, excess-profits, or estate taxes, appeal to the Board of Tax Appeals and secure an impartial and disinterested determination of the issues involved. In the consideration of the appeal both the Government and the taxpayer will appear before the Board to present their cases, with the result that each member of the Board will sit solely as judges and not as both judges and advocate. . . . The divisions of the Board will sit locally throughout the United States to enable taxpayers to argue their cases with as little inconvenience and expense as is practicable. This proposal meets all the objections that have been raised as to the existing system and at the same time provides for a flexible and informal procedure which will permit the Board to determine expeditiously the cases brought before it on appeal.

The function of the Board is to determine from the statute whether the tax assessed by the Commissioner is properly due; it is concerned with the regulations only to the extent that such regulations validly interpret the Revenue Act in question.[1] Indeed, the Board has already held that although it is not bound by the rulings promulgated by the Bureau of Internal Revenue, it will look to the statute and regulations properly interpreting the law.[2] Under such circumstances one cannot help feeling that the taxpayer, whatever the amount of his income, has a very valuable check upon the rulings of the Treasury; that the Board acts as a buffer between the judgment of the Treasury and the Judiciary, thereby saving much of the annoyance and expense that would necessarily result from regular court action.[3]

[1] See Holmes and Brewster, *op. cit.*, pp. 107-108, and Appeal of B. B. Todd, Inc., 1 B. T. A. 762, Dec. No. 282, Docket No. 707.

[2] *Ibid.*, p. 107 and Appeal of Cleveland Home Brewing Co., 1 B. T. A. 87, Dec. No. 47, Docket No. 73 (A).

[3] For political checks upon the Treasury in making rulings, see the discussion in chapter viii as to the method of making administrative rules.

CHAPTER VI

Administrative Legislation: Safeguards

I

The facts indicate that it has been impossible, whatever the causes may be, for the electorate, acting directly through the ballot-box or indirectly through law-making assemblies, to supply its own demand for effective social and industrial legislation; that this failure has resulted in actually shifting much of the burden for meeting this demand to the shoulders of the Executive; and that the Judiciary has, after much muddling, succeeded in reconciling the redistribution of powers to the separation theory supposedly found in the American constitutional system. There remains, however, a very important problem to be discussed, viz., that of holding the law-making Executive responsible to the electorate for the exercise of discretionary power. The term "safeguards"[1] is employed to express the methods which are or may be used in accomplishing this important purpose.

It is not unlikely that the Supreme Court early envisaged the great problem of checks connected with entrusting legislative discretion to the Executive when it included the following essay in a decision upholding an important delegation of contingent legislation to the President:[2]

> It is no answer that such power may be abused, for there is no power that is not susceptible to abuse.

[1] In the discussion which follows, this term connotes not only absolute restraint, but restraint that is directive in character.

[2] Martin *v.* Mott, 12 Wheat. 19 (1827).

The remedy for this, as well as for all other official misconduct, if it should occur, is to be found in the Constitution itself. In a free government the dangers must be remote, since, in addition to the high qualities which the Executive must be presumed to possess, of public virtue, and the honest devotion to the public interests, the frequency of election, and the watchfulness of the representatives of the nation, carry with them all the checks which can be useful to guard against usurpation or wanton tyranny.

II

For purposes of convenience, the important restraint upon executive discretion exercised by the Judiciary will first be discussed. It is through legal remedies that the individual is guaranteed his security against the arbitrary legislative acts of the Executive. The popular safeguards considered later may, and do in the long run, guarantee conformity of rule-making to the will of the people as expressed in statutes. Judicial remedies, however, are those which can be enforced and which are, in large part, relied upon in this country to protect the individual person from all agencies of government purporting to have authority.[1]

In Kendall *v.* Stokes [2] the Supreme Court made the following statement:

The executive power is vested in a President. So far as his powers are derived from the Constitution, he is beyond the reach of any other department, except in the mode prescribed by the Constitution through the impeaching power. But it by no means follows that every officer in every branch of that department is under the exclusive direction of the President. Such

[1] Hart, *op. cit.*, chapter xi, and Appendix, covers the entire subject of safeguards. The writer acknowledges the use of some of this material. Almost all of it, however, has been worked up independently.

[2] 12 Pet. 524 (1838), used as a case under mandamus; see also Freund, *Cases on Administrative Law*, p. 434.

principle, we apprehend, is not and certainly cannot be claimed by the President. There are certain political duties imposed upon many officers in the Executive department, the discharge of which is under the direction of the President. But it would be an alarming doctrine that Congress cannot impose upon any executive officer any duty they may think proper, which is not repugnant to any rights secured and protected by the Constitution; and in such cases the duty and responsibility grow out of and are subject to the control of law, and not to the direction of the President.

Although these words were uttered in a case upholding a mandamus against the Postmaster-General acting in a ministerial capacity, they have value here because they indicate that the President, while in office, " is beyond the reach of any other department, except in the mode prescribed by the Constitution through the impeaching power ", an authority largely political in nature. The important point is that the President is thought to be free from all judicial control over his person while he is in office, an attitude that is consistent with the view that one department of government cannot behead another. This is further evidenced by the refusal of the Judiciary to hold the President in contempt of court [1] or to issue an injunction to restrain him from executing certain Reconstruction Acts.[2] Certainly the President could

[1] Beveridge, *Life of John Marshall*, vol. iii, chap. viii, cited in Hart, *op. cit.*, p. 303, note 38.

[2] Mississippi *v.* Johnson, 4 Wall. 475 (1866). Although special consideration is given to the President's position here, it appears that an injunction against any department head would not issue under similar circumstances. In the case of Georgia *v.* Stanton, Secretary of War, 6 Wall. 50 (1867), the Supreme Court refused to issue an injunction against the Secretary whose duty it was to enforce the Reconstruction Acts in Georgia—not because of the character of the officer but because of the nature of the rights to be protected, viz., political. See Freund, *Cases on Constitutional Law*, pp. 397-399, note 5. For a clear discussion of this question as to state executives, see 35 *Har. Law Rev.* 185-189, and Melville F. Weston, " Political Questions," 38 *Har. Law Rev.* 296 *et seq.*

not be enjoined from issuing a regulation or proclamation, compelled by mandamus to issue the same,[1] indicted in criminal proceedings,[2] sued in damages [3] for the issuing of such executive legislation, or compelled to testify [4] in any case involving legislation that he has made.

From the quotation given above it is seen that although the Supreme Court acknowledges that the heads of departments or independent agencies may be subject to the political control of the President, and, of course, are free from judicial checks, yet it refuses to admit that these immediate aids of the President are free from the control of law, especially where there is no discretion involved. But from the very fact that administrative officers, under the President, are exercising discretion when they issue regulations or general orders, it would apparently follow that mandamus would not lie to compel them to issue such regulations.[5] For the reason that the acts of a legislative character here considered are also of a discretionary nature, the logical conclusion is that the President's aids and advisers are free from writs enjoining them from issuing such legislation. Indeed, it

[1] Hart, *op. cit.*, p. 304, note 43.

[2] *Ibid.*, note 44.

[3] *Ibid.*, note 45.

There seems to be no precedent in the United States for an action against a chief executive [President or Governor] during his term of office to recover damages for an alleged wrongful act done in his official capacity or in connection with his office.

For such an action, brought after the expiration of the term of office, see Livingston *v.* Jefferson, 1 Brock. 203, Fed. Cas. No. 8411, which was, however, dismissed on a point of venue. Freund, *Cases on Administrative Law*, p. 284, note 8.

[4] Hart, *op. cit.*, p. 304, note 46.

[5] *Cf.* Decatur *v.* Paulding, 14 Pet. 497 (1840). Although the court can easily find discretion, whenever it decides it is lacking, mistaken duty or honest or dishonest intention, will not save an officer from being mandamused. Amy *v.* Supervisors, 11 Wall. 36 (1870).

would seem that no court would convict such officers in criminal proceedings for fraud or bad motive in exercising this power, or, except in extreme cases, hold them for damages for the same. To be sure admitted arbitrariness on the part of an officer might cause the court to hold an officer liable in damages. In Spalding v. Vilas [1] the principle was laid down that heads of departments are exempt from payment of damages claimed against them for mere excess of jurisdiction. The court, however, was unwilling to hazard an opinion as to what would happen where jurisdiction was lacking altogether. In Robertson *v.* Sichel [2] it was held that the heads of departments are not liable for damages for acts of their subordinates where no personal fault on their part can be found.[3]

III

The President, while in office, cannot be controlled by any compulsory process, and his chief aids can only rarely be held liable for the exercise of discretion in the making of secondary legislation. These facts might lead one to the conclusion that there is little relief the courts can give in protecting individuals from arbitrary or mistaken action of the various authorities who exercise this exceedingly broad power. It is not the case, however, for the courts have methods of attacking all legislation issuing from all administrative authorities.[4] A few of the conditions under which

[1] 161 U. S. 483 (1896); also 5 Ops. Atty. Gen. 759 (1823). Freund, *Cases on Administrative Law*, pp. 284, 290.

[2] 127 U. S. 507 (1888); Freund, *op. cit.*, pp. 344-345.

[3] See Hart, *op. cit.*, p. 305.

[4] Mississippi *v.* Johnson, 4 Wall. 475: "The Congress is the legislative department of government; the President is the executive department. Neither can be restrained in its action by the judicial department though the acts of both, when performed, are, in proper cases, subject to its cognizance."

the Judiciary may bring such legislation under question will be discussed in the following pages.[1]

Criminal proceedings may be brought against an administrative authority who, in enforcing a piece of delegated legislation, is committing a crime defined in the statutes of the United States. A superior officer, because of his office duties, would rarely, if ever, be the victim of such a situation. It is the subordinate officer politically bound to enforce the regulations of his superior who is the one most likely, however unjustly, to suffer. The collectors of customs are prohibited by statute, under a penalty of $200,[2] from making a charge for any appraisement of imported goods not permitted by law. A certain collector, contrary to this statute, demanded an extra fee for re-appraisement of an importer's goods. The additional charge was made under Article 472 of the Treasury Regulations of 1884. After imposing the penalty upon the collector, the Court said:[3]

> In matters of this kind . . . there is no other way to reach the departures from the statute and to check and prevent petty impositions, than some such mode as this. There are various general statutes like that under which this action is brought, designed, by the penalties imposed, to afford both a compensation to the persons aggrieved and a check against exactions beyond which the law allows. The object of this statute is evidently the protection of the public. It may operate harshly considering a single transaction, but this is the only way to make it felt.

Again, when Congress makes the violation of an executive legislative act a crime or a misdemeanor, any person prosecuted for violating such an act may set up its illegality or

[1] See Hart, *op. cit.*, pp. 306-313.

[2] U. S. Rev. Stat., sec. 2636.

[3] Iselin *v.* Hedden, 28 Fed. 416 (1886).

unconstitutionality as a defense. Under such circumstances the court will have to pass upon the validity of the legislation. This is a very common means of affording a remedy. There is always the plea that a particular delegation has gone beyond what the court considers the constitutional boundary line. There is the further possibility that the issuing officer has exceeded his authority, failed to recognize his lack of authority, or omitted some essential step or steps in the procedure laid down in the law. A review of the entire question of the constitutional right of Congress to make the violation of an administrative regulation a penal offense was brought up in the leading case of United States *v.* Grimaud.[1] In the case of Illinois Central Railroad Company *v.* McKendree [2] a railroad corporation was prosecuted for violating a cattle quarantine regulation of the Secretary of Agriculture. The plea set up was the unconstitutionality of the regulation. The Court found in favor of the appellee on the ground that the executive rule was trying to accomplish, at least in part, what Congress itself could not, viz., the regulation of purely intrastate commerce. In the case of United States *v.* George [3] a party was protected against the serious charge of perjury by pleading the illegality of an administrative rule naming the content of a land oath.

Any person may apply for a writ of *habeas corpus,* if he is held under restraint by authority of, or for the violation of, a rule or proclamation of the Executive. The court, in such case, must inquire into the validity of the executive action. For example, a Chinese person, claiming American citizenship, was held for deportation upon his arrival at a port of the United States. A petition for a writ of *habeas*

[1] 220 U. S. 506 (1911).

[2] 203 U. S. 514 (1906).

[3] 228 U. S. 14 (1913). See also Selective Draft Cases, 245 U. S. 366 (1917); Avent *v.* U. S., 266 U. S. 127.

corpus resulted in a review of the alleged illegal procedure by which he was denied entrance.[1] The Supreme Court found that the immigration authorities had not observed the rules of procedure laid down by the Department of Commerce and Labor for all hearings. Mr Justice Holmes, speaking for the Court, went so far as to say, "The courts must deal with the matter somehow, and there seems to be no way so convenient as a trial of the merits before the judge."

A ministerial officer enforcing a particular legislative act of the Executive which is contrary to a statute or to the Constitution may be held in damages or in money. This ruling arises from the principle firmly rooted in American public law that the state itself cannot be sued without its consent.[2] If the United States is exempted from suit, unless it consents thereto, its officers are not free from personal liability to parties whose rights of property have been unlawfully violated.[3] In practice, however, this safeguard usually works against subordinate officers, who are the persons that enforce legislation in particular cases.

[1] U. S. *v.* Sing Tuck, 194 U. S. 161 (1904). See also Chin Yow *v.* U. S., 208 U. S. 8 (1908); Sibrony *v.* U. S., 282 Fed. 795 (1922). Perhaps the most arbitrary action of the Department of Labor, unearthed as a result of a petition for *habeas corpus*, was exposed by Judge Anderson in Colyer *v.* Skeffington, 265 Fed. 17 (1920). Rules of the Department relative to deportation hearings were changed over night in order "to get" the men wanted. It might be inferred from Jan Fat *v.* White, 253 U. S. 454 (1920), that arbitrary unwritten rules of procedure in handling Chinese exclusion cases may be questioned on a petition for a writ of *habeas corpus*.

[2] For statutes permitting suit see U. S. Comp. Stat. (1901), pp. 734, 745; 3 Stat. 692 (1822). For decisions enunciating this principle in American public law see Lanford *v.* U. S., 101 U. S. 341 (1879); U. S. *v.* Lee, 106 U. S. 196 (1882).

[3] Belknap *v.* Schild, 161 U. S. 10, 18; Tindal *v.* Wesley, 167 U. S. 204; Scranton *v.* Wheeler, 179 U. S. 141; U. S. *v.* Lee, 106 U. S. 196.

Perhaps the leading case is The *Flying Fish.*[1] An embargo law prohibited any vessel in which an American had a direct interest from sailing to ports under the jurisdiction of France. The President was given power to enforce this prohibition by means of the navy, even on the high seas. Seizure and condemnation in admiralty constituted the penalty. Half of the proceeds of the capture were to go to the captors. The Navy Department gave orders to captains of armed vessels to exercise sound and impartial judgment in preventing all intercourse between the ports of the United States and those of France, and to seize all vessels, really American, bound to or from French ports. The *Flying Fish,* a vessel not bound to a French port, was seized by Captain Little and brought to the United States for adjudication. Even an American ship could not have been legally seized under such circumstances. The Court, after making the following statement of the main question, held the captain liable in damages:

These orders, given by the Executive, under the construction of the Act of Congress made by the department to which its execution was assigned, enjoin the seizure of American vessels sailing from a French port. Is the officer who obeys them liable for damages sustained by this misconstruction of the act, or will his orders excuse him? If his instructions afford him no protection, then the law must take its course, and he must pay such damages as are legally awarded against him. . . .

Two additional cases seem to establish the liability in damages of subordinates in carrying out illegal rules of their superior. In each case certain imported goods, in accordance with the orders from the Secretary of the Treasury, were so classified as to make the duty higher than the terms

[1] 2 Cranch 170 (1804). See Freund, *op. cit.*, sec. 37, p. 332 *et seq.* Perhaps the rule that the captor gets all or part of the capture made the court here the more ready to check up on the captor's personal interests.

of the tariff law permitted—a duty so high, in fact, that the importer, unable to give bond, had to leave his goods to deteriorate in the customs house. In the first case [1] the Court said:

The collector of the customs is a ministerial officer. He acts under the instruction of the Secretary of the Treasury, who is expressly authorized to give instructions, as to the due enforcement of the revenue laws. Do these instructions, when not given in accordance with the law, afford a justification to the collector, or exonerate him from the payment of adequate damages for an injury resulting from his illegal acts? . . . The Secretary of the Treasury is bound by the law; and although, in the exercise of his discretion, he may adopt necessary forms and modes of giving effect to the law, yet neither he nor those who act under him can dispense with, or alter, any of its provisions. It would be a most dangerous principle to establish that the acts of a ministerial officer, when done in good faith, however injurious to private rights and unsupported by law, should afford no ground for legal redress.

In the second case [2] the customs officer had actually collected under orders from his superior a larger duty than the law permitted and, although the importer had protested at the time of payment, had turned the money into the treasury. Action was brought to recover the overpaid amount. The Court, in the course of the opinion, used the following words: [3]

This question must be answered in the affirmative, unless the broad proposition can be maintained that no action will lie against

[1] Tracy *v.* Swartwout, 10 Pet. 80 (1836). See Freund, *op. cit.*, sec. 35, p. 314.

[2] Elliott *v.* Swartwout, 10 Pet. 137 (1836). See Freund, *op. cit.*, sec. 35, p. 316.

[3] Gelston *v.* Hoyt, 3 Wheat. 248, is a particularly interesting case, cited by Hart, *op. cit.*, p. 311, corroborating the same general principle.

a collector to recover back an excess of duties paid him, but that recourse must be had to the government for redress. . . .

From this view of the cases, it may be assumed as the settled doctrine of law that, where money is illegally demanded and received by an agent, he cannot exonerate himself from personal responsibility by paying it over to his principal, if he has had notice not to pay it over. The answer, therefore, to the third point, must be that the collector is personally liable to an action to recover back an excess of duties paid to him as collector, under the circumstances stated in the point, although he may have paid over the money into the Treasury.

In each of the cases cited the superior officer lacked altogether any authority for the rules which a subordinate carried out at his own peril. This may account for the harshness of the decisions. On the other hand there are circumstances under which a subordinate officer may not be held liable in damages or money. As early as 1851 a state court held to the principle that a ministerial officer in carrying out the will of superior officers who had jurisdiction over the matter involved, but who might have erred in the exercise of such jurisdiction, could not be held for damages.[1] In 1872 the Supreme Court adopted the same principle in the case of Erskine *v.* Hohnbach.[2] Here the collector of internal revenue was sued for the seizure of property owned by Hohnbach. The collector claimed that he had acted as an official of the government in enforcing the collection of an assessment duly made and certified to him by his superior who had jurisdiction over the matter. The Court, in holding the collector not liable under the circumstances, said:

[1] Chegaray *v.* Jenkins, 5 N. Y. 376. See Freund, *Cases on Administrative Law*, pp. 339-341.

[2] 14 Wall. 613. This case is cited, together with Stutsman County *v.* Wallace, 142 U. S. 293 (1892), by Freund, *op. cit.*, p. 341, note 46, as being in accord with the Chegaray *v.* Jenkins Case. See also Hart, *op. cit.*, p. 312.

It is well settled now, that if the officer or tribunal possess jurisdiction over the subject-matter upon which the judgment is passed, with power to issue an order or process for the enforcement of such judgment, and the order or process issued thereon to the ministerial officer is regular on its face, showing no departure from the law, or defect of jurisdiction over the person or property affected, then in such cases, the order or process will give full and entire protection against any prosecution which the party aggrieved thereby may institute against him, although serious errors may have been committed by the officer or tribunal in reaching the conclusion or judgment upon which the order or process is issued.

Finally, where the interests of private persons are affected by the arbitrary or mistaken legislative action of national administrative officers, the question of its validity might be raised in a civil suit. If so, the courts would have to pass upon the regulation before the rights of the parties in dispute could be determined. This is illustrated in the case of Swendig *v.* The Power Company.[1] Under a statute of 1901 [2] the Secretary of the Interior was given the power, under proper regulations, to grant rights of way for water power lines. He granted such a right of way in 1902 to a power company through the Coeur d'Alene Reservation. Under a law of 1906 [3] the President by proclamation was allowed to, and did, throw open for settlement certain portions of this reservation for entry. It happened that the right of way noted above cut through the land entered by Swendig, for which he had been granted a clear patent. When friction arose the power company brought suit to keep the patentee from interfering with the power line. The Court had to consider both the regulatory power of the

[1] 265 U. S. 32 (1924).

[2] 31 Stat. 790.

[3] 34 Stat. 335.

Secretary of the Interior and the power of the President to open the land to entry before the rights of each party could be determined.[1]

IV

In addition to the judicial safeguards which inevitably play a large part in the American constitutional system there are what may becalled political safeguards. In a sense the latter are by far the more important. As they are more or less general in nature, they touch a greater number of people; they constitute the checks which forestall, in most cases, the necessity for the individual application of the former, or assure that evils not remedied by law will be removed. For a democracy, at least, the play of public opinion upon the agencies directly or indirectly responsible for all control over personal rights and property is the most logical and wholesome safeguard against arbitrary action. A state whose people are willing to depend entirely upon the Judiciary for protection may ultimately find that its power has been delegated to an "aristocracy of the robe".

When political responsibility, in its general form, is to be treated as a check upon the Executive as a maker of subordinate legislation, the particular form of government obtaining in a state must be considered important. In this country direct political responsibility for administrative law-making is less real than in other Anglo-Saxon countries. Under the presidential system as it exists in the United States the popularly-elected Chief Executive is, in theory, held politically responsible both for the exercise of legislation delegated to him, which he exercises personally or subdelegates to his subordinates, and for the exercise of legis-

[1] According to Hart, *op. cit.*, p. 307, there is still another method of action: where a right is claimed under delegated legislation which a ministerial officer refuses to apply or enforce before the right can be realized, a writ of mandamus may issue to force the administrative officer to act.

lative discretion directly delegated to departmental officers or to the independent agencies. Responsibility in the latter has resulted from his power to appoint and remove, or from the political pressure which few inferiors can resist.[1] In practice, however, the Chief Executive, always occupied with primary legislative policies and the "dignified" activities that go with his office, has found it utterly impossible to keep close scrutiny on the ever-expanding legislative activities of his subordinates. Only to the most important cases. has he given his attention.[2] Consequently, there does not exist, in practice, that solidarity which is so important in holding the Executive responsive to public opinion.[3] It is just at this point that the parliamentary system of other Anglo-Saxon countries has the advantage. There the Prime Minister subjects all ministers, as well as all other administrative officers, to his will.

No one will deny that his direct popular responsibility has played a part in tending to check, generally, the discretion of the Executive. The President as head of his party must answer at the polls for bad or unwise acts. Although he may satisfy the criticism of accomplished acts by pleading ignorance, he must give his promise of closer control in the future.[4] Discontent with specific administrative laws does

[1] For a concise discussion of the political relation between the President and his subordinates, together with cited cases and individual testimony, see Hart, *op. cit.*, chap. viii.

[2] E. g., proclamations under the Tariff Act of 1922. See *Ninth Annual Report of the Tariff Commission*, pp. 84-85. But see the *Hearings of the Senate Committee on Public Lands and Surveys*, pp. 177-286, 68th Cong., 1st Sess. (1923-1924), as to the signing of the naval oil lease order.

[3] Woodrow Wilson, *Constitutional Government in the United States*, pp. 75-81, quoted in Hart, *op. cit.*, p. 295, note 10.

[4] E. g., the Republican Campaign Committee's position in 1924 on the navy oil lease situation as brought out by the Senate Comm. on Public Lands and Surveys, *Hearings* on S. R. 147, 67th Cong., 4th Sess. and 68th Cong., 1st Sess. (1923-1924).

not, as a rule, affect a large group of voters at any one time. But an accumulation of irritations may make the party suffer. Perhaps the airing of complaints against administrative officers, were such officers permitted to discuss and defend their acts involving legislative discretion in either house of Congress, might result in a wider play of opinion as well as in a closer supervision by the President.[1]

There is not the indirect political responsibility of the Executive in the American system that is found, for example, in the parliamentary system of Great Britain. In other words, Congress, the governmental body closest to the people, has no political power to dismiss the Executive from office, as has the House of Commons. The only means by which the national legislature can act directly in the interest of the people is that of impeachment. Whether the Fathers intended that this method should be used as a political weapon, as it was in England preceding the establishment of responsible cabinet government, is not known. Certainly the phrase "impeachment for, and conviction of, treason, bribery, and other high crimes and misdemeanors" would lead one to believe that criminal acts alone invoke such action.[2] Since everything that Congress does, however, is tinged with politics, it is conceivable that officers, individually, not collectively, might be impeached and convicted for wilful abuse, or even unwise use, of delegated legislative discretion.

[1] A Senate committee favored this closer relation—but on a wider basis—as early as 1881. See Senate Report, No. 837, 46th Cong., 3rd Sess. President Taft put the general idea again before Congress in a special message in 1913. In 1921 the budget law debate was not free from suggestion of this idea. President Lowell, *Essays on Government*, pp. 25-45, decries such a change, lest in going too far it destroy our form of government in action. See Beard, *American Government and Politics*, pp. 218-221.

[2] The Constitution, Art. II, Sec. 4; see also Art. I, Sec. 2, par. 5, and Sec. 3, par. 6.

In practice this power over administrative officers has been of slight importance.[1]

V

Theoretically Congress has a complete and decisive political check upon the use of delegated discretion in that it may withdraw from the Executive the power which it bestows and withhold the funds which are necessary for effecting the legislation upon which the Executive may determine. But according to the discussion that has gone before such political control would be begging the whole question. It has been insisted that Congress, in order to accomplish desirable purposes, has found in most cases that administrative agencies are an invaluable and indispensable instrument for breaking incomplete and contingent legislation onto the back of the public. Hence the withdrawal of such delegated power or the denial of enforcement funds would be likely to result in a more severe blow to the interests of those affected by the law or laws concerned than the particular acts of the Executive against which there might be complaint.

Although this great power is always in the background it is likely in practice to be called into action only where the evils of executive legislation are greater than the good accomplished. Congress has anticipated the abuse of legislative discretion many times by declaring in advance the withdrawal of the delegation thereof, especially in near-war or war emergencies. This tendency can be seen from an examination of the statutes bestowing legislative power under such circumstances.[2] Then, too, Congress might well withdraw a great amount of discretion from the Executive after the involved problems which prompted the delegations have

[1] See D. Y. Thomas, "The Law of Impeachment in the United States," *Pol. Sci. Quar.*, May, 1908, pp. 378 *et seq.*

[2] E. g., 1 Stat. 372; 1 Stat. 577; 13 Stat. 376; 40 Stat. 76; 40 Stat. 556.

been reduced to such simple formulas that the laws themselves might incorporate them. If this calling in of the older delegations were resorted to, the sum total of discretion would be greatly lessened, and dangers of abuse anticipated. Thus, Secretary Jardine, after the attitude of the cattlemen concerning grazing regulations was ascertained by a series of hearings held by a sub-committee of the Senate Committee on Public Lands and Surveys,[1] came to the conclusion that Congress should resume certain discretion which had been exercised by the Forest Service. His words follow:[2]

I favour a provision of law that will authorize firm contracts or licenses for periods of ten years, to be binding upon the Government as long as their conditions are met, and under which the requirements to be observed by the range users, the possible reductions in numbers of livestock, and the provision for grazing fees shall be specifically set forth.

VI

The remainder of this chapter will be devoted to a consideration of publicity as a means of safeguarding the people from arbitrary or misguided acts of the Executive in its exercise of law-making power. Presumably, if all acts resulting from the sub-letting of such an important power were formally presented to Congress, that body could be reasonably held responsible for them. One might even expect special consideration of a portion of such legislation, especially if the individuals or groups affected by it were to

[1] *Hearings of the Sub-Committee of the Senate Committee on Public Lands and Surveys*, 69th Cong., 1st Sess. (1925), held pursuant to S. Res. 347.

[2] *Annual Report of Secretary of Agriculture*, p. 87 (1925). See also *Hearings of the Senate Finance Committee*, 68th Cong., 1st Sess. (1924), relative to H. R. 6715 (revenue bill); Report of Joint Comm. on Postage on Second Class Mail Matter and Compensation for the Transportation of Mail, 63rd Cong., 2nd Sess. (1914).

notify their representatives of any unsatisfactory conditions therein. Any discussion of grievances would get into the *Congressional Record,* and possibly might appear in the press. A study of the Statutes at Large reveals, however, that although Congress has from the first demanded an occasional accounting to itself by its agents who wield legislative power, this demand appears only spasmodically.[1]

Thus the President has been given the power by statute to reduce the weight of copper coin of the United States, but when he does he must both make his acts known by proclamation and " report to Congress at the next session ".[2] The Secretary of the Navy was authorized to prepare the necessary rules and regulations for the government of the Marine Hospital and " report the same to Congress at the next session "; [3] likewise for the government of the Navy Department.[4] All purchases of supplies for the Navy are required to be made under such directions and regulations as the Executive may make; but all rules so made must be " laid before Congress ".[5] The President may prescribe fees to be charged by consuls for all official services; but he must report annually to Congress the fees established.[6] The Secretary of the Treasury may make certain regulations for the appraisal of goods; but he must report them directly to Congress, together with the reasons for so doing.[7] The Presi-

[1] *Cf.* the English law requiring reports of similar executive acts to Parliament: Rules Publication Act (1893), 56 and 57 Vict. c. 66, vol. i, Chittys Stat. (6th ed.), pp. 21 *et seq.* See Carr, *Delegated Legislation,* p. 33.

[2] 1 Stat. 440.

[3] 2 Stat. 650.

[4] 3 Stat. 203.

[5] 5 Stat. 535.

[6] 11 Stat. 57.

[7] 15 Stat. 110. In considering the Revenue Bill (H. R. 6715), the clause

dent may by regulation prescribe the procedure and modes of proof in cases before all military tribunals provided that " all the rules made in pursuance of this article shall be laid before Congress annually ".[1]

VII

Congress has methods of eliciting from the departments and special agencies information relating to their legislative activities other than that of a specific demand for accounting contained in the delegation clause. There is a general provision concerning the content of annual reports to be made by all the departments to Congress;[2] and there are specific provisions calling for annual reports from particular departments and agencies.[3] These reports usually give extended, and sometimes very detailed information, as to the legislative activities that have been carried on during the year which the reports cover. These valuable documents are not only filed with the legislature but are available to press and private

"and all such rules and regulations and all amendments thereto shall be annually reported to Congress," was added by the House. The Solicitor of the Bureau of Internal Revenue made this comment thereon: "There is no necessity in the world for this . . . clause; it was put in on the floor of the House." See *Hearings of the Senate Finance Committee* on H. R. 5716, 68th Cong., 1st Sess., p. 47 (1924).

[1] Rev. Stat., Sec. 1342, as amended by 39 Stat. 656. Some regulations, e. g., those issued under 1 Stat. 440, are also to be promulgated by the President. Other regulations are to be promulgated but not officially reported to Congress. See 1 Stat. 577; 43 Stat. 1961, a proclamation under 40 Stat. 755. Of course, a proclamation is intended in itself to give information to the public and has value as a general check.

[2] Rev. Stat., Sec. 195: "Except where a different time is expressly prescribed by law, the various annual reports required to be submitted by the heads of Departments shall be made at the commencement of each regular session, and shall embrace the transactions of the preceding year."

[3] E. g., Rev. Stat., Sec. 257, the Treasury; Rev. Stat., Sec. 445, Department of the Interior; Rev. Stat., Sec. 429 for the Navy; 24 Stat. 379, Sec. 14, as amended by 25 Stat. 855, for the Interstate Commerce Commission.

citizens.[1] Congress may also, by concurrent resolution or by resolution of one or the other of the chambers, call for special information from the Executive relative to the exercise of legislative functions. In this way a series of Senate resolutions once called for copies of all rules and regulations issued respectively by the Secretaries of the Interior, Treasury, Agriculture, and by the Postmaster-General.[2] The result was a more or less complete compilation of the formal regulations governing the activities of these agencies.

As a matter of fact, however, even if the report be fairly complete it is a most unsatisfactory method of getting at the truth of what is going on within the various administrative offices. To get the spirit and the subtle practices a more intimate contact is necessary. Hence it has been the habit of Congress to get in touch with executive officials who make and enforce delegated legislation and with the representative parties or groups actually affected by such legislation. This is done through regular or special committees of Congress.

According to Mr. Luce [3] Congress sets committees at work to accomplish one or the other of two distinct purposes, viz., to secure information for the purpose of making laws or to learn whether the laws already made are being properly executed. The hearings on proposed statutes, however, actually result in disclosing the attitude and practice of officials concerned in the making of administrative legislation under former statutes of similar nature, or, where the

[1] E. g., see the annual reports of the following executive departments and agencies: I. C. C., 1921; Secretary of the Treasury, 1924; Department of the Interior, 1909; Department of Agriculture, 1922; U. S. Shipping Board, 1923 and 1924. The reports of the subdivisions of departments, although made for inclusion in the general report of the department, are more detailed; they are also available to all.

[2] For resolutions, see *Cong. Rec.*, vol. 41, pt. 3, p. 2064, 59th Cong., 2nd Sess.

[3] *Legislative Procedure*, ch. viii, especially p. 170.

bill under consideration deals with an absolutely new policy, the contemplated action of such officials. While the enforcing agency is eager to relate its past experience, the groups affected are quite ready to present their criticisms as to what executive officials have done or may do under delegated discretion. The hearings are usually open to the public and all the facts and opinions are preserved in written form. Thus the hearings held by the Senate Finance Committee on the Revenue Bill of 1924 contained some of the material relating to previous regulatory practices which, in turn, appeared in the records of a special investigating committee.[1]

The hearings that attract the most attention are those under the direction of regular or special committees whose duty it is to investigate the administration of laws.[2] "Armed with the omnipotence of a subpoena", such committees, or subdivisions thereof, may force attendance and testimony at Washington or in any locality under the jurisdiction of the United States. Attorneys and advisory experts may appear for the committee, for the administrative

[1] *Hearings* on H. R. 6715, 68th Cong., 1st Sess. (1924). See also *Hearings* of the House Judicial Comm. on H. R. 6645 to provide a Bureau of Prohibition in the Treasury, 68th Cong., 1st Sess. (1924); *Hearings of the House Committee on Merchant Marine and Fisheries*, pp. 22-103, 68th Cong., 1st Sess. (1924); *Hearings of the Senate Finance Committee* on the tariff bill of 1922, 67th Cong., 1st Sess., pp. 23-151 (1921), for viewpoint of Tariff Commission. The summary of such hearings in the form of committee reports, although frequently partisan in nature, are sometimes enlightening. See Report of Joint Committee on Postage of Second Class Mail Matter and Compensation for the Transportation of Mail, 63rd Cong., 2nd Sess. (1914), for an elaborate presentation of postoffice practices brought to light after a period of some nineteen months of arduous labors; also the facts brought out by the House Ways and Means Committee in Report 852, p. 6, on H. R. 2123, to amend 38 Stat. 277.

[2] Administration of laws includes the making and changing of rules and regulations, Luce, *op. cit.*, p. 175.

agency under investigation, and for parties who have complaints or commendations to give relative to executive legislation affecting them. These committees, sitting as informal tribunals, listen alike to the story of the most humble citizen, to the explanation of technical officials or advisory experts, and to the legal points raised by the lawyer. It is evident, however, that a good bit of testimony is given the turn that a majority of the committee prefer. This lessens the value of many specific facts brought out in the investigation. Still there is usually sufficient material assembled to form the basis for direct political checks upon officers or indirect political checks by congressional action.[1] Public hearing, recorded testimony, exposure of the most secret practices of executive-legislative officers, sterling defense or forced confession of wrong on the part of such officers, charges and counter-charges of private individuals and groups in the presence of their oppressors or friends, as the case may be—all tend to lend force to the plea that such investigations do

[1] The following are some of the investigations which illustrate the general statement made in this paragraph: (a) *Hearings of the Senate Judicial Committee on the Activities of the Department of Justice in Deportation Cases*, pp. 398-419, 66th Cong., 3rd Sess. (1921); (b) *Hearings of Senate Committee on Public Lands and Surveys on Leases upon Naval Oil Reserves* (41 Stat. 912), 67th Cong., 4th Sess., and 68th Cong., 1st Sess., pp. 177-286 (1923-1924); (c) *Hearings of the Sub-committee of the Senate Committee on Public Lands and Surveys on the Administration of Public Lands*, parts 11, 12, 13, 14, 15, 69th Cong., 1st Sess. (1925). These hearings took place in the various public land states of the West; (d) *Hearings of the House Select Committee on the Policies and Affairs of the U. S. Shipping Board*, especially pp. 194-201, 68th Cong., 1st Sess. (1924); (e) *Hearings of the Senate Select Committee to Investigate Bureau of Internal Revenue*, beginning 68th Cong., 1st Sess. (1924), and extending through 68th Cong., 2nd Sess. (1925). See also Senate Report No. 27, 69th Cong., 1st Sess. (1926); (f) *Hearing of the Senate Select Committee for the Investigation of the Tariff Commission*, 69th Cong., 1st Sess. (1926). Data secured from *New York Times*, Jan. 17, Mar. 24, 1926 and Apr. 1, 2, 1926.

result in emphasizing or changing opinions already formed or in creating new opinions. If this is so, publicity finds its justification.

Although concrete results from the exposure of administrative practices are not always at first apparent, they do usually appear in some change of policy on the part of the Executive through its own efforts or through Congressional action. As has already been shown, the Secretary of Agriculture has picked out the three or four weakest points of the Forestry Service's grazing policy and has asked Congress, by definitizing the law, to take away a large part of that agent's discretionary power. This action resulted from the hearings of the Senate Public Land and Surveys Committee.[1] The inquiry into the administration of Section 15 of the Tariff Act of 1922, although it has not as yet resulted in the modification or abolition of the Tariff Commission or in the elimination of the flexible provision of that law, has succeeded in indicating the political rather than the scientific character of the Commission's actions. Likewise it has brought to light the secret recommendations of this body relative to the tariff on sugar, butter, and the like, which the President had refused to make public before the Committee began its work.[2] The Senate Judiciary Committee got to the bottom of the arbitrary action of the Department of Labor in its secret change of procedure in deportation hearings with a view to deporting whomever it desired, without due process of law.[3] It is likely to be a long time before that department will abuse its power in such a manner again. The investigation of the complaint that Section 28 of the Merchant Marine Act, if put into operation by the Shipping

[1] See p. 191, note (1), subdivision (c); *Annual Report of the Secretary*, p. 87 (1925).

[2] See p. 191, note (1), subdivision (f).

[3] See p. 191, note (1), subdivision (a).

Board, would seriously discriminate against certain ports of the United States and would disrupt the rate schedules of the Interstate Commerce Commission, put an end to the indecision of that Board and led to further consideration by Congress of the wisdom of the law itself as well as of the policy of turning such great power over to a subordinate.[1] The extended inquiry into the actions taken by certain departmental officers relative to the conservation of the Navy oil-bearing lands led to one resignation, to civil suits and criminal prosecutions, and to a solemn promise by the official head of the government that a closer supervision would in the future be maintained over such valuable public assets.[2] The Committee on the Investigation of the Bureau of Internal Revenue felt a certain satisfaction in recounting a number of instances in which the Bureau " had faced about " as a result of the public disclosures in both its general and particular practices. Secrecy of regulations, revised procedure in collecting excise taxes and in compromising income taxes, and improved internal supervisory organization were some of the cases cited where improvements had resulted.[3]

[1] See p. 191, note (1), subdivision (d). See also *Hearings of the House Committee on Merchant Marine and Fisheries*, 68th Cong., 1st Sess., pp. 19-103 (1924).

[2] See p. 191, note (1), subdivision (b).

[3] See p. 191, note (1), subdivision (e), pp. 3401, 3381-3389, 3665 and Senate Report No. 27, 69th Cong., 1st Sess. (1926), pp. 17, 96, 223-225 and 227-228. Partly as a result of this investigation the House inserted a section (Sec. 1203) in the Income Tax Law of 1926 which provided for a joint commission, consisting of five members from each house and five from the public whose duty was set forth as follows:

> To investigate and report on the operation, effects and administration of the federal system of income and other internal revenue taxes and upon any proposals or measures which, in the judgment of the commission, may be employed to simplify or improve the operation and administration of such systems of taxes, and to make and report upon their investigations in respect to such system of taxes as the commission may deem necessary.

One might well agree with Bryce that the American committee device has a real advantage over the usual European system of checking the administration by interrogating the ministers on the floor of the popular chamber only, however, when it is publicly and continuously employed in exposing and criticizing the defects of the Executive. On the other hand, when it is considered that this system is only an occasional political method of bringing publicity to the discretionary acts of administrative officers—at times nothing more than an up-to-date method of "fishing"—one is inclined to agree with Woodrow Wilson, who expressed the belief that resolutions calling upon officials to give testimony before committees are a much clumsier and less efficient means of eliciting information than is a running fire of questions addressed to ministers constantly in their places in the popular chamber to reply publicly to all interrogatories.[1]

VIII

Finally, in fairness to the groups affected directly by delegated legislation as well as to the public at large, publicity ought to be given to all such legislation. Although this, as Mr. Carr says, is post-natal in character,[2] it is essential in that it gives an opportunity for individuals and groups to know what the law is—a necessary condition precedent if political reaction is to precede actual application of policies that may be thought injurious to those affected.

It has been shown that many practices affecting the rights and duties of individuals are unknown until applied; it remains to indicate that many people are unable to ascertain with reasonable facility most of the administrative legislation that is to be put into effect. The presumption is that every citizen or inhabitant of the United States who has

[1] See Luce, *op. cit.*, p. 200, for the opinions of Bryce and Wilson.

[2] *Delegated Legislation*, p. 36.

reached the years of discretion possesses knowledge of the primary federal laws. Theoretically, ignorance of the law stands in no stead as a defense. This means that if Congress passes an Act, everyone, in theory, has passed it, that everyone knew the original content of the bill, sat in at the committee hearings and deliberations, listened to the arguments for and against the committee report, acquiesced or not in any motions to amend, had full knowledge of the content of the bill as finally passed and, above all, knew the actual time when the law would go into effect. The same reasoning applies to the repealing or amending of such legislation. This presumption is in part justified in that all of the primary laws of the national government may be found in official or unofficial compilations that are within easy reach of all lawyers and of almost all private citizens.[1]

But such is not the case with almost all of the mass of federal administrative legislation that daily affects a large proportion of the people of the United States. To be sure, all proclamations since 1873 [2] are supposed to have been printed in the Statutes at Large and from that time are as accessible as the primary laws. Almost all of the executive orders since 1905, moreover, may be found in at least two places, the Department of State and the Library of Congress at Washington.[3] It is difficult, however, to see how such a monopoly on the part of the Capital can inure to the benefit of the general public. With these exceptions, if the execu-

[1] Statutes at Large; U. S. Rev. Statutes; U. S. Compiled Statutes; Federal Statutes Annotated, with supplements; Barnes's Federal Code, with supplements, etc.

[2] See Statutes at Large: also letter from the Division of Publications of the Department of State, quoted in Hart, *op. cit.*, p. 317, note 10.

[3] See Gaillard Hunt, *The Department of State* (1914), and the letter from the Department of State to Mr. W. C. Ford, at one time head of the Department of Manuscripts, Library of Congress, printed in the first volume of *United States Executive Orders*.

tive orders may be counted as a unit, there is absolute confusion in the matter of publicity. The discouraging element about it all is that no serious attempt has been made by the federal government to remedy the situation. One private publisher in 1918 made an effort to compile all general rules and regulations made pursuant to national laws. But no supplements have been found since that time.[1]

The result is that a presumption of knowledge of the secondary law (regulations), and even of the primary law (statutes) can no longer go unquestioned, even from a theoretical viewpoint. There is no standardized compilation of the former, including amendments; and the latter cannot be applied in many cases without the former.[2] Publication is tied up with, and dependent upon, the particular agency possessing the power to enforce the statute under which the sub-legislation issues. One must, therefore, be able to identify the enforcing agency, and then seek from it the law which names his rights and duties. Usually such law is printed in pamphlet form, sometimes with innumerable loose-leaf amendments setting aside partially or wholly some regulation; occasionally a valuable compilation of the rules and practices, with or without annotations, is published by individual departments or agencies.[3]

[1] J. A. Lapp, *Federal Rules and Regulations* (1918).

[2] "A citizen desiring to obey the laws would search the acts of Congress in vain to find that grazing sheep upon a forest reserve without the permit of the Secretary of Agriculture is a criminal offense. It has been suggested that the acts under which indictment is drawn give notice that the Secretary may make rules and regulations, and that search would not be complete and inquiry concluded until it be ascertained whether he has made such rules and regulations, the violation of which it is expressly declared shall be a criminal offense. U. S. *v.* Mathews, 146 Fed. 306 (1906).

[3] E. g., *Military Laws of the United States*, 2 volumes (1921); George Smelling, *Laws Relating to the Navy* (1921); Bureau of Mines, *Mining Laws Annotated*, 2 volumes (1915); *Postal Laws and Regulations* (1913).

Professor John A. Fairlie[1] has made a penetrating, first-hand study of the technique of publication. Between the lines of his discussion, however, one can see that his main purpose is to secure adequate publicity for all delegated legislation. A summary of the main suggestions which he gives for accomplishing this purpose may well be given as a fitting conclusion to the above discussion;[2]

(a) An official Bulletin of Executive Ordinances should be issued from time to time containing and keeping up to date all ordinances and other executive acts of the government. In this Bulletin differences of form should indicate differences of content.

(b) Better arrangements should be made for the distribution of rules of a particular kind or type to the officials upon whom they are binding, and for making them available to the private persons to whom they apply. They should to this end be issued, not only *seriatim*, but periodically in collected and revised form, with adequate indices, digests and summaries. This should supplement the general collection of all types in the Official Bulletin.

(c) There should be uniformity in the methods of issuing amendments to rules and regulations and to other ordinances.[3]

These are generally made at the request of Congress. Private initiative has greatly helped in the case of particular laws. E. g. see Montgomery, *Income Tax Procedure*.

[1] "Administrative Legislation," 18 *Mich. Law Rev.* 183 (1920).

[2] This summary is taken from Hart, *op. cit.*, p. 321.

[3] *Cf.* these suggestions with the English practice, as presented by Carr, *op. cit.*, chapters iv and v.

CHAPTER VII

Political Safeguards: Group Opinion in the Framing of Administrative Legislation

I

No one who has studied the process—formal and actual—of law making at Washington has any doubt that a great deal of pressure from the outside is effectively exerted on any bill of consequence introduced in Congress. Pressures have always reached members of the national legislature, regardless of the avenues of approach. Few will deny that opinion must be largely concentrated upon a representative group of those who come from the electorate—a committee, which, for the most part determines the content and the life or death of any particular bill. A report that goes to the whole house is a precipitate of the highly diluted solution of the opinions of all, or a part of, the groups interested in a certain measure. Hearings, formal and informal, which have come to be an approved method of focusing this opinion, have the decided advantage of being on record, or at least capable of being recorded. As a result reasons and justifications for the content of the measure can be given to all. This reflection of opinion upon the legislature and the response made are in harmony with the theory of popular sovereignty. They have become a part of the political *mores* of the American democracy.

But if this expression of opinion as to what policy the law-making authorities should adopt stops with the signing of a bill by the President, or its passage over his veto, interested persons have failed to "follow through". That which further concerns the person interested in the actual legislative process is the question of what action takes place regarding incomplete or contingent laws between the time they are enacted and the time they begin to touch the individual citizen. What influences are brought to bear upon the single administrator or the commission in framing supplemental legislation or in pushing the button by which conditional laws are set in motion? Is this the strategic place for the bureaucrat of democracy?

It is natural, perhaps, for one to look even here for a continuation of the reflection of restraining opinion. In fact, a readier response at this point is possible and practicable than in the general legislative field. The Executive is better organized to reach out for the more timid and modest opinions, and for the sifting of the bolder and more aggressive types. It may be that administrative officials do not actually hold formal or informal hearings from which subordinate legislation issues. Many times the formulator of the law is the official who has gained, through many contacts and wide experience, the attitude of the interests concerned—an attitude he must harmonize with the public's welfare. This intermediate-executive-legislative (and often-judicial) authority is looked upon as a buffer between greedy monopoly and the poor individual; between an indifferent, slow-moving, or incapable Congress and a deserving, though often neglected, group of citizens.

This last statement, however, does not express the whole truth. Pressure groups must not be looked upon merely as expressing their opinion to an administrative legislator whose only desire is to effectuate their every wish. Although a relation of such a character between official and group may be thought to exist in some cases, it is, for most purposes, too simple a description of the process. These same group forces must be looked upon as furnishing a political check upon a powerful Executive with discretion to put into effect or to suspend laws in particular cases, to turn the purpose of Congress in directions not contemplated by that body, or to create privileges and rights as well as to take them away. It is the larger aspect of the question of executive checks that is to be emphasized, i. e., the compelling force of organized opinion to make a careless or arbitrary officer respond to, and to bring a sympathetic officer into harmony with, the groups affected.

In recent years many of the statutes authorizing delegated legislation have included provisions to the effect that a hearing must be held before such legislation can legally issue.[1] Perhaps a large majority of laws do not call for such hearings. The administrative authorities see to it, however, that those chiefly interested and sufficiently clamant get their viewpoints presented.[2] Indeed, when the law provides for such focusing of public opinion there are instances where fuller opportunity has been given than Congress contemplated.[3] Whatever begets the impulse to hear those interested, the official who finally embodies the results of hearings and conferences into regulations for a busy department is of necessity a thoroughly harassed person. The Chief Solicitor, in his 1909 report to the Secretary of Agriculture,

[1] E. g., 37 Stat. 315, Secs. 5, 7, 8 (1912); 39 Stat. 728, Sec. 23 (1916); 41 Stat. 1063, Sec. 20 (1920); 42 Stat. 1435, Sec. 3 (1923).

[2] 34 Stat. 35 (1897); 41 Stat. 437, Sec. 30 (1920).

[3] Federal Water Power Act, 41 Stat. 1062 (1920); see *infra*, pp. 239-46, and the permanent records of Fed. Power Comm., designated as File, F. P. I., "L", Regulations, for numerous hearings in addition to formal hearings. Forest Reserve Act, 34 Stat. 35 (1897). For non-mandatory hearings, see Regulation G-3, *Use Book*, and pp. 207-11, *infra*; Plant Quarantine Act, 37 Stat. 315 (1912), and S. R. A.—Fed. Hort. Board 72, pp. 15-16 (1922). National Park Service Act, 39 Stat. 535 (1916), and Proceedings of National Park Conference (1917).

says that any examination of the statutes, the administration of which is committed to the Secretary, will disclose how far-reaching, diverse, and intricate are the powers of this important official in the promulgation of regulations to effectuate those statutes; and how much care must be exercised in properly drafting the regulation to meet both the demands of the groups affected and the tests applied by the courts.

Just what the procedure is in any particular department or special agency at any one time is difficult to get at; departmental practices are not for the outsider. A governmental employee of the classified or unclassified service sometimes gives a glimpse of what actually happens. Usually such glimpses, since they are given with an initial cautiousness and a final finger-on-the-lip sign, are of little documentary value. Few departments give freely. Annual reports of special agencies and departments, or of their subdivisions, have contributed something toward a knowledge of the procedure in question; hearings before congressional committees and specific requests from Congress itself or from any individual member of that body give some additional insight into the process. Private persons or organizations help out now and then with facts obtained at hearings on certain rules and regulations. Altogether the writer has garnered not a little information from the so-called silent sources, and has been permitted to follow in some detail the record of the actual workings of one or two agencies in formulating subordinate legislation.

The remaining pages will be devoted to the presentation of cases in which various administrative agencies, endowed by Congress with legislative discretion, have actually been influenced or checked in their exercise of such discretion by the force of political pressures or by the pressure of group opinion. This chapter will deal with the processes by which the legislative activities of the Department of Agriculture are touched by the force of group opinion. The succeeding chapter will take up the study of the same processes in a number of other departments or agencies.

II

The Department of Agriculture, perhaps, has more contacts with individual persons than any of the other governmental agencies—with the possible exception of the Treasury. Its experience in adjusting by regulation many of the duties that the government of late years has assumed has given it an attitude toward the individual and the government which has gained the confidence of both.[1] Laws for the protection of the health of the people, for the prevention of commercial frauds, for the preservation of the national resources—plant, animal, and mineral—for bringing about and maintaining constructive policies of production and marketing, and for many other purposes that have to do with the welfare of the individual and the group, have been assigned to this Department for execution. The late Henry C. Wallace, while Secretary of Agriculture, made the following general statement when questioned concerning the method by which the rules and regulations applicable to the various laws enforced by his Department were promulgated:

There is no established procedure which can be said to be

[1] Of course there are, and have been, decided objections to regulations by certain interested parties. The criticisms, perhaps, are growing in number and intensity. See criticism by Dr. W. T. Hornaday of the Biological Survey's administration of the Migratory Bird Treaty Act, *New York Times*, August 12, 1925, p. 1; the Fed. Hort. Board's administration of the Plant Quarantine Act, *Atlantic Monthly* for June (pp. 775-785) and August (pp. 241-245), 1925; *infra*, pp. 214-216; the administration of the public lands by the Forest Service and the Department of the Interior, *Hearings of Sub-committee of Senate Public Lands Committee*, 69th Cong., 1st Sess., parts 1-15 (1925).

uniform or applicable to every set of rules and regulations in every particular. The laws themselves have pronounced variations in character. The nature of the regulations issuing under them and the considerations given to the preparation of such regulations as well as their purpose vary correspondingly. Some of the acts, such as those which attempt to control interstate traffic in certain commodities by the imposition of penalties in the nature of fines, have regulations which are general in character and which it has been unnecessary to modify or alter except very infrequently. Other laws, which contemplate control on an entirely different basis through an exercise of prohibitive measures, such, for instance, as quarantine, have regulations more specific in their nature dealing extensively with particular conditions, such as plant pests and animal diseases, and prescribe in a definite way the precise restrictions or limitations that are expected to be effected through the terms of the act itself. In the latter case changing conditions and developments of various kinds make it necessary to modify, amend, or alter these regulations comparatively frequently.

It may be said as a general proposition that all of these regulations are predicated upon a thorough investigation which has for its purpose the determination of the need for the exercise of that type of control defined in the regulations.[1]

III

That part of the public domain now known as the National Forest Reserve Lands was at one time used by individual stockmen without restriction for grazing purposes, somewhat in the way that the unreserved lands of the national government are used to-day. Later it became necessary for the stockmen to institute some sort of coöperative scheme for

[1] Letter from former Secretary Wallace to Senator Morris Sheppard dated Oct. 18, 1923, in reply to a letter from the latter dated Sept. 27, 1923, making both a general and a specific inquiry relative to the rule-making procedure. The letter, due to the courtesy of Senator Sheppard, is in the possession of the writer.

getting the best use from these lands. Without such a system they recognized that the live-stock industry would be endangered. Late in the nineteenth century the national government began to take a decided hand in controlling the uses to which private persons and organizations might put such reserves. The protection of reserves from destruction, and the ranchmen from one another, was the intent of Congress, as evidenced by the following excerpt:

> The Secretary . . . may make such rules and regulations . . . as will insure the objects of said reservations, viz., to regulate their occupancy and use and to preserve the forests thereon from destruction; and any violation of this Act or such rules and regulations shall be punished [by $500 fine or twelve months' imprisonment, or both] as is provided in the Act of June 4, 1888, amending section 5388 of the Revised Statutes of the United States.[1]

Since 1905 the actual task of administering forest reserves for grazing, as well as for other uses, has fallen upon the Secretary of Agriculture. This officer in 1920 remarked that no directive policy had been laid down by Congress for the guidance of the department in the exercise of the administrative discretion, with which it had been invested for fifteen years, to determine the conditions under which the use of the range might be permitted ".[2] To effectuate the will of

[1] 34 Stat. 35 (1897). This is the basis for the famous case of U. S. *v.* Grimaud, 220 U. S. 506 (1911). The primary uses of the forest reserves are to produce continuous supplies of timber and to regulate water flow. Grazing is subordinate. This may be the reason for the attitude of the Court and the zeal of the Service.

[2] In his annual report for 1920, p. 48, the Secretary of Agriculture makes this statement:

> Even in the absence of legislation, the Department will make a classification of the ranges and fix a new scale of charges, to be imposed in 1924, under which the fees will represent the actual grazing value of the particular portion of the range used by each permittee or group of permittees. Before a new scale is determined,

Congress as expressed in such general terms the Department, through the Forest Service, has been forced to develop a highly trained staff of experts, who, in turn, have had to evolve a plan of management which would not only safeguard the productivity of the forage crop but would permit the most economic operation of the hundreds of ranches dependent in whole or in part upon the national forest ranges.[1] Consequently, not only has Congress had to defer to its administrative agency in the handling of this important work but the agency itself has also been compelled to defer in large measure to the expressed will of the cattle-raising industry. Such delegation has been necessary if rules and regulations were to be designed in the interests both of the national government and for the private economic interests

> an opportunity will be given the local associations of the national forests users to submit any data regarding the fairness of the proposed fees which they desire to present.

The Forest Service seems to be more considerate of the ranchman than Congress itself. In 1918, it made leases for a five-year period and at a certain rate. At once Congress wanted to raise the rate by legislation more than fifty per cent. The Secretary evidently thought that his policy was the better one and that Congress should keep its hands off until the old licenses had expired. Since the reserves were not being ruined it seemed to him it was worth while to lose income when the confidence of the grazing industry in the Forest Service was at stake.

[1] *Report of the Forester* (1924), p. 24. *The National Forest Manual For Grazing*, effective March, 1924, pp. 103-104, states that a technical staff was created to aid the administration, to assist the permittees and to conduct investigations along the following lines:

(a) Improvement of the range by artificial re-seeding.

(b) National re-vegetation and methods of range management which will insure the perpetuation and maximum production of forage with a minimum loss through non-use.

(c) The distribution and economic importance of plant life in the national forests.

(d) Climatic characteristics of vegetation belts in certain forests.

(e) Carrying capacity of the ranges.

(f) Proper seasons for grazing national ranges.

(g) Improved methods of handling stock under range canditions, etc.

concerned. The ranchman knows that the Secretary of Agriculture has authority to permit, to regulate, or to prohibit grazing in the National Forests; the Forest Service, acting for the Secretary, knows that it must temper this power to the actual needs of the ranchman.

A veteran member of the Forest Service indicated to the writer the philosophy that has guided the Service in the administration of the national forest laws: the primary duty of the Forest Service is to protect against individual desires certain resources that the government has reserved for the public good. Acting as the custodian of Congress this agency has not adopted a policy of denying to individuals anything left to them by implication or definitely by the terms of the law. This it cannot do. On the other hand, with the government's interest dominant, the outsider gets the benefit of any doubt as to his legal rights only when the Service feels that the dominant interest is not adversely affected. The burden of proof is always upon the individual.[1] The Secretary himself implies this same viewpoint when he begs Congress to exclude from forest reservations, national parks and the like, all public lands that sooner or later will be opened up for legitimate economic exploitation. He says that any areas the private uses of which cannot be made incidental to the public interest should not be reserved. Evidently a philosophy embodying the public interest in terms of free individual exploitation of the national resources cannot be reconciled with a philosophy the very essence of which identifies the public weal with the preservation of such resources by social force.[2]

[1] Mr. Mangan, an attorney long with the Forest Service.

[2] *Report of the Department of Agriculture* (1920), p. 47. Perhaps the earliest and fullest statement of the policy of the Department of Agriculture is given in a communication of the Secretary to the Chief Forester, Feb. 1, 1905, at the time the National Forests were placed under the Department. See R. H. D. Boerker, *Our National Forests*, Introduction, pp. xxix-xxx.

Cooperation must and does exist between the government forest officials and the stockmen. Such cooperation is officially recognized in the *Use Book* issued by the Forest Service, which contains regulations and instructions to field employees. Regulation G-3 provides for advisory boards.[1] These boards are the official representatives of local, state and national live-stock associations; their agreements made with the proper officials of the Forest Service, a sub-division of the Department of Agriculture, are binding upon their principals. Locals are classed as majority or minority associations, depending upon the ratio of the membership to the total number of a particular class of permittees or to the total number of permittees of all classes using a national forest or a portion thereof. Among other things these boards, with the approval of the forest supervisor and the district forester, may make special rules of general interest to meet local conditions (*intra vires*); such rules, when once made, are binding upon all users of the particular grazing area concerned. Whenever a state live-stock association appoints an advisory board it may be recognized by the district forester and consulted in regard to matters which affect the general administration of the national forests within the state. Such an association may also appoint advisory boards for any particular forest in the state in which the association's membership includes a majority of the users. National live-stock associations representing the owners of any kind of stock using the national forests may appoint an advisory board. This board will be recognized by the Secretary of Agriculture and consulted annually in reference to matters affecting the use of all of the national forests at such time and place as may be agreed upon. According to Mr. Will C. Barnes,

[1] *Use Book, Grazing Section* (1921), p. 13 *et seq.* Such associations were first officially recognized by the Forestry Service in the Forest Rules of May 31, 1906.

Assistant Associate Forester, and Mr. C. E. Rachford, Inspector of Grazing, there are about 7,500 associations of stockmen which have advisory boards.[1]

From a personal interview with certain Forest Service officials [2] and from perusal of the " Minutes of the Grazing Conference " held at Ogden, Utah, March 4-12, 1923, the writer was able to learn the essentials of the process by which the revised *National Forest Manual for Grazing*, effective March, 1924, was worked out.[3]

At the outset it must be held in mind that the Forest Service has an intelligent field force constantly in touch with the numerous live-stock associations and their individual members. This field force, stationary and traveling, is con-

[1] Interview, Jan. 2, 1925, with Mr. Will C. Barnes and Mr. C. E. Rachford of the Central Office of Forest Service. The stock raisers evidently hold such boards in high esteem. Recognized for the first time in 1906, there were 84 in 1913 and 7,500 twelve years later. For the 1913 data, see A. F. Potter, " The Administration of Grazing in the National Forests," *American National Livestock Ass'n Reports* (1913). In *Hearings of Subcommittee of Committee on Public Lands and Surveys*, 69th Cong., 1st Sess. (1925), part 10, pp. 2928-2929, Senator Gooding of Idaho approves of the early cooperation of live stock organizations with the Forest Service officials, and bemoans its lack at the present time (1925). In the same *Hearings*, part 11, pp. 3126-3130, different stockmen of Wyoming praise such active cooperation, and a Forest Service man gives an excellent account of its technique, p. 3136 *et seq.* In part 12 of the *Hearings*, p. 3292, tribute is paid to the practical value of such mutual understandings.

[2] See note (1), *supra*.

[3] These regulations and instructions are still in mimeograph form, probably because of the inability of the live-stock interests and the Government to get together on a few important questions, such as grazing fees and the vested interests of the older stockmen. The final regulations are not likely to be issued until Congress has acted positively or negatively on the results of the *Hearing of Subcommittee of the Senate Committee on Public Lands and Surveys*, 69th Cong., 1st Sess. (1925), parts 1-15, especially part 14, p. 3780. These important hearings reveal clearly the attitude of the eleven western grazing states affected by the Forest Service regulations.

tinuously furnishing the central office at Washington with information as to the needs and desires of all parties interested in the national forest grazing lands.[1] In addition, the associations are regularly and directly advising with the central officers. The result is that the central office becomes a perennial clearing-house for the ideas, plans and suggested policies emanating from various points of the law's incidence.[2]

The central office initiated the formal process of revising the rules for grazing by sending out a set of tentative regulations dealing with the more important problems of administration. The circular had a twofold purpose: setting the live-stock associations to thinking, and provoking criticism on the part of the various forest district officials. The central officials profited from the reaction of the field forces, as well as from the various interests concerned. The Chief Forester then sent invitations to all stockmen, chiefly through their organizations, to meet at Ogden the first week in March for the purpose of considering closely the tentative regulations with the purpose of bringing order out of chaos. All

[1] This had been going on as early as 1906, according to *Forest Reserve Orders*, No. 13, Oct. 15, 1906. Forest field officials were instructed by the Acting Forester, Mr. Wm. Hall, to make suggestions that would help to clarify existing regulations, to advise revision of all regulations where the policy was questionable, and to recommend new rules that might be considered advisable. It was also urged upon the field officers that such suggestions be attended to carefully, since they were the ones best acquainted with the local situations and most interested in the administration.

[2] In 1906, when the advisory boards were first officially recognized, they were given the privilege of receiving notice of, and of being heard relative to, (a) the increase or decrease in the number of stock to be allowed on any particular forest area for any one year, (b) the division of a particular range between the different kinds of stock and (c) the adoption of special rules to meet local situations. A. F. Potter, "The Administration of Grazing in the National Forests," *American National Live Stock Association Reports* (1913).

of the local, state and national live-stock associations were represented; many of them had already been working together in framing their programs for presentation to the government officials. It was intimated that the packers and the commission-men had advocates at this conference.[1] The Forest Service men were divided into ten committees, each committee considering a different phase of the general question of forest grazing—such as grazing fees, supervision and range improvements. Each committee early began the consideration of changes in the current regulations applicable to its special field. The work consisted largely of hearings at which the interested parties—some of whom were requested to appear and others of whom came of their own accord—testified.

On the fifth day of the hearing the Chief Forester, Col. Greeley, had what was known as a free-for-all stockmen's day meeting. He stated that while the committees were going over point by point the important features of the government's grazing policy and regulations, as well as the details of instruction, it would be well to hold an open meeting so that any stockman or group of stockmen might elaborate particular viewpoints. The agenda for the day had been prepared but was not adhered to. Questions of principle and policy were discussed freely by the live-stock interests.

The various committees presented the results of their week's work to a committee of the whole. Each report in which there had been a split vote gave both minority and majority views, together with supporting reasons; each report, for the sake of unity of policy and law, had the written approval (with comments) of the Chief Forester, who all the while had the Solicitor at his elbow. The com-

[1] Personal interview with Mr. Will C. Barnes and Mr. C. E. Rachford, Jan. 2, 1925.

mittee voted on the reports by sections; there was evidence in many cases of differences of opinion. Two or three days were then spent by the proper committees in fitting the various recommendations into the Manual. When this had been done and order had been brought out of chaos, the chief inspector for the Service, Mr. Rachford, together with all the supervisors of grazing, met for three days in Denver with a committee representing all the stockmen for a careful review of the results of the conference. This committee for the most part approved the conference suggestions for revision of the Manual. The unchanged principle set forth by the government, viz., that "the grazing interest is not a property right" and the principle underlying the grazing fees could not be agreed upon. The stockmen later had their opportunity to speak on these very points to the Sixty-ninth Congress.[1]

It might be asked why the government agencies having control over water-power sources and grazing lands within areas actually owned by the national government should listen so closely to claims set forth by interested parties; better examples of working together are hard to find. The answer is that in the case of grazing the public lands have always been and are now becoming more necessary for maintaining the live-stock industry itself so vital to the people as a whole that in order to promote it or even to save it from destruction, the interests and viewpoints of the ranchmen themselves must be closely considered in establishing governing rules.[2]

[1] *Hearings of Subcommittee of Senate Committee on Public Lands and Surveys*, 69th Cong., 1st Sess., pts. 1-15 (1925).

[2] Another case which proves the close contact of the Forest Service with interested groups is that of the Kaihab National Forest deer situation. Reduction of the deer herds had to be made in some way. The procedure to determine the method included soliciting the opinions of large groups of sportsmen. Heywood Cutting of the Boone and Crockett

IV

To the Department of Agriculture has been assigned many duties in connection with the care and development of industries having to do with plant and animal life. The fostering of plant life was especially provided for, at least in general terms, by the Plant Quarantine Act of 1912.[1] All plant diseases and insect pests not already widely spread in the United States are according to the terms of the statute to be kept out and uninfected domestic areas protected from infected areas insofar as the foreign and interstate commerce power can make it possible. Provision for the entry of foreign nursery stock, if properly certified by the country of origin, is made; if not so certified, entrance must be according to the regulations of the Secretary. Whenever the Secretary determines that unrestricted importation of plants and plant products, not included under nursery stock, is dangerous to domestic plant life he may announce his deter-

Club, T. Gilbert Pearson of the National Association of Audubon Societies and National Parks Association, T. W. Tomlinson of the American National Live-stock Breeders Association and John B. Burnham of the American Game Protection and Propagation Association were appointed to assist the Department in determining the possible steps to be taken. This they did after personal investigation and numerous hearings. The Department was moved to bring in outsiders to give an impartial view of the situation because a considerable sentiment against the Government's proposed measures had been created. Needless to say, the Committe's recommendations were followed, especially since they simply corroborated the Department's views. The point is that when the leaders of the great game organizations of the country put their approval on governmental action, the groups themselves are content. *Annual Report of the Forest Service* (1924), p. 28; *Special Committee's Report of Oct. 1, 1924* (mimeograph).

[1] 37 Stat. 315 (1912). Unsuccessful bills of a similar character had been introduced in the 54th Cong., once, in the 55th Cong., five times, in the 56th Cong., six times, in the 57th Cong., three times, in the 60th Cong., twice, in the 61st Cong., twice, in the 62nd Cong., nine times.

mination and the restrictions on nursery stock will apply.[1] Furthermore, whenever the Secretary shall deem it necessary, because of the existence of plant disease or insect pests in a foreign country or a part thereof, he may place an absolute ban upon importation of any or all plants therefrom.[2] Domestic quarantine against the shipping in interstate commerce of plants and plant products from states or their subdivisions may be established by the Secretary " when he shall determine the fact " that a dangerous plant disease or insect infestation " new to or not theretofore widely prevalent " within the United States exists in such district or state.[3]

When the Secretary of Agriculture can place unrestricted plants and plant products under the restrictions to which the nursery stock is subjected; when he can set up a foreign quarantine against any or all plants and plant products from any exporting country where certain plant diseases and dangerous insects exist; when he can except plants from

[1] *Ibid.*, Sec. 5. See S. R. S.—Fed. Hort. Board 1, p. 5 (1914), and 4, p. 26.

[2] 37 Stat. 854 (1913), amending Sec. 7 of 37 Stat. 315 (1912) and allowing any plants or plant products under the ban to be imported " for experimental or scientific purposes by the Department of Agriculture upon such conditions and under such regulations as the Secretary . . . may prescribe ".

[3] 37 Stat. 315 (1912), Sec. 8, amended by 39 Stat. 1165 (1917), to read " when he shall determine that such quarantine is necessary ". The basis for the promulgation of a quarantine order is thereby changed from establishing the fact of the existence of such disease or insect infestation to " whenever he shall determine it best ". This difference is noted in the 1917 *Report of the Fed. Hort. Board*, p. 1. The same amendment extends the power of the Secretary over " any class of stone or quarry products or any other article of any character whatsoever capable of carrying any dangerous plant disease or insect infestation " specified in the notice of quarantine, regardless of the use for which such articles may be intended. The Board recognizes the significance of this broad power, as shown in its 1917 *Report*, pp. 1-2. An example of its application is found in S. R. A.—Fed. Hort. Board 31, p. 1 (1916).

such quarantine under his own rules; when he can establish a domestic quarantine against plant diseases and insect infestation, prohibiting thereby all commodities which may carry such diseases or insects from entering interstate commerce, he has a power of determination which vitally affects the interests of many people. What are the steps by which he arrives at such regulations or determinations? Certain directions laid down in the law he must follow out literally. First of all, he must appoint five experts from certain scientific divisions of the department. These officials form the Federal Horticultural Board which is the real administrative authority for effectuating the purposes of the Act.[1] The statute then provides that before the promulgation of a change in the classification of plants or plant products and before the promulgation of foreign or domestic quarantines the Secretary " shall, after due notice, give a public hearing, under such rules and regulations as he shall prescribe, at which hearing any interested party may appear and be heard, either in person or by attorney ".[2]

The Department, however, has not merely carried out the letter of the law by holding formal hearings. There is recorded evidence to show that especial care has been taken to incorporate the wishes of the interested parties into the regulations issued under the Act. It might be added that when the interests of a powerful trade, supported by the sentiment of thousands of persons, point to regulations in harmony with their welfare, administrative officers are more or less likely to give heed. Such is the case whenever a foreign plant quarantine, with its attendant regulations and

[1] The normal composition of the Board calls for two from the Bureau of Entomology, two from the Bureau of Plant Industry and one from the Forestry Service. C. L. Marlatt of the Bureau of Entomology has been the chairman since its organization.

[2] 37 Stat. 315 (1912), Secs. 5, 7, 8. See S. R. A.—Fed. Hort. Board 1, p. 7 (1914).

conditions, is declared. Quarantine No. 37, with amendments, has aroused more criticism from an active minority than any other quarantine under the statute. In October, 1922, Chairman Marlatt of the Federal Horticultural Board felt called upon to refute a statement [1] by importers to the effect that Quarantine No. 37 had been promulgated hastily, without an opportunity for conferences and had come as an element of surprise to the trade and other interests involved (it is to be noted that conferences are looked upon as an additional, though customary, right which the authorities must grant on demand over and above the formal hearing required by law). His statement was as follows: [2]

(a) The necessity for restrictions similar to those involved under Quarantine No. 37 had been the subject of discussion and recommendation by resolution over a period of several years at annual meetings of the various trade associations, national and regional.

(b) On the basis of such resolutions, the board had asked the advice of the Bureau of Plant Industry concerning such proposed quarantine and the report of that scientific bureau recommended such action on February 26, 1918.

(c) On March 28, 1918, notice of a public hearing to be held two months later relative to the proposed quarantine was sent to nurserymen, permittees, and others interested who were on the department's mailing list, and was published in the leading horticultural and trade papers of the country.

(d) The hearing was well attended by the officials and other representatives of the principal trade societies related to horticulture and by a large state representation of technical and practical men. A stenographic record of the proceedings was

[1] S. R. A.—Fed. Hort. Board 72, p. 15 (1922).

[2] S. R. A.—Fed. Hort. Board 72, pp. 15-16 (1922). This defense of the quarantine regulations was given before a general conference on No. 37 held at Washington, D. C., May 15-16, 1922, and is given at length here because of its description of procedure.

kept on file. The pages of this record indicated a practically unanimous point of view in favor of a quarantine even more drastic than the one actually promulgated by the department.

(e) Following the hearing the board, in cooperation with the Bureau of Plant Industry, made a thorough-going and country-wide investigation of the subject over a period of three months, consulting with prominent nurserymen and florists in different parts of the country.

(f) Subsequent to this period of investigation, Quarantine No. 37, with regulations and conditions, was provisionally drafted substantially along the lines on which it was afterwards promulgated and was sent in this form for consideration and criticism to the trade journals and societies represented at the formal hearing and to all persons in attendance as well as to many others who had manifested any interest in the subject—with a view to a later conference for the purpose of discussing the quarantine and the regulations thereunder.

(g) Such a conference, after due notice, was held October, 1918, and resulted in developing a need in the judgment of the Department for only minor modifications of the regulations as provisionally drafted.

(h) After an additional month of examination and conference, within and without the Department, the quarantine was promulgated in November, becoming effective six months later.

(i) Without going back farther than the formal public hearing of May, 1918, there were eight months of publicity, hearings, and conferences, and six additional months before the quarantine itself became effective.[1]

[1] Between June 1, 1919, and May 15, 1922, many private conferences were held relative to specific changes in regulations and several resulted in amendments. For later conferences, see *Annual Report of the Department of Agriculture* (1923), pp. 14-15. It should be noted, however, that a by-product of the regulations established under both the formal and informal procedure has been a more or less effective protection of domestic growers from the competition of foreign growers. When the by-product becomes the main product of such regulation, if it ever does, Congress should take the matter of policy in hand.

In another instance the Secretary was asked to give in writing the procedure used in arriving at the Pink Bollworm Quarantine, No. 46, and the regulations governing the importation of cotton and cotton goods, revised to 1923. He replied that the formulation and issuance of such regulations, like others under the Plant Quarantine Act, could be illustrated by the following procedure [1] established by the Horticultural Board:

(a) Presentation of the need of the quarantine to the board by experts both within and without the Department.

(b) Preliminary conference conducted by the Board with the department experts and any others available.

(c) Public conference, after notice, with the commercial interests involved. (This, although optional, is often done.)[2]

(d) Formal notification of public hearings as required in the Act.

(e) Public hearing.

(f) Drafting of quarantine and regulations by the Board.

(g) Re-submittal of quarantine and regulations to the trade and other interests for criticism and suggestions (optional, but often done).[3]

(h) Review of quarantine and regulations by the Solicitor of the Department.

(i) Review of the quarantine and regulations by the Department and, if approved, their promulgation.

The Pink Bollworm Quarantine No. 46 [4] is a good illus-

[1] Letter, former Secretary Wallace to Senator Sheppard, Oct. 18, 1923, in reply to the latter's letter of inquiry, Sept. 27, 1923. The writer has this letter in his possession. Later the same procedure was found in large part in S. R. A.—Fed. Hort. Board 72, p. 17 (1922).

[2] E. g., Quarantine No. 37.

[3] *Ibid.*

[4] S. R. A.—Fed. Hort. Board 67, 68, 70, 71 (1920) give the story. Quarantine No. 46 was revised as No. 52, Sept., 1923.

tration of an important domestic quarantine. The bollworm situation, in its foreign aspects, had become, as early as 1917, the headline of the Board's circulars. By 1920 the new cotton pest had found its way from Mexico into parts of Texas and Louisiana. Notice of a public hearing on the question of quarantining these two states was duly made and the hearings held in Washington, April, 1920. Both states had political and technical officials present; the cotton interests too were well represented. All of the other cotton states sent representatives to look out for their welfare. The chief discussion centered round the areas to be quarantined (the states as a whole or only the areas infected) and the things to be quarantined (cotton and its products only or all contaminated objects). The Board bargained with Texas and Louisiana officials by placing in the draft a proviso according to which quarantine restrictions were to be limited to areas infected within the states, provided the states would cooperate—i. e., that they would adopt federal regulations and enforce them under the supervision of federal officers. This was the alternative, so far as interstate commerce was concerned, to a complete quarantine of the state. Texas legislation of June, 1920, although it provided for cooperation, proved very unsatisfactory to the federal authorities. A general conference was called at Washington, D. C., the following July, to which all cotton states sent representatives. Those present agreed to harmonize their actions with the national regulations according to the terms of the revised quarantine which was promulgated the latter part of July, becoming effective as No. 46 ten days later. By its terms not only would the affected states be quarantined as a whole, but all states not affected would quarantine against Texas and Louisiana, should those states fail to cooperate. The conditions were too much for Texas to meet. On May 16, 1921, still another conference was called at the national capital and further pressure brought to bear. With the expectation that Congress would help in compensating farmers for stopping the use of their lands in the so-called non-cotton zones, Texas enacted a better law of cooperation. At last the Horticultural Board was able to extend its regulations to intra-state affairs and all cotton and cotton products, together with all property suspected of being capable of harboring the bollworm, were brought under the watchful eye of the federal authorities. The opinion of the entire cotton industry as expressed at the various conferences, the sanction of Congress as expressed in a subsidy law, state legislation and regulations, all tended to show that administrative officers can do indirectly that which they cannot do directly.

V

The Cotton Futures Act [1] is another source of legislative power which affects at many points the business interests of private individuals. The administration of this law, in as much as it is technically one for the production of revenue, the Secretary of Agriculture shares in part with the Treasury. Section 9 gives the Secretary of Agriculture power to establish and to promulgate, from time to time, standards of cotton by which its quality and value may be judged including grade, length of staple, strength, color, and "such other qualities, properties, and conditions as may be standardized in practical form", to be known as the "official cotton standards of the United States". Freedom is given to adopt, change, or replace standards, provided that any standard adopted or promulgated shall not be changed within

[1] 38 Stat. 693 (1914), declared unconstitutional in Hubbard *v.* Lowe, 226 Fed. 135 (1915), on account of the house of origin, a decision which the Supreme Court refused to review. See Low *v.* Hubbard, 242 U. S. 654, No. 309 (1916). This law was re-enacted Aug. 11, 1916, as 39 Stat. 476.

less than one year after adoption or promulgation.[1] No directions are given in the Act as to the process of arriving at the official standards.

As early as 1909 the Secretary had been given power to establish permissive standards for nine grades of American white cotton. To aid in their establishment a committee of nine men prominent in the various branches of the cotton trade, together with three practical expert classers from the chief markets of the country, was set to work. With samples furnished by the experts, by domestic and foreign exchanges and by farmers of the cotton belt, a high-grade classification was made, but was never promulgated for permissive use because it was not acceptable to the trade. As a result of the influence of the English cotton industry an attempt was made in 1913 to get the Secretary to adopt the Liverpool standards. He had already found out that the classification of 1909 would never prove satisfactory either to the domestic or to the foreign trade. Upon the passage of the first Cotton Futures Act the Secretary, knowing the conditions much better as the result of five years of advice and experience, made an almost superhuman effort to meet all valid objections in arriving at the United States official standards. In answer to the statement by a dissatisfied element of the trade relative to the standards finally promulgated under the Act, to the effect that no rules or regulations had been given out by the Department prior to the effective date of the Act, the Secretary made a defense which may be summarized as follows: [2]

The Act was passed August 18, 1914, and from that date to November 1 the time was spent by the Department, aided some-

[1] See S. R. S.—Markets, Nos. 1, 4, 5, 7, 10 (1915-1916) for a discussion of the acts and the making of the standards.

[2] S. R. A.—Markets 4, pp. 30-31 (1915).

what by the Treasury, in preparing tentative regulations. About November 1, the two Secretaries jointly announced, through the press and otherwise, that a public hearing would be held in the national capital, November 12, to consider the rules and regulations proposed under the Act. Simultaneously there was distributed to the interested public, including producers, cotton merchants, members of exchanges, manufacturers, bankers, carriers, and warehousemen, more than 12,000 copies of the tentative regulations, together with the text of the Act itself. At the same time, all were invited to be present and discuss orally the proposals, while those who could not come were asked to send written criticisms. Stenographic records show that representatives of the New York Cotton Exchange and many others were given full opportunity to present their views on any and every section of the proposed regulations and that numbers of written criticisms were read. Few alterations, however, were suggested either orally or in writing. In the rules and regulations as finally adopted (1915), only four changes were made in the hearings draft. In order that the new regulations might reach the persons concerned at the same time, proof sheet copies, together with the request that they be posted on the exchange bulletin boards, were mailed to the chief officers of the leading cotton exchanges on dates that would guarantee February 12 delivery at each exchange. Then followed copies to members of every future and spot cotton exchange in the United States and to thousands of other interested parties.

The regulations under the 1914 Act, especially those setting up the official cotton standards, were simply duplicated under the reenacted law of 1916 and remained unchanged up to June, 1922.[1] Pursuant to a demand of the trade, the Bureau of Markets, later known as the Bureau of Agricultural Economics, made a tentative revision of the cotton standards. It then chose a committee of the cotton

[1] For a detailed history of the changes following this date, see S. R. A.—Agr'l Economics, Nos. 72, 80, 82 (1922-1924).

trade to cooperate with the Department in making a final revision. The committee of twenty-four, composed of merchants, spinners, classifiers, farmers, exchange members and cotton factors, met June, 1922. Virtually two tentative sets of standards were before the committee, in addition to the one in force. Agreement was reached a month later and promulgation of the revised standards, effective August 1, 1923, was made soon after.[1]

There were still essential differences between the standards and regulations of European exchanges and those of the Department of Agriculture. The movement towards making the American standards the "universal standards" began to be emphasized by those who were jammed between the American and European regulations. A conference of American producers, shippers and spinners met in Washington, D. C., April, 1923, to attempt a harmonization of American and European staple lengths. Tentative revisions of the regulations to go into effect the following August were made as a result of the conference. Then public hearings were held in all important cotton centers of the South and East during April and May. At their conclusion a conference of international scope took place at Washington to discuss cotton grade standards. In addition to representatives of the American government and the domestic trade there were men from all the European exchanges under the leadership of the Liverpool Cotton Association, which had taken the initiative in calling the conference. All saw the real difficulties in harmonizing the old and the new. The Department, with the conference viewpoints in mind, spent

[1] S. R. A.—Agr'l Economics, Nos. 72, 80. The statute which replaced the original, with amendments, 42 Stat. 1517, Sec. 6 (1923), had a proviso that "the official standards established, effective August 1, 1923, under the Cotton Futures Act, shall be the official U. S. cotton standards until changed or replaced under this Act" or until the Secretary shall see fit to make any modifications.

the following month in an extensive inquiry among the home trade interests as to the desirability of revising the federal standards to meet the Liverpool demands. A final conference was then called together on July 17, 1923, for the purpose of revising the standards: European exchanges, domestic shippers, traders and producers and the Department itself were all well represented. After changes were agreed upon the revised standards were promulgated on July 30, 1923, to take effect one year later.[1] Thus the opinion of interested groups had caused the administrative officials to postpone for another year a set of standards (modified, to be sure) almost on the very day on which that set, under the law, was to have taken effect.

VI

The Department of Agriculture touches also the large trade interest where "corn is king". It has entered this regulatory field under the Grain Standards Act of 1916.[2] Shipments in interstate commerce, tied up closely with the Warehouse Act,[3] allow a large field for regulation on the part of the Executive. Although nothing in the law calls especially for consultation with the grain interests concerned, yet such interests, especially those of certain grains, are, like those of the cotton trade, very powerful. Then, too, the intent of the law is to conserve, not to destroy, the grain and

[1] S. R. A.—Agr'l Economics 82 (1924). Official U. S. wool standards were set up only after full expression by all the trade. S. R. A.—Agr'l Economics 75 (1923). These standards issue from the Warehouse Act, 39 Stat. 486, Sec. 19 (1916), one unit of the triplets known as A, B, C, of the Agricultural Appropriation Act for 1917 (39 Stat. 446). See *infra*, p. 226, note 3.

[2] 39 Stat. 482 (1916). See Harold W. Samson, "The March of Standardization," *Agricultural Year Book* (1920), pp. 353-362, for the steadily-growing demand for such activity on the part of government.

[3] 39 Stat. 446, 486 (1916).

allied industries. The Department has had the most difficulty in establishing wheat standards.[1]

The Bureau of Markets spent the five months following the passage of the Act in preparing tentative standards for domestic wheat.[2] The basis for the proposed standards was found in the facts collected by the Department during the preceding ten years of intensive investigation of every step of the production process, from the time the wheat leaves the field until it reaches the ultimate consumer. Field, threshing machine, country elevator, carriers at central markets, terminal elevators and mixing houses, domestic and foreign ports, mill—all were sources of information. The great markets likewise disclosed their practices to the Bureau experts. In addition, the laws and regulations of the states were a mine of suggestion.[3] Notice of a series of public hearings was sent out in January, 1917, along with the tentative standards. During the month of February a series of preliminary hearings, each of one or two days' duration, was provided for at all the grain markets of the country. This series culminated in the final hearings at Washington, D. C., some ten days later. Millers, producers, manufacturers, bankers, grain inspectors, members of exchanges, warehousemen, carriers and others attended these hearings—or at least had the opportunity of doing so.[4] The Depart-

[1] Sec. 2: The Secretary is authorized to investigate the handling, grading, and transportation of grain and "to fix and establish as soon as may be after enactment hereof standards of quality and condition for corn (maize), wheat, rye, oats, barley, flaxseed, and such other grains as in his judgment the usages of the trade may warrant and permit". He shall have power to alter or modify such standards when he thinks there is need. Notification of the original and revised standards must be given to the public three months before they are effective.

[2] S. R. A.—Markets 19 (1917).

[3] S. R. A.—Markets 35, p. 2 (1918).

[4] S. R. A.—Markets 19 (1917).

ment, after embodying the constructive criticisms brought out at the various meetings, promulgated the final wheat standards on March 31, to become effective some five months later.[1]

War conditions and the price-fixing policy of the government caused the Bureau of Markets to give notice of renewed public hearings for the purpose of ascertaining whether the wheat standards in force were meeting the current marketing conditions; and if not, whether the "attached tentative standards" would meet the conditions. It was stated in the notice that eighteen public hearings had already been held throughout the United States during November and December; that much advice and many suggestions had been received through the media of letters and personal conferences; that the opinions ascertained indicated revision along the lines specified in the draft; that before final action was taken, further advice and suggestions would be asked for at a series of five hearings set for March, 1918, at five of the great grain centers. The revision was promulgated to take effect July 15.[2] Additional conferences and hearings

[1] S. R. A.—Markets 22 (1917).

[2] S. R. A.—Markets 32 (1918) and 33 (1918). In reply to a charge by the Commissioner of Agriculture of No. Dak., that the farmers had had no voice in this revision, the head of the Bureau of Markets replied that he was surprised that anyone could be of such an opinion, since the Bureau had taken special steps to provide producers an opportunity to be present at the hearings and to express their views; the number of hearings had been increased and the locations had been made as accessible as possible; all such hearings had been attended by large groups of farmers, many of whom led the discussions; numerous written suggestions had been received and considered; and contact with the farmer by the many agencies of the Department gave other means by which their attitude could be judged. The additional statement was made that the Department had to consider the grain standards from the point of view of every interest concerned, all along the road from farmer to consumer. S. R. A.—Markets 34, pp. 7-8 (1918).

in the spring of 1920 failed to convince the Department of the need for further revision.[1]

The United States Warehouse Act, 1916,[2] is not a compulsory law. Until a person desires to convert his private warehouse into one conforming to the terms of the Act or until some person wants to store agricultural products in such converted warehouse, the regulations of the Department of Agriculture do not apply. Advantages accruing under the Act to both the shipper and the warehousemen, however, have brought many of them under its terms and regulations. Rules and regulations for the storage of each product, as well as general rules for all products, are permitted under the Act. Although standards for all agricultural products that can be stored in such warehouses may be set up by the Department, those that have already been set up under other laws are applicable for the purposes of the Act.[3] The statute does not require securing the advice of the industry or trade concerned either with regard to the making of standards or as to the formulation of the rules and regulations governing the conditions of storage.

Under this Act regulations, standards, or both have been adopted, amended and superseded relative to cotton, grains, wool, tobacco, peanuts, potatoes, dry beans, dried fruit, broom corn and sirups. The regulations for warehouses for each of the first four products were formulated after the

[1] S. R. A.—Markets 62 (1920). In addition to hearings on wheat there is written evidence that oats standards (S. R. A.—Markets 39, 1918) and rice standards (S. R. A.—Markets 59, 1920) received the thorough consideration of the entire trade concerned. It seems that the Department used its technical knowldge largely in shelled corn standards (S. R. A.—Markets 11, 1916) and rye standards (S. R. A.—Agr'l Economics 73, 1923).

[2] 39 Stat. 486, as amended July 24, 1919 (41 Stat. 266), and Feb. 23, 1923 (42 Stat. 1282).

[3] Sec. 19, closely related to the U. S. Grain Standards Act (39 Stat. 482). For wool standards under this Section, *supra*, p. 223, note 1.

experts of the Department had made tentative drafts, given due notice of hearings to those interests immediately concerned, and distributed the proposed drafts by selected mailing lists. Merchants, dealers, bankers, warehousemen, producers and others interested were placed on such notification lists. A series of preliminary hearings, ten to fifteen in number, were held in the most convenient places for the trade concerned. In all the dates set for the first series of hearings the Department took particular pains to arrange each meeting so that a résumé of the one immediately preceding could be had by each chairman. Through this arrangement the climax of the final hearing lay in the clash of minds in the general group rather than in the findings. All this search for the views of the interested groups had been preceded by thorough research on the part of the technical members of the departmental staff, accompanied and supplemented by written criticisms and suggestions.[1] Regulations under the Act having to do with peanuts, potatoes, broom corn, dry beans, dried fruit and sirups apparently had no such formal hearings. The Bureau of Markets in working them out, however, searched carefully the minds of those who dealt in such products.[2]

VII

When the Secretary of Agriculture was asked by Senator Sheppard to give the steps in the process of formulating Bureau of Animal Industry Order 273 (1921), which dealt

[1] Cotton, S. R. A.—Markets 27 (1917), regulations only for standards adopted under Cotton Futures Act; grain, S. R. A.—Markets 53 (1919); wool, S. R. A.—Markets 57 (1920); tobacco, S. R. A.—Markets 66 (1920).

[2] Peanuts, S. R. A.—Agr'l Economics, No. 81 (1923); Potatoes, No. 83 (1924); broom corn, No. 84 (1924); Dry beans, No. 87 (1924); dried fruit, No. 88 (1924); sirups, No. 89 (1924). On Feb. 23, 1923, Secs. 2 and 19 of the original Act were amended to include agricultural products in general, whereas the unamended sections limited the Act to cotton, grains, wool and tobacco; hence the new products standards.

with the interstate movement of live stock, he did not reply so definitely as he had in the case of the plant quarantines.[1] After observing that the process in each case was similar, he wrote:

A thorough investigation of existing conditions is made by the appropriate subdivision or subdivisions of the Bureau. As a result of such investigations suitable rules and regulations are prepared by the Chief of the Bureau. Where there is an outbreak of contagious, infectious and communicable diseases of live stock which requires the cooperation of federal and state authorities, these regulations are submitted to the state officials for their consideration and approval. If their control under the regulations relates to restricted importation, such regulations are submitted to the Secretary of the Treasury for his approval. In the case of all regulations the judgment of a competent legal officer of the Department is obtained before issuance.[2]

The Bureau of Animal Industry just referred to by the Secretary has to do with all departmental activities relating to the live-stock industry such as the investigation, control and eradication of animal diseases, the inspection and quarantine of live stock, the inspection of meat and meat products, and animal husbandry.[3] This work embraces regulatory, research and educational features, the two latter reacting directly or indirectly upon the first. One of the leading scientists of the Bureau, in speaking of the more

[1] *Supra*, page 217, note 1, and page 217.

[2] "All orders and regulations of the Secretary promulgated under statutory authority and affecting the public are examined in advance by the solicitor and in many cases are wholly or partly prepared by him. This division of the work of the office is one of the most important and exacting of all duties assigned the solicitor." *Report of the Secretary of Agriculture* (1909), p. 783.

[3] *28th Annual Report of the Bureau of Animal Industry* (1910), p. 525.

technical regulations, informed the writer that the process of supplementary rule-making was, in broad outline, about as follows: the inspectors report, with supporting facts, all situations that in their opinion need regulatory attention; if the facts need further verification special investigations are made; the scientific experts then indicate in writing the best methods of handling the situations that their own experiments or those of outside experts in all countries have proved most effective;[1] if the situation is a novel one or one that has never been successfully met, experts are set to work to find a method; the scientific data are turned over to the Solicitor and the Bureau head for form, law and policy and even to the Secretary now and then for general consideration. Of course continued research, added experience and changing

[1] The Bureau's experts are constantly being aided by those of the states that have intra-state supervision over similar conditions. Specific problems are being worked out by many of the scientists in private and public institutions. Researches under the direction of local, national and international associations are supplementing the work of the Bureau. The control of bovine tuberculosis, for example, has absorbed the attention of the American Veterinary Medical Association for years (Bur. Animal Industry Circular 175, 1911). Where the Bureau experts are doubtful as to the best method specific outside aid has been drafted by the Secretary. This was done in 1907, after Order No. 137, Sec. 15, had been questioned and fought by packers. The commission, with Dr. Welch of Johns Hopkins at its head, was authorized to consider and advise relative to those portions of the meat regulations which dealt with carcasses affected with various diseases and abnormalities. The commission found that if there was any error, it had been made in favor of the public rather than the butchers and packers. Specific suggestions of the commission were taken up by the Bureau in revising Order No. 137 (*Report of the Chief of the Bureau of Animal Industry*, 1907, p. 7). It is not uncommon for the Bureau to adopt outright foreign regulations that have proved effective in handling certain conditions. If one could trace the origin of many so-called purely American regulations in this field, he would be likely to find adoption or adaptation rather common. See, for example, *Report of the Chief of the Bureau of Animal Industry* (1891), p. 89.

conditions often make it necessary to modify or set aside such regulations. Order 271, for example, which deals with the southern cattle fever, is reviewed annually so that it may be made more conformable to actual conditions, and therefore more effective.

It would seem, then, that where, as here, the promotion of the physical conditions of man and animal is concerned—even to the point of protection of life—and where the means is to be found bound up closely with the technicalities of science, the regulations have to be made to carry out the law without devoting much time to the consideration, at first hand, of the opinions of the groups concerned.[1] The actual process seems to be that regulations are made by experts and put into effect. Thereafter, or perhaps before they actually become a part of the law, a process of education is carried on by the Department, tending to show that it is only by means of such regulations that people can hope to realize the larger policy as expressed in law. This has been doubly necessary because of the almost inevitable cooperation between the state and the national agencies. The Chief of the Bureau has insisted on acquainting stockmen with the constructive side of the regulatory work by printed and verbal messages.[2] The inspectors in the ordinary course of their work, and the special representatives of the Bureau at the associations of cattlemen, are always explaining the purpose of the technical regulations. A common message is that disease eradication, after all, is the basis of ample production and, in the final analysis, the basis of liberal consumption and proper nutrition. What serious objection can a democratic constituency make to such a procedure? To get the approval of interested groups before issuing regula-

[1] E. g., 26 Stat. 416, Sec. 8 (1890), and 21 Ops. Atty. Gen. 460 (1897).

[2] *Report of the Chief of the Bureau of Animal Industry* (1919), p. 5.

tions frequently consumes as much time and energy as securing the same approval after the issuing of regulations. Proof of benefit is often more convincing than assertion of benefit; a few obviously good results accomplished in interstate commerce, if necessary by force, will convert where the explanations of science would but confuse. At all events, the results will probably be the same, i. e., the trade or interest concerned will be likely to make its own wishes conform to those of the rule-making authority—else the rules will never be adopted; or if adopted, they will never be obeyed.

VIII

Congress has recently conferred upon the Secretary of Agriculture authority relative to naval stores. Section 3 of the Naval Stores Act[1] empowers him "to establish and promulgate standards for naval stores for which no standards are herein provided". At least three months' notice of the proposed standards must be given the trade and "due hearings or reasonable opportunities to be heard" must be afforded those favoring or opposing the new draft. The standards finally decided upon cannot become effective until three months after their promulgation. In addition, the standards laid down in the Act, or those promulgated by the Secretary under its terms, may be modified by him whenever, in his opinion, the trade conditions demand such modification. Six months' notice and six months' effective date after promulgation are required.

As a matter of fact the Bureau of Chemistry, as early as 1915, had set up permissive standards for rosin which the trade had gradually adopted.[2] In 1922 the Bureau, largely as a favor to the trade, set up tentative standard types for

[1] 42 Stat. 1435 (1923).

[2] *Annual Report of the Department of Agriculture* (1915), p. 200; *Report of the Chemist* (1924), p. 17.

four commercial grades of turpentine. The naval-stores groups, represented by the Turpentine and Rosin Producers' Association, the National Paint, Oil, and Varnish Association, the state supervisors of naval stores and others, tried to secure voluntary adoption of the standards. Since the law of 1913 practically adopted these standards, the trade felt secure in allowing the Bureau to add to or to revise any of the group.[1] A tentative draft of all regulations, with a statement of the standards, was sent out to the trade in October, 1923, for criticism. Announcement was then made that hearings in accordance with the law would later be held.[2]

The statute itself represents the up-to-date wording of delegated legislative power; it represents also, perhaps, the best way of arriving at any ordinary form of regulation which does not call for immediate action: the securing, through voluntary action on the part of the leading interests concerned, of certain types of conduct desired by the government and the making of such conduct legally binding later through law and regulations. In other words, the executive departments have created, in this case, a demand for legal regulations through a demonstration of their value by means of previous voluntary experiment.[3]

IX

A decided step, although one of doubtful legality, was taken in 1913 to conserve the wild bird life of the country. Conservation education had reached the point where Congress dared to push through the so-called Migratory Bird

[1] *Report of the Chemist* (1922), pp. 16-17.

[2] *Savannah Naval Stores Review and Trade Journal*, Oct. 20, 1923; *Report of the Chemist* (1924), p. 17.

[3] 42 Stat. 1289, 1313 (1923), providing for certificate of quality and condition of perishable farm products; it is now voluntary for all purposes; later, however, it may develop into a compulsory law for interstate shipments.

Act on the back of the Annual Appropriations Bill.[1] Section 1 of the Act authorized the Department of Agriculture to make suitable regulations to carry the purposes of the law into effect. Direction was given that after the preparation of such regulations the Department should cause them to be made public, allowing a period of three months in which they might be informally examined and considered by the parties affected before final adoption. Public hearings were left to the discretion of the Secretary. After the Department had perfected the regulations they were to be "engrossed" and submitted to the President for approval. Opportunity for criticism by interested parties certainly is possible under such a scheme. But the Department went further: it allowed the Biological Survey to create an unofficial Advisory Board of fifteen members. This body was to offer criticisms of all regulations made under the Act before they were to be put into effect; in practice, many of the regulations were drawn up or suggested before even a draft had been made. The practice of holding hearings in different parts of the country was carried out, great care being taken to avoid any appearance of arbitrariness.

The chief complaint, if the public records are to be trusted, came from the state game-commissioners. Some of these men felt that the state authorities, whose cooperation was absolutely necessary, were not sufficiently represented on the Advisory Board. They did not hesitate to accuse the federal authorities of packing that body against them. An analysis of this Board, made in 1915, showed that one-fourth

[1] 37 Stat. 847 (1913), 31 Stat. 187 (1900) and 32 Stat. 285 (1902) were earlier acts giving the Secretary regulatory powers for the conservation of bird life. The 1913 Act was held unconstitutional in 1915 by a federal court in U. S. *v.* McCullogh, 221 Fed. 288, in so far as it tried to give the national government complete control over migratory birds. The attempt to conserve bird life was then taken up through a treaty, supplemented by an enforcing statute.

of its membership was taken from the National Association of (State) Fish and Game Commissioners, while the remaining three-fourths were made up of men from New York City and its environs. One of the complainants, evidently for purpose of emphasis, stated that the states had no representation at all—since those chosen from them were either non-sportsmen or were paid representatives of the American Association of Audubon Societies. Furthermore, he claimed that not only were the states' representatives ignored as such, but that recommendations and criticisms made at hearings by state officials were usually barren of results.[1]

This information came out before the House Committee on Foreign Affairs in 1917 when it was considering one of the bills for making effectual the Migratory Bird Treaty. The National Association of Fish and Game Commissioners insisted that the law should provide for an advisory committee to aid in the making of regulations one-third of whose members should under its terms consist of state game wardens chosen by the Department from a group nominated by the Association or its representatives. Only in this manner did the states' representatives think that their interests could be protected from the overzealous Audubon federated societies which were supported by the powerful arms and ammunition manufacturers of the country.[2] The

[1] *Hearings by Committee on Foreign Affairs*, House of Reps., on Migratory Bird Treaty Bill, H. R. 20080, 64th Cong., 2nd Sess., parts 1-2, Feb. 3, 7, 1917.

[2] *Ibid.* The committee Report (No. 1430, Feb. 6, 1917) added this section to the bill as prepared and presented to it by the Department of Agriculture: "... all rules and regulations made and adopted by the Secretary of Agriculture to carry out the provisions of this Act, shall before being put into effect, be submitted for consideration to an advisory board, appointed by him, consisting of 15 members, at least 5 of whom shall be appointed by the Secretary from a list of 10 state game wardens to be recommended by the National Association of Game and Fish Commissioners."

law on the statute books providing for the enforcing of the treaty contains no provisions either mandatory or directory concerning any advisory committee, the publication of a preliminary draft of regulations, or the holding of hearings.[1] The Biological Survey, nevertheless, has carried over the idea of an advisory committee in the administration of the new law.

This unofficial Committee is made up at present of twelve state commissioners of game and fish; seven men from sporting groups such as the American Protection and Propagation Association, the National Association of Audubon Societies, the Camp Fire Club of America; and three well-known sportsmen without affiliation. The personnel is thus representative not only of the national groups directly interested but of those coming from the major geographical areas of the country. Although provision is always made for an annual meeting of this Committee with the Biological Survey, call meetings are in order at any time. Whenever a conference is held it is greeted with numerous requests from one or more sections of the United States asking for changes in, additions to, or exceptions from, the current regulations. These pleas are sent in by national officers, state or local game officers, game organizations and private individuals. Of course each group on the Advisory Committee acts as a collector of suggestions and has frequently made an investigation as to the facts back of such suggestions before its conference with the government authorities. It is evident that much of the same ground is covered by each group. The Biogolical Survey does not merely wait for suggestions to come in to the central office nor does it accept the Committee's statement of conditions touching wild fowl life; it actually makes independent investigations for itself, as is evidenced in the following statement:

[1] 40 Stat. 755 (1918).

During the latter part of 1924 and in the early months of 1925, the Biological Survey made an extended investigation, by personal conference and by correspondence, of the entire United States in regard to the migratory wild-fowl situation. Information on the subject was received from thousands of people. The reports indicate that wild fowl are present in enormous numbers in the greater part of the country, many reports stating that there have been unprecedented flights of birds. . . . The information as a whole indicates the continued existence of vast numbers of migratory wild fowl.[1]

It is difficult to see how group opinion could better be focused on the supplementary law-making authority for regulating the taking of such wild game. The Biological Survey and the Advisory Committee work out the best rules possible in the light of the many facts secured: the former accepts the suggestions of the latter when there is good reason for doing so. Those who are in a position to know state that most, if not all, of the recommendations made by a majority of the Committee or by those members of that body who represent a majority of the sportsmen of the country, are sure to find their way into the regulations of the Secretary. If this is so, it is due to the fact that both the government and private authorities are collectors of facts and opinions that seem to harmonize with the best interests of all.[2]

[1] *Farmers' Bulletin* No. 1466, p. 2 (1925).

[2] This information comes from a conversation with Mr. Dort of the American Game Protection and Propagation Society, 233 Broadway, New York City, in August, 1925. Mr. Dort reported the personnel of the Advisory Committee to be as follows: W. C. Adams, Mass. official; W. E. Albert, Iowa official; Brooke Anderson, Chicago Camp Fire Club; J. B. Burnham, Pres. Amer. Game P. and P. Ass'n; Alva Clapp, Kansas ex-official; W. L. Ginley, Ore. official; E. H. Forbush, Mass. official; J. F. Gould, Minn. official; G. B. Grinnell, Pres. Boone and Crockett Club; W. T. Hornaday, Director Nat'l Ass'n Audubon Soc.; Clarke McAdams, St. Louis sportsman; Marshall McLean, Camp Fire Club of America; T. N. Marlow, Mont. official; Lee Miles, Ark. official; I. S.

X

The Packers and Stockyards Act of 1921,[1] together with the regulations of the Secretary of Agriculture, touch directly or indirectly the interests of practically all persons connected with the live-stock industry—so much so, indeed, that the United States Supreme Court has remarked that the businesses proposed to be regulated were of real public concern.[2] Title III of the Act, having to do with stockyard owners, market agencies and dealers in their daily conduct of business, had to be administered through executive rules and regulations. Consequently, tentative general rules were prepared and, for the purpose of securing suggestions and criticisms, furnished to all classes of persons interested. Public hearings followed shortly afterwards in each of the five principal stock markets of the country. After full consideration had been given to the information received through the media of hearings and correspondence, formal rules were issued in November, 1921.[3] No directive or mandatory provision of the law calls for such consideration by the persons concerned in the making of the general rules—although hearings are demanded for the making and altering of rates and practices of the businesses that come within the terms

Myers, Ohio sportsman; F. M. Newhart, Calif. official; T. G. Pearson, Pres. Nat'l Ass'n Aud. Soc.; I. T. Quinn, Ala. official; L. Rathbun, Wash. State official; A. A. Richardson, So. Car. official; Geo. Shiras, American Game P. and P. Ass'n; G. M. Willard, Ariz. official.

[1] 42 Stat. 159 (1921).

[2] Stafford *v.* Wallace, 258 U. S. 495 (1921).

[3] *Report of the Department of Agriculture* (1922), pp. 37-38; Circular No. 156 (1921), Dept. Agric. The proposed rules and regulations of Oct. 22, 1921, included invitations "to live-stock producers' organizations, shippers' organizations, live-stock and trader's exchanges, stockyard companies, market agencies and dealers, and other persons concerned in the marketing and handling of live stock" to be present at any or all hearings.

of the Act. Perhaps the reason for this free play of ideas in formulating the regulations is explained by a statement of the Secretary to the effect that the dominating thought in the working out of the rules was " to bring about harmony and cooperation and remove cause for antagonisms, misunderstandings, and irritations, to the end that confidence in the manner in which live stock is marketed shall be established ".[1]

[1] *Report of Department of Agriculture, op. cit.*

CHAPTER VIII

Political Safeguards: Group Opinion in the Framing of Administrative Legislation, Continued

I

Perhaps the most complete account of the procedure taken by administrative authorities in the formulation of rules and regulations can be found in connection with the enforcing of the Federal Water Power Act.[1] Consequently it is easier to see here the checking influence of the different groups upon the final action of the executive agency. The statute is administered by the Federal Power Commission which has an ex-officio personnel and a permanent executive secretary. In general, the Commission is empowered to make such administrative and interpretative regulations, not inconsistent with the Act, as are necessary and proper for carrying out its purpose—i. e., to utilize the public resources in such a manner as to improve navigation and develop water power.[2] In particular, authority is given to regulate rates, services and securities and to prescribe rules and regulations for the establishment of a system of accounts and for their maintenance by the licensees.[3] Any licensee or any other person wilfully failing or refusing to comply with any regulations contained in the licenses or with any other regulations made in accordance with the Act, is, upon conviction, to be heavily fined.

[1] 41 Stat. 1063 (1920).

[2] *Ibid.*, Sec. 4 (h).

[3] 41 *Stat.* 1063 (1920), Secs. 4 (h) and (g), 20, 25. Hearings are required in advance in making rules governing rates, services or securities.

Mr. O. C. Merrill, Executive Secretary of the Commission, issued the statement on July 20, 1920, that before any regulations were finally adopted full opportunity would be given to those interested in their operation to confer with the staff committee or with the Commission for the purpose of presenting their views concerning such regulations.[1] Two years later (March 18, 1922) this same official issued a memorandum in which he said that the fullest opportunity had been given all parties interested to present their views before action had been taken, or even recommended by the technical staff to the Commission.[2]

After the staff had framed preliminary regulations for certain sections of the Act, the leading interested parties were invited to attend an informal hearing August 12, 13, 1920. The National Electric Light Association, the Electric Bond and Share Company and others were present. A satisfactory conference resulted and a committee of the Light Association, representing a large part of the private electric power industry, was retained for daily consultation with the government staff. The conclusions reached were presented to the Water Conservation Committee of the Engineering Council of America for its review of questions of policy. Meanwhile, government officials interested in public health, Indian rights, forest preservation, etc., were being consulted by the Commission and were aligning their public groups with the purpose of seeing to it that all regulations were kept in harmony with these interests. It was not until Septem-

[1] File "L", Fed. Power Comm. Regulations: correspondence and memoranda pertaining to draft of regulations 1-10, 11-20. This File is the original source of all statements made relative to the process of making rules and regulations by the Federal Power Commission, and may be found in the permanent records of that body.

[2] A mimeographed memorandum of the Hearings before the Fed. Power Comm., Nov. 21, 1921.

ber 3, 1920, that the first section of the general regulations were approved and put into effect.

Along with this section of the regulations there was considered a second group having to do with the intricate problems of finance. On September 7, 1920, the Executive Secretary sent to the War Department a letter inclosing a copy of suggestions for such regulations tendered by the committee of the Light Association. This message also contained the statement that arrangements had been made to have the Engineering Council's Conservation Committee sit as technical advisers to the government staff in a conference to be held the following Friday on regulations dealing with rental charges, allocation of earnings, amortization and depreciation reserves. The Executive Secretary intimated that it was highly desirable to have the staff hold several meetings before the assembling of the conference in order that the members might have in mind the matters which should be discussed, as well as suggestions of their own to offer.[1] The tone of the communication seemed to indicate that the pressure from without was becoming formidable. In the meantime the Engineering Council Committee had had a meeting of its own. It agreed that the controlling principle for framing the regulations should be one of liberality on the part of the government in regard to all financial matters.[2]

The prearranged conference was held, as well as numerous others with interested persons present. On January 1, 1921, Mr. Merrill sent the preliminary drafts to the Commission asking for criticisms and setting February 10-15 as the dates for a formal hearing for all interests. The chief accountant

[1] Letter dated Sept. 7, 1920, Secretary Merrill to Gen. E. H. Crowder, Judge Advoc. Gen'l., War Dept., File "L", Fed. Power Comm.

[2] Memorandum of the Conference of Water Conservation Committee of the Engineering Council, held at the Cosmos Club, Washington, D. C., Sept. 10, 1920, to consider regulations 1-4 and covering notes proposed by Secretary Merrill, Aug. 26, 1920, File "L", Fed. Power Comm.

of the Commission had already secured a tentative draft proposal of uniform classification of accounts for electric companies from the National Association of Railway and Public Utilities Commissioners. He had also asked the Light Association to give the viewpoint of the private utilities companies on this draft. Because of serious criticisms by the latter Association, changes had been made in some of the draft regulations. After calling in experts and holding further conferences with interested associations and individuals and sending revised drafts to half a hundred private persons and many government field experts (with notice of the formal hearing) the technical staff spent about ten or twelve days in listening to informal criticisms and observing rifts in the great electric group over the proposed regulations.

On February 10 and 11, 1921, after the completion of the first tentative draft of the regulations, conferences were held between the staff of the Commission and certain representatives both of the Light Association and of the Empire State Gas and Electric Association of New York. As a result of the recommendations presented at these conferences changes were made in the draft: the amended document was then submitted to the Commission for approval. Mutual agreement, however, had not been reached; on the request of the Empire State Association a hearing on the proposed regulations was granted by the Commission itself. This was held on February 25. The Commission dismissed all charges of unsoundness of principle and *ultra vires* made against the regulations, refused to suspend action, and on February 28, formally approved the regulations.[1]

[1] Memorandum on Hearings of November 21, 1921, by O. C. Merrill, pp. 6-7. Nos. 1-10, approved Sept. 3, 1920, were superseded by the corresponding Nos. of Regulations 1-20, approved Feb. 28, 1921, and printed as Orders No. 9.

The "Phantom Public" is the political "Flying Dutchman" in

A new administration came in on March 4. The personnel of the Federal Power Commission was, of course, changed, although the technical staff remained the same. On March 5, the Light Association through one of its committees requested a re-hearing on the regulations as adopted on February 28. Permission was granted and the hearing held March 25. Following it, at the request of the Commis-

America today. In questions that have a political bearing, one is told that three groups should be represented, viz., the government, the interested parties, and the public. One might well ask who represented the public in the various water-power hearings. The writer asked this pertinent (or impertinent) question of the Executive Secretary of the Federal Power Commission. He made the following reply in a letter, dated Feb. 1, 1926:

> With regard to the participation in making the regulations, the Commission is authorized and empowered to make them. In so doing, it and its staff represent the public as other governmental agencies represent the public in performing the duties with which they are charged by law. It may be added that the hearings on the regulations were public and that it would have been proper for persons to appear on behalf of the public and give the Commission the benefit of their views, just as *amici curiae* appear in civil cases to give judicial tribunals [sic] where the questions at issue are thought to be of public concern.

If the Federal Power Commission represented the public, then all the state water-power commissions referred to in File "L", Fed. Power Comm., *op. cit.*, did also. Is not the government a representative of all interests? Has it an interest all its own? Gifford Pinchot, of the National Conservation Assn., was called upon for advice. (File "L", Fed. Power Comm., *op. cit.*, p. 38). Does the National Conservation Assn. represent the public? The Natl. El. Light Ass'n has its Water-Power Conservation Committee. Why does it not represent the public? Whatever problem may be up for consideration, there is no definite answer to this question. It seems the public is represented for practical purposes by organized groups that identify their interests with that of the public. An individual person of one particular group, organized for one general purpose, may be a member of a number of other groups that happen to have different purposes in view. It seems that public interest must be identified with one or more group interests; for this discussion it is so considered.

sion, a conference was arranged between the technical staff and representatives of the Light Association. This conference extended over a two weeks' period. At the request of the Executive Secretary a committee of bankers, representing such institutions as Lee, Higginson and Company and the Electric Bond and Share Company, was invited to sit in. A most thorough review was then made of all regulations, amendments were agreed upon, objections were withdrawn, and as finally amended, they were adopted by the Commission on May 28, 1921, and promulgated by Orders No. 11, the following June 6.[1]

Before the adoption of the general rules and regulations on February 28, 1921, work had been begun on the draft of a system of accounting. A tentative draft was prepared, printed, and on June 7 distributed among interested persons for consideration and criticism. The following October a hearing before the Executive Secretary was called to consider the tentative draft at which there appeared, among others, the Accounting Committee of the Light Association and certain representatives of its Water Development Committee. Although many detailed suggestions were made no agreement could be reached until Regulation 16 of the general rules had been amended to harmonize with the viewpoint of these interests. According to Mr. Merrill, whatever had been agreed to by the Light Association on May 28, was here repudiated by that organization through the influence of the Eastern representatives, especially those of the Consolidated Gas Company of New York.[2]

At any rate, the Commission granted a hearing, November 21, 1921, with respect to depreciation, amortization and accounting, on Regulations 16, 17, 20, and on the tentative system of accounts in course of preparation. Four formal

[1] Memo. of Hearings, Nov. 21, 1921, O. C. Merrill.

[2] *Ibid.*

hearings, three before the Commission itself, and many informal meetings had been held relative to these regulations since their preparation had been begun in July, 1920. Every facility was given to all interested persons for presenting their views. But not a single new argument or reason was offered on November 21—so thoroughly had all matters been canvassed in preceding conferences. The record shows that while minor changes have since been made as a result of outside pressure in some of the general regulations and in those establishing a system of accounts, the "big three" (Regulations 16, 17, 20) owing to the greater weight of opinion among the directly interested business organizations of the country and the wisdom of the technical officials of the Commission, have held their own up to the present.

In this particular case of the exercise of rule-making power, the interested persons had great influence in shaping the rules—whether such rules were regulative and had the force of law or whether they were merely interpretative in character with the possibility of adding to or subtracting from the law. The policy of the Federal Power Commission, under the direction of Congress, has been to encourage the development of water power through private enterprise; there has been a tendency therefore to give considerable heed to the desires of the licensees. On the other hand there is abundant evidence to show that the government should never listen too carefully to the most insistent of the interested groups. There still exist two different philosophies of government in the United States, the individualistic and the collectivistic. The former seems now to have its center in the East, at least in so far as the water power interests are concerned. A report of the Commission's chief accountant indicates that the persons most insistent at all the hearings could be classed into three groups: (a) representatives of the Consolidated Gas Company of New York, determined to check all governmental evaluation methods; (b) representatives of financial corporations dealing in securities of electric power companies and other public utilities, as for example, the Electric Bond and Share Company; and (c) representatives of corporations which operate and manage but do not own electric power companies and other utilities, and which also deal in the junior securities of such utilities. The lines of control all lead to the East.[1]

No record of administrative law-making tends more to confirm one in the conviction that the government official can and must be an impartial umpire between rival group ambitions, even when it is the avowed policy of Congress to permit the individual group great latitude in the general field of public resource exploitation. This balancing of interests must be entrusted to some agency; the more ponderous and less capable legislative body is quite unequal to the task.

II

In the administration of the public domain the Department of the Interior in the past has held to the policy of distribu-

[1] File "L", Fed. Power Comm. Executive Secretary Merrill, in his Memorandum of Hearings, Nov. 21, 1921, goes further into detail. He says that of the nine men who appeared for the Water Power Development Committee of the Light Association, which approved the rules of May 28, 1921, seven were officers of operating hydro-electric concerns, five were from the Pacific Coast States, eight were officers of corporations which were either applicants, permittees, or licensees of the Commission. Of the eleven men who appeared for the Accounting Committee of the Association, eight were from N. Y., two from Mass., and one from Cal. Only two were officers of corporations which were either applicants, permittees, or licensees of the Commission, while five, including the chairman, were officers of the Consolidated Gas Co., of N. Y. "It is believed that more weight should be given to the opinion of [actual] licensees and ... [state commissions] than of those whose relation to the Water Power Commission is largely academic, and it is recommended that the [regulations] be prepared with [that] in view".

tion rather than to that of reservation.[1] If anything, the administration, however, has been more alert than Congress to the dangers of distribution. During the era of sale (1789-1860), the individual person, when the law permitted any privilege or right, was always given the benefit of the doubt. The era of development of free homes, although there were continued protests on the part of a few of the great administrators of the Department, saw a continuation of this advantage. As early as 1871, and repeatedly thereafter, the reports of the Department contained prayer after prayer to the source of all national legislation for laws that would guarantee a comprehensive system of reserved forests. But Congress was too responsive to the wishes of the interested individualists; and the more or less permanent group in the Department had come to have a soul of its own in harmony with the philosophy of the time. As a result of the insistence of state officials who saw their resources going, of state and national forestry associations, and of widely scattered groups and individuals, however, Congress in 1891 gave the President power to reserve forest lands;

[1] Mr. Mangan, an attorney long connected with the Forestry Service, in a conversation with the writer, insisted that the Land Office nearly always leaned toward the individual's side at the expense of the public's. He cited the stand taken by that Office in the famous Hyde-Benson cases, e. g., 33 Land Dec. 639 (1905) and 40 Land Dec. 284 (1911). He probably overemphasized this idea because of the historical background, although the same conclusion is reached by Louis F. Post, in *Administrative Decisions in Connection with Immigration*, p. 251. Mr. Mangan claimed that the Forest Service under the Dept. of Agric. always took the side of the public. Historically, the idea of public land conservation originated and gradually developed as a policy within the Forest Service of the Public Land Office; its good tradition was transferred to the forest scientific service already established in the Dept. of Agric. where there was guaranteed a scientific atmosphere in which the conservation idea could thrive without being choked by the fumes and smoke of politics (33 Stat. 628, 1905). The transfer was recommended by the Commissioner of the General Land Office in his *Report* (1904), p. 50. See, also, J. P. Kenney, *Forest Law in America*, ch. vii (1919).

but no authority was set up by law for the protection of such lands. Finally in 1897 a statute was passed giving the Secretary of the Interior power to protect the reserved forests. This was not accomplished until Hoke Smith, then Secretary, asked the Forestry Committee of the National Academy of Science to make an exhaustive report to the Department upon the conservation of the national forest lands.[1]

It still remains true that the Department of the Interior, especially through the activities of the Land Office, is a distributing agency for the public resources. That is its bent; that is the intent of a majority of the laws to be enforced. Still there is a sufficiently large opinion in the United States to set the Public Lands Committee of the Senate to work investigating all the agencies having to do with the public land administration.[2] The Land Office and the Bureau of Mines are not likely to be greatly annoyed; it is the Park Service and the Indian Service that will have the most trouble—since their policy is avowedly against individualism in the use of governmental resources, as is that of the Forest Service in the Department of Agriculture.[3] One would naturally suppose that a department, or subdivision thereof, which emphasizes the rights of individuals would give willingly and eagerly all possible opportunities for

[1] *Annual Report of the Dept. of Agriculture* (1909), p. 55; *Report of the Commissioner of the General Land Office* (1900), p. 110; pp. 72-80 (1893); p. 99 *et seq.* (1902); p. 55 (1901), where it is said that the Timber and Stone Act of 1878 (20 Stat. 89), if not repealed or amended, "will result ultimately in the complete destruction of timber on the unappropriated and unreserved lands". Forests of live oak and red cedar were early reserved for naval purposes; it was made unlawful to cut such timber anywhere, on or off of such reservations for certain purposes (3 Stat. 347, 1817).

[2] *Hearings of Subcommittee of Senate Committee on Public Lands and Surveys*, 69th Cong., 1st Sess., pts. 1-15 (1925).

[3] *Supra*, pp. 206-207.

private interests to be heard in the making of rules and regulations governing the public domain; also that the reverse would apply to the administrative agency that has the collective interest more at heart.

It has already been shown that the Forest Service gives close attention to the private interests affected.[1] In apparent contrast the Land Office officials make many sets of regulations without formally inviting the interests concerned to present their side of the case. This is true chiefly in connection with the older laws, such as the Timber and Stone Act,[2] and the Alaska Timber Act.[3] Many of the regulations under these laws are technical and have been added to as a result of many years of experience recorded in the files of the Department. A Solicitor of the Interior Department made this statement to the writer, relative to Circular Number 289 of the General Land Office: "A lawyer sat down and wrote these rules out and they were approved by the Secretary and promulgated at once." The attorneys, through continued contact with the experts in the various branches of the public land service and through private experts that come into the courts, have accumulated in addition to their legal lore a great store of expert knowledge which they use in making regulations. Another observation relative to such exclusively intra-departmental rule-making is that the Land Office not only makes the regulations under the law but also interprets both the law and the regulations pertaining to it.[4] In this way the Land Office or the Depart-

[1] *Supra*, pp. 206-207.

[2] 20 Stat. 88 and the series of regulations issued thereunder between 1878 and 1903 (Circular 85, 1916), Land Office.

[3] 30 Stat. 409 and regulations (29 Land Decs. 572).

[4] 1881 is the beginning of Land Decisions of the Dept. of the Interior. In part 2 of the Digest of Decisions, vols. 1-40 (1913), the acts of Congress (p. 244), the rules and regulations made under the acts (p. 285), and the rules of practice (309) are construed and cited by the Department.

ment can and does temper the rules to the particular case, time and place. Secretary Work doubtless expressed fairly accurately, even if rather generally, the Department's process of making rules when he said:

It may be stated . . . that the rules and regulations pertaining to the work of the respective bureaus and offices . . . are usually prepared in the respective offices to which they relate under the general supervision of the head thereof. Thereafter, they are forwarded to the Department where they are considered either by the Secretary or by one of the Assistant Secretaries, under whose assignment of work the bureau or office may come, and when the circumstances of the case warrant, are also referred to the Solicitor for his views before they are signed by the Secretary and promulgated.[1]

III

In 1920 Mr. Clay Tallman, Commissioner of the General Land Office, maintained that the Mineral Leasing Act of 1920 is the most important change in the national policy of a century.[2] Under its provisions exploitation of coal, gas, phosphate, oil shale and sodium on the public domain must be carried on under a lease to which many regulations are attached, dealing with questions of diligence and skill in carrying on operations, the prevention of undue waste, the safety and welfare of miners and the fair and just measurement of miners' daily output. Although the holding in fee simple by private individuals has passed the national policy of encouraging private development is still present under the Act; it is being carried on through the Bureau of Mines.

[1] Secretary Work to Senator Sheppard, Oct. 2, 1923, in reply to the latter's letter of Sept. 27, 1923. The letter is in the possession of the writer.

[2] 41 Stat. 437 (1920); see also *Report of Commissioner of the General Land Office* (1920).

To accomplish the purposes of the Act the regulations must not be too strict; the individual must be given all the advantage the law allows, and must have some part in the making of the regulations.[1]

The Land Office asked the Bureau of Mines to aid in the preparing of leasing forms and general leasing regulations for the various minerals under the Leasing Act. The latter agency, long in contact with the mining interests of the country, took up the task of preparing operating regulations for oil and gas through its Petroleum and Gas Division, and for coal and other minerals through its Mineral Division. Representatives of all petroleum and gas associations which had any interest in the exploitation of the public domain were invited to a conference to consider operating regulations. The governor of each public land state sent officials to the conference to guard the local interests. An agreement was quickly reached; the regulations had the approval of the Secretary by March, 1920.[2] In a similar manner the operating regulations for the coal leases were prepared and submitted to the leading coal associations and to the governors of the public land states.[3] Although phosphate and sodium regulations were prepared no statement has been found as to the extent of the influence of interested parties.[4] Further to fit the regulations to the needs of the private exploiting groups—in the case of oil and gas, for example—the Department is attempting to insure that the terms and the spirit of the regulations be met in the manner of the best

[1] The leasing of unalloted Indian lands for farming, grazing, mining, etc., had been provided for by law much earlier, e. g., 30 Stat. 85 (1897) and 39 Stat. 128 (1916); Alaskan territory also had leasing regulations.

[2] Circular 672, Land Office.

[3] *Annual Report of the Director of the Bureau of Mines* (1920), p. 34, and Circular 679 (1920), Land Office.

[4] Land Office Circulars 696 and 699 (1920).

practices of the local areas. This liberality is increased by making the rules broad in scope, leaving details to the interpretation of the supervisor and of the local deputies who are "empowered to alter or modify them as conditions may warrant".[1] This is almost equivalent to the old method of issuing regulations as tentative, for the most part, and fitting them to the conditions by actually applying them in a workable way.

IV

The Act creating the National Park Service provides that this agency shall "promote and regulate the use of the federal areas known as the national parks, monuments, and the reservations hereinafter specified by such means and measures as conform to the fundamental purpose" thereof, which purpose is "to conserve the scenery and the natural and historical objects and wild life therein and to provide for the enjoyment of the same in such manner and by such means as will leave them unimpaired for the enjoyment of future generations".[2] The policy of former Secretary Lane was based upon certain broad principles: (a) that the national parks must be maintained in absolutely unimpaired form for present and future generations; (b) that they are set apart for use, observation, health, and pleasure of the people; and (c) that the national interest must dictate all decisions affecting the public or private interests in the parks. This policy means that the parks and monuments must not be commercialized; cattle grazing is not to be permitted except in the most isolated places—not even there if any of the natural features or man-made improvements are in danger; and the cutting of timber is to be permitted, under the guidance of landscape engineers, for local building purposes,

[1] *Bureau of Mines Bulletin 232* (1923), which gives a revision of the first set of regulations of 1920.

[2] 39 Stat. 535 (1916), amended by 41 Stat. 731, 732 (1920).

for scenic effects and for protection from injurious insects only.[1]

Although Congress has usually reserved to itself the specific task of creating national parks, it gives to the Secretary of the Interior power to expel trespassers and to make regulations for the preservation from injury or spoliation of all timber, mineral deposits, natural curiosities or wonders in the parks and for the retention of the natural condition of such reservations.[2] The control of roads and trails, of traffic, of concessioners, of animal life, of public utilities, of timber, minerals, forage and water power exposes the Park Service to the wails of the inconvenienced tourist, to the hunter's passion, to the jealousy of unsuccessful concessioners, and to the political pressure of the powerful livestock, mining and lumber industries. The Water Power Act of 1920 was amended in 1921 to put the burden of allowing power development in national parks upon Congress, thus relieving the Service of direct pressure.[3] Of the three general classes of public lands—the unappropriated or unreserved, the reserved forest, the reserved park and monument—the last subordinates wholly the interests of the individual to that of the national group, the first emphasizes the

[1] *Annual Report of the Director of the National Park Service* (1918), pp. 273-276. This is a classic statement by the former Secretary relative to the national park policy; it has been repeated in many of the documents of the Park Service.

[2] 39 Stat. 535, Sec. 3, gives general power of this character, while each act creating national parks gives specific authority. The specific power is taken from the Act of 1872 creating the Yellowstone National Park. National monuments may be created by a proclamation of the President and when so created the Park Service regulatory power applies (34 Stat. 225, 1906).

[3] *Report of the Director of the National Park Service* (1917), p. 14; (1923), p. 14; (1924), p. 20. The 1924 *Report*, p. 5, indicates that whenever lands on the outer edges of parks are of greater economic value than of park value, Congress should and does cut off such property from the parks.

individual rights and privileges, and the second gives the first chance to the public.[1]

If the parks are so exclusively for the public, what is the process by which the public interest is protected through the making of rules and regulations? Certainly the Director does not carry out such a difficult task by himself. In 1911 the Secretary of the Interior, Mr. Walter L. Fisher, called a National Parks Conference to consider the question of park administration.[2] The records show that this conference was, in fact, a hearing under the direct leadership of the Secretary himself. All national park superintendents, representatives from the Land Office, the Forest Service, the Public Health Service, the Steamboat Inspection Service, the Geological Survey, the Bureau of Entomology—all agencies of the national government that could possibly aid in perfecting the administration—, the leading western railroads, park concessioners, landscape architects and others were present by invitation. Such problems as opening the parks to automobiles, with their numerous attendant questions, the letting of concessions—whether they should be monopolistic or competitive—the kinds of camps, the control of passenger boats, the timber uses, live-stock grazing and road construction were considered. The discussions were based upon experience and theory. Whether the interests represented were public or private the expert was at hand, and because of the already-developing park policy, practically all interests had by necessity a quasi-public character. This conference, followed by others in 1912 and 1915, formed the basis for the modernization of the early park rules and regulations.[3]

[1] *Ibid.* (1924), p. 5: "the principle of complete conservation governs the parks and monuments."

[2] *Proceedings of the National Park Conference* (1911), especially pp. 20-40.

[3] *Proceedings of the National Park Conference* (1912 and 1915). The

The National Park Conference of 1917 was called to put the existing policies, rules and regulations in harmony with the Act of 1916 creating the National Park Service and unifying the entire national park system of administration. A fresh consideration of the whole subject became necessary. The best thinking and experience of the country were summoned to aid the Department in revising and perfecting the administration. There were present members of Congress who had specialized in the subject of public parks, representatives of cooperating clubs and associations, specialists in forestry, natural science and wild life conservation, and men and women interested in the recreational and economic phases of the question. From all these the Department got its information. It was a more thorough hearing than had ever before been held. Regulation of accommodations, of fishing, of wild animal life, of timber uses, of roads and traffic—all were discussed in open session.[1]

These general hearings, the specific experiences of the various members of the Service, the cooperation with every other department having had experience in some special phase of a problem with which the administration has to deal—all have tended, by giving the viewpoints of the variously interested private groups and individuals, to keep down the arbitrariness of the Director. In fact all the opinion brought to bear upon the Forest Service's timber and grazing regulations, upon the Biological Survey's handling of wild life or upon the administration of the national fisheries by the Bureau of Fisheries would naturally have its influence upon the park regulations dealing with these questions.

purpose of the 1915 meeting was "to consider all questions that arise in the administration of the parks in order that the Department might be able to make such changes in the regulations and to foster such development as might be for the best interest of the public" (p. 3).

[1] *Proceedings of the National Park Conference* (1917).

V

The Treasury Department has had wide experience in framing both administrative and interpretative regulations. Congress has seen fit to entrust this agency with the task of enforcing laws whose chief purpose is that of securing revenue or of handling the nation's finances, as well as applying laws whose chief aim is the national welfare. The variety of contacts which the Treasury Department has with the vital needs and strong desires of individuals and groups is well illustrated by the statutes dealing with internal revenue,[1] customs,[2] prohibition,[3] habit-forming drugs,[4] adulterated butter [5] and public health.[6] One might expect that it would be forced to listen to the opinions of those affected before it finally established supplementary regulations. This expectation is not so readily realized, however, at least in so far as recorded evidence goes. The reports of the Secretary and of his subordinates indicate that although group opinion does have a share in the framing of rules, administrative and interpretative, details are lacking. Occasional statements of individual officers or testimony brought out in congressional investigations add something to the record. It is believed that the technical character of many of the revenue statutes has led to a great amount of independent rule-making on the part of departmental experts.[7] This belief may be discounted, however, for two

[1] 40 Stat. 1057 (1918).

[2] 36 Stat. 97 (1909).

[3] 41 Stat. 305 (1919).

[4] 38 Stat. 784 (1914).

[5] 24 Stat. 209 (1886); 32 Stat. 194 (1902).

[6] 27 Stat. 449 (1893); 28 Stat. 372 (1894); 26 Stat. 31 (1890); 31 Stat. 1086 (1901); 34 Stat. 229 (1906).

[7] An official of the Bureau of Internal Revenue made the following statement relative to a certain set of Treasury regulations:

The regulations were written to a large extent by attorneys in the

reasons: first, when a tax law expresses absolutely new policies, there is usually some play of opinion upon the rules enforcing such policies: secondly, a large part of each new set of regulations is a renewal of regulations of the past that have proved efficacious, upon which public opinion once played. In other words the revenue system is one into which new laws are made to fit through old regulations, or through original regulations upon which opinion has had some influence.

The Revenue Act of 1916, as amended October, 1917,[1] seemed to many to be impossible of enforcement, especially in connection with its new features. The Commissioner of Internal Revenue insisted, however, that the intent of Congress could be ascertained and effectuated by regulations provided the interests chiefly affected could be brought to offer their assistance. The Secretary of the Treasury, accepting this suggestion, called to the Commissioner's aid a group of men prominent in, and representative of, agriculture, manufacturing, trade, finance and accounting. This group was reinforced by experts in the fields of economics, sociology and governmental administration. The temporary advisory board thus assembled sought information, advice and suggestions from tax payers by all known means. Hearings were conducted for the purpose of securing an oral dis-

office of the Solicitor of Internal Revenue. An employee of the Income Tax Unit was detailed to the Solicitor's Office to assist in the preparation of the regulations and they were reviewed by the Deputy Commissioner in Charge of the Income Tax Unit and by the Head of the Technical Division, Income Tax Unit. In the preparation ... no person outside of the Internal Revenue rendered assistance.

Memorandum of C. R. Nash, Assistant to the Commissioner, sent to Senator Sheppard, Oct. 15, 1923, who very kindly put it in the possession of the writer. Mr. Nash did suggest that many of the regulations were those made by a former Commissioner of Internal Revenue.

[1] 39 Stat. 756, as amended by 40 Stat. 300.

cussion of the law and the proposed regulations intended to effect its purpose. Parallel with, and supplementary to, this thoroughgoing investigation the Commissioner was busy receiving the opinions of numerous individual taxpayers relative to the less important regulations. After months of thorough and painstaking consideration of proffered suggestions both administrative and interpretative regulations were promulgated. As a result of this deliberative procedure business and industrial conditions and practices were disturbed to the least possible extent and the Treasury kept the confidence of the taxpayers of the country.[1]

Under the Revenue Act of 1918 an elaborate procedure of ascertaining the views of the taxpayers seemed unnecessary. Much of the information secured in 1917 still held good. However, a fresh viewpoint on old questions was secured indirectly through men who, because of their desire to render war service, had come to the Department from the various taxpaying groups of the country. Business men, lawyers and expert accountants were able to pass judgment upon the work of the regular Treasury experts. The resulting regulations were considered fair.[2] On strictly new policies these same men were exerting their influence. Evidence was brought out in 1924 to show that in the drafting of certain new oil regulations, large groups of "patriotic" experts had been brought to Washington from all parts of the

[1] See *Report of the Commissioner of Internal Revenue* (1918), pp. 9-10; also *ibid.*, pp. 8, 36, for the methods of obtaining criticisms of the regulations. But see Geo. O'May's criticism of these regulations in *Hearings of Senate Special Committee on Investigation of Bureau Internal Revenue*, 68th Cong., 1st Sess. (1924), pp. 262-263.

[2] *Report of the Commissioner of Internal Revenue* (1919), pp. 12-15. This officer makes much of the fact that his legal service is made up at all times of men "of sound legal training and experience, whose contact with the business world is such as to deal intelligently with the broad problems of business law daily presented".

country; that some ninety of them, guided and led by Mr. Ralph Arnold of California, had actually framed the regulations.[1] In addition to the representation which the interested parties had within the Bureau and the Advisory Board on Oil Regulations, the Act itself provided for an advisory board [2] whose existence should be limited to a maximum of two years and whose purpose should be the giving of adequate attention to the viewpoint of the taxpayer. This body of expert men taken, with one exception, from men outside the departmental personnel, was chiefly busied by the task of making regulations to enforce the excess profits provisions of the law. Its work was accomplished largely through formal and informal hearings and conferences. Although many of its regulations were explanatory in character, they formed the basis for, and determined the play of, the necessary administrative rules.

The Treasury Department, in a memorandum giving the process by which certain prohibition regulations had been formulated, made this statement: [3]

> The original issue of 1920 was prepared by a major committee consisting of an Assistant Deputy Commissioner experienced in such work, especially designated for the purpose, the then Head of the old Distilled Spirits Division, and an attorney from the office of the Solicitor of Internal Revenue. The actual work was largely performed by a sub-committee consisting of a section chief and a former section chief in the old Distilled Spirits Division, which division was abolished in December,

[1] *Hearings of Senate Special Committee on the Investigation of the Bureau Internal Revenue*, 68th Cong., 1st Sess. (1924), p. 344.

[2] 40 Stat. 1057 (1918), Sec. 1301 (d). The personnel of the Board was made up of Dr. T. S. Adams, economist; J. E. Sterrett, accountant; Fred T. Field, lawyer of the Bur. Int. Rev.; Stuart W. Cramer, manufacturer.

[3] Memorandum made for Senator Sheppard, dated Oct. 15, 1923, and now in the possession of the writer.

1919. All persons participating in this, except the attorney from the Solicitor's Office, had had long and varied experience in the preparation of regulations . . . pertaining to intoxicating liquors.

Numerous hearings were granted to persons who were interested in the subject, such as homeopathic pharmacists, manufacturers of proprietary medicines, manufacturers of U. S. P. and N. F. preparations, manufacturers of flavoring extracts, retail druggists, rabbis and others.

This last statement is more or less corroborated by the testimony before the House Judiciary Committee in 1924.[1] The Association of Retail Druggists, although admitting that the regulations of 1920 concerning intoxicating liquors had been framed with its own close collaboration, charged that of late the Prohibition Unit had been refusing its offer of advice and that, as a result, the prohibition agency had lost the confidence of all retail druggists.

Similar statements were made by the National Wholesale Druggists and by the Interstate Manufacturing Association.[2] Mr. Britt, Counsel for the Prohibition Unit, on the other hand, stated that an unofficial advisory committee, representing the alcoholic and allied trades, had been appointed by the Commissioner of Internal Revenue with the approval of the prohibition officials. This body was constantly being consulted by the Prohibition Unit. " We have deferred regulations ", said Mr. Britt, " week after week, from month to month, from quarter to quarter, and would not finish them until they either had their [the committee's] approval or the question had been fought to a finish and a decision made ".[3]

[1] *Hearings* on H. R. 6645, 68th Cong., 1st Sess., pp. 70-71 (1924).

[2] *Ibid.*, pp. 158-160.

[3] *Ibid.*, p. 185.

VI

When the Tariff Act of 1922 was passed it contained provisions naming, in a more or less general way, the procedure by which the President was to act in exercising his exceedingly large discretionary powers. Whenever he was to adjust rates of duty to carry into practice the principle of equalization of costs of production—thereby potentially controlling within broad limits practically all imports other than those on the free list [1]—or to name rates for, or to employ the embargo against, foreign goods as penalties for unfair practices or discriminatory acts,[2] he was to have the aid of the Tariff Commission as an intermediary between the parties concerned and himself.[3] The following parts of the 1922 Act indicate the procedure in arriving at executive action:

Section 315 (c). Investigations to assist the President in ascertaining differences in cost of production under this section shall be made by the United States Tariff Commission, and no proclamation shall be issued under this section until such investigation shall have been made. The Commission shall give reasonable public notice of its hearings and shall give reasonable opportunity to parties interested to be present, to produce evidence, and to be heard. The Commission is authorized to adopt such reasonable procedure, rules and regulations as it may deem necessary.

Section 316. (b) That to assist the President in making any decisions under this section the United States Tariff Commission is hereby authorized to investigate any alleged violation hereof on complaint under oath or upon its initiative.

[1] Section 315 of Tariff Act of 1922, 42 Stat. 858.

[2] 42 Stat. 858 (1922), Secs. 316, 317.

[3] The outsider does not know, of course, what forces play directly upon the President or how these forces are exerted.

(c) That the Commission shall make such investigation under and in accordance with such rules as it may promulgate and give such notice and afford such hearing, and when deemed proper by the Commission such rehearing with opportunity to offer evidence, oral or written, as it may deem sufficient for a full presentation of the facts involved in such investigation; that the testimony in every such investigation shall be reduced to writing, and a transcript thereof with the findings and recommendations of the Commission shall be the official record of the proceedings and findings in the case, and in any case where the findings in such investigations show a violation of this section, a copy of the findings shall be promptly mailed or delivered to the importer or consignee of such articles. . . . (d) The final findings of the Commission shall be transmitted with the record to the President.

Section 317 (g). It shall be the duty of the United States Tariff Commission to ascertain and at all times to be informed whether any of the discriminations against the commerce of the United States enumerated in subdivisions (a), (b), and (e) of this section are practiced by any country; and if any, when such discriminatory acts are disclosed, it shall be the duty of the Commission to bring the matter to the attention of the President, together with recommendations.

Since the President has discretionary powers affecting the general schedules, especial notice must be taken of the procedure under Section 315. The Tariff Commission, as already noted, must, after making an investigation, report as a condition precedent to executive action. The Commission is required to give to persons interested reasonable public notice of its hearings, reasonable opportunity to be present, to produce evidence and to be heard. The Commission is, in this connection, authorized to adopt such reasonable procedure, rules and regulations as it may deem necessary. But the fact must not be lost sight of that it is upon the President that the statute expressly confers the power to ascertain the differences in costs of production, to determine and proclaim the changes in classification or increases or decreases in rates necessary to equalize the same and to find and to make public the facts upon which the basis of assessment is changed from foreign value to the American selling price. By subdivision (e) of Section 315, the President is authorized to make all needful rules and regulations for carrying out the provisions of the Section. The Chief Executive, in accordance with this authority, issued under date of October 7, 1922, the following order:

> It is ordered that all requests, applications, or petitions for action or relief under the provisions of Sections 315, 316, and 317 of Title III of the Tariff Act approved September 21, 1922, shall be filed with or referred to the United States Tariff Commission for consideration and for such investigation as shall be in accordance with law and the public interest, under rules and regulations to be prescribed by the Commission.[1]

The Commission, following the law and its supplement (the executive order quoted above) framed its rules of procedure for all three sections which they then made public. These provide, *inter alia,* that applications for an investigation under these sections may be made by any person, partnership, corporation or association. Although no special form is required, each application must be in writing and signed by, or on behalf of, the applicant; it must also contain a short and simple statement of the relief sought with the grounds therefor. No investigation can be ordered unless

[1] Treas. Dec. 39283. Pres. Harding on April 21, 1923, after a conference with the Commission, issued a statement interpreting the order for investigations upon the initiative of the Commission under Sections 315 and 316, regardless of the filing of an application or a petition by an interested party. See *Seventh Annual Report of the U. S. Tariff Commission,* pp. 34, 35. For an elaboration of the spirit of the rules, see former Vice-Chairman Culbertson's address of Oct. 26, 1922, quoted from McClure, *A New American Commercial Policy,* pp. 55-56.

the application for a preliminary investigation indicates to the Commission good and sufficient reason under the law for so doing. The applicant may, at the will of the Commission, amend his application.

According to the rules laid down by the Commission the procedure under Section 315 departs in some respects from that under the other sections. There are apparently two main parts to the process: the investigation proper, and the hearing.[1] The rules prescribe a particular form of order instituting an investigation. The notice of such investigation is made by posting a copy of the order for thirty days both at the principal office of the Commission in the City of Washington, D. C., and the branch office in the port of New York, and by publishing a copy for two successive weeks in *Treasury Decisions* and in *Commerce Reports.* The order thus published is to contain a notice that persons interested will be given an opportunity to be present, to produce evidence, and to be heard at the office of the Commission or at some convenient center on a date thereafter to be fixed, of which thirty days' public notice shall be given by publication in *Treasury Decisions* and in *Commerce Reports.*[2] At times the public notice of an investigation is to be accompanied by a notice fixing the date for a public hearing at which parties will be given an opportunity to produce evidence and to be heard. Usually this hearing is of a preliminary character designed to elicit from interested parties information upon the various aspects of the investigation and to shed light upon the proper scope and method of the inquiry.[3]

[1] See the *Seventh Annual Report of the Commission*, p. 35.

[2] E. g., see Investigation No. 47, *re* edible gelatin, Treas. Decs., vol. 48, no. 7, Aug. 13, 1925; Investigation No. 45, *re* granite, Treas. Decs., vol. 48, no. 5, July 30, 1925. Seattle was the place for hearings on spruce and halibut. See *Ninth Annual Report of the Commission*, p. 14.

[3] Straw hats investigation, 1924, and the vegetable oils investigation, 1924. See *Ninth Annual Report of the Commission*, pp. 14, 26, 73 and also *Report to the President on Wheat and Wheat Products*, Mar. 7, 1924.

Since the provisions of Section 315, also of Section 316. are designed to be applied in the public interest—not at the suit of private parties in their own private interests—the Commission has to be very careful as to which applications are actually investigated.[1] Under the present practice every application is submitted to the chief economist who transmits it to the chief investigator who, in turn passes it on to the expert of the proper commodities division, with comments and directions, for a preliminary report.[2] This report summarizes all relevant material available in printed form such as statistics, hearings before committees of Congress, former tariff surveys and manuscript material collected by the Commission in the course of its inquiries, surveys and investigations. The members of the Advisory Board then review the preliminary report, individually or collectively sending their conclusions to the Commission. This body determines finally whether the data collected calls for the initiation of an investigation under Section 315 or, perhaps,

[1] Applications are in no sense regarded as pleadings. The Commission proceeds upon the theory that the whole matter is one of general public interest, affecting not only the particular applicant, but, on the one hand, all other parties concerned and, on the other, the ultimate consumers of the article. *Eighth Annual Report of the Commission*, p. 9.

D. Culbertson, former Vice Chairman of the Tariff Commission, told the Senate Committee for Investigating the Tariff Commission, May 21, 1926, "The President [Harding] was beginning to pay the penalty for having indicated a desire that he be consulted before the Commission ordered investigations on its own initiative." The same person later remarked, "How many influences, direct and indirect, through political leaders and others, were brought to bear upon him nobody will ever know." See *New York Times*, May 22, 1926, p. 6.

[2] Investigations contemplate the collaboration of technical, economic, accounting and legal experts. The advisory board set up by the Commission, composed of the Chief of the Economics Division (chairman), Chief Investigator, Chief of the Legal Division, Chief of the (appropriate) Commodities Division, and an assigned economist, forms this expert element in the investigation. See *Ninth Annual Report of the Commission*, pp. 5-6.

under Section 316.[1] In the event of such a determination a complete plan for the investigation is worked out with the approval of the Advisory Board and the Commission. Conferences are held with foreign and domestic representatives of the industry under consideration to acquaint them with the character of the data required to ascertain the costs. Then field crews are sent out to bring in the information, which is carefully reviewed in Washington.[2] After tabulation and analysis of all such data have been made by the Advisory Board and approved by the Commission—as far as is consistent with the statutory prohibition against disclosure of trade secrets or processes—a summary of the tentative results of the field investigation is usually made and submitted to the interested persons, in advance of the public hearing.[3]

At least thirty days' notice is given of all regular public hearings under Sections 315 and 316. The chief purpose of a public hearing under Section 315 is to subject the cost and other data collected by the Commission to the closest scrutiny. Interested persons are free not only to present affirmative evidence of their own, but to discuss all cost factors in the light of their own experience. They may also indicate additional sources of information unexplored by the experts. The chief value of this kind of information is to place the Commission on guard against data which, in the view of interested persons, are considered inadequate or which fail to take into account all aspects of the inquiry. Testimony at the hearings is given under oath, a steno-

[1] *Ninth Annual Report of the Commission*, pp. 37-38 (1924).

[2] *Ibid.*, pp. 17-20. The Commission complains that the proper data cannot be secured in certain cases outside the territory of the U. S. and that the indirect means used to ascertain such costs are questionable under the terms of the law.

[3] *Ibid.*, pp. 6-7; also *Seventh Annual Report of the Commission*, p. 40.

graphic record of which is made for the central office. After the evidence has been obtained in this manner interested persons are given opportunity to criticize it orally or in writing. The Commission has taken the same viewpoint relative to hearings that it has held with regard to applications for investigations, viz., that they are not contests between parties litigant or interested as plaintiff and defendant, but are a part of proceedings in the public interest to determine whether a change in classification, a decrease or an increase in the rate of duty, should be made with respect to a particular article of importation. Although the Commission does not spend a great deal of time in holding hearings in any particular case, the information and views brought forward have proved of great value in the final consideration of data upon which a report is made to the President.[1]

The Commission's published reports to the President under Section 315—i. e., those upon which the Chief Executive has taken action—seem to follow the procedure as described above. Usually each report lists all or almost all of the following documents used by the Commission in the formation of its conclusions and recommendations on the article concerned: applications for increase or decrease of duty or for both; the public summary of information for the use of interested persons at the hearing; the stenographer's minutes of the public hearing or hearings held; the briefs of interested persons presented after the evidence has been taken; and the Advisory Board's final confidential summary. Reference is specifically made, as the report develops, to the appropriate document. It is interesting to note that the Commission often relies directly upon public hearings for its facts. In many cases, when the experts' reports are relied upon, the information is that secured from documents

[1] *Ninth Annual Report of the Commission*, pp. 13-16.

of general knowledge and from testimony of public-interest agencies as well as from that of private-interest agencies.[1]

It has been stated above that the procedure under Section 316 for the most part followed that under Section 315. There seem, however, to be some differences. When the Commission makes a preliminary finding upon the basis of an application complaining of unfair methods the evidence is submitted therewith. This really corresponds to the preliminary investigation made under Section 315. If it is determined by it that the entry of any goods should be forbidden pending further investigation, the President may order the Secretary of the Treasury to issue an *ad-interim* order forbidding the entry of such goods into the United States pending such further investigation.[2] The Act leaves it to the Commission to afford such hearing as it may deem sufficient for a full presentation of the facts involved; but the practice of the Commission has been to accord a full public hearing in every case of investigation.[3] The detailed procedure in the case involving the simulation of Smith and Wesson revolvers illustrates the identity of the public hearing procedure under the two sections. The hearings under Section 316, by reason of the subject matter, are more quasi-

[1] Data are taken from the following special reports of the Commission to the President: Sodium Nitrite, May 6, 1924; Barium Dioxide, May 19, 1924; Barbital or Veronal, Nov. 14, 1924; Oxalic Acid, Dec. 29, 1924; Live Bob White Quail, Oct. 3, 1925. Further evidence can be found in the annual reports of the Commission.

[2] Sec. 316, subdivision (f). Whenever the President has reason to believe that any article is sought to be offered for entry in violation of this section, "but has not information sufficient to satisfy him thereof, the Secretary shall, upon his request in writing, forbid entry thereof until such investigation as the President may deem necessary, shall be completed". A good example of this action is found in the alleged simulation of the Smith Wesson revolver noted in the *Ninth Annual Report of the Commission*, Appendix 2, p. 93.

[3] *Ninth Annual Report of the Commission*, pp. 14-15.

judicial in character. However, the establishment of an unfair method under the general terms of the law, as well as the raising of the duty on, or the excluding of the articles involved, is a legislative determination of penalty.[1]

The rules of the Commission governing investigations and hearings under Section 317 are stated in a general way as follows:

> If in any investigation under Section 317 it becomes necessary in the judgment of the Commission to order a hearing, a notice shall be given and hearings shall be had, as provided with respect to hearings under Sections 315 and 316.[2]

From this statement it would appear optional with the Commission whether it will use the procedure already outlined or not. In 1923, it set about to find out whether discriminations against American commerce existed and to obtain data as to the practical effects of any discriminations that might be found. Questionnaires were sent to more than a thousand leading manufacturers and exporters in all lines of trade, asking them to report upon the existence and effects of discrimination against United States products in their respective lines of business. Information was also obtained through personal interviews with exporters.[3] By the end of the fiscal year 1925 there had been about thirteen applications for investigations, most of them doubtless coming as a result of the initial action of the Commission. Each case is reported as an "investigation undertaken".[4] In answer to the question as to what reports had been made by the Commission to the President, the Secretary replied, "Such reports under Section 317 have been submitted in confidence and

[1] *Ninth Annual Report of the Commission*, pp. 8, 14-15 and 90-115.

[2] *Seventh Annual Report of the Commission*, p. 54.

[3] *Ibid.*, p. 42.

[4] *Ninth Annual Report of the Commission*, table i, pp. 83-84.

have not been made public ".[1] The hearings, if any, seem to be protected against public scrutiny—or at least they will be until the President has acted.[2]

[1] Letter from the Secretary of the Commission to the writer, dated Mar. 25, 1926.

[2] Further illustrations of political checks through group opinion upon the making of administrative legislation can be found in the following citations:

(a) Department of Commerce: Steamboat inspection, *Annual Report of the Department of Commerce and Labor* (1905), p. 35 *et seq.*; Alaskan fisheries, *Annual Report of the Department of Commerce* (1915), p. 115 *et seq.*, and *ibid.* (1922), pp. 14 and 172; load line regulations, *Department of Commerce Bulletin*, Dec. 27, 1916.

(b) Interstate Commerce Commission: Car demurrage rules, *Service Circular* No. 2412, American Railway Association (1923); safety appliance standards, *Twenty-fourth Annual Report of the Commission* (1910), p. 42 *et seq.*; transportation of explosives, *Thirty-fourth Annual Report of the Commission* (1920), p. 74 *et seq.*

(c) U. S. Shipping Board: *Tentative Tariff Regulation* (1917).

INDEX

Adams, T. S., quoted, 162
Administrative legislation, general, 9-11; causes for development, 11-15; advantages claimed, 15-17; disadvantages claimed, 17-18; limited treatment, 19; distinguished from: basic law, 21; statutes, 21-22; treaties, 22-25; independent law making of President, 22-25; interpretative regulations, 28-29; complementary class: definition, 26; varied nomenclature, 27; contingent class: general, 26, 30; definition, 31; varied nomenclature, 32-33; why called legislation: involves discretion, 33-41; considered by courts, 41-47; considered by Congress, 48
Administrative rules, *see* Administrative legislation
Advisory boards, in Bureau of Internal Revenue, 167-69; in Biological Survey, 233, 235-36; Tariff Commission as, 262; in Tariff Commission, 265, 266-67
Aldrich, Senator, favors delegation, 82-83
Allison, Senator, on delegation, 83-84
Animal quarantine, *Order 273*, 227-31
Arnold, Ralph, member of Oil Advisory Board, 259
Association of Retail Druggists, pressure group, 260
Audubon Societies, pressure group, 234

Barnes, Will C., Forest Service, referred to, 207
Barnett, James D., referred to, 116
Board of Tax Appeals, recommended to Congress, 168; independent body, 168; functions, 169
Boske *v.* Comingore, quoted, 136
Brandeis, Justice, quoted, 47
Brig Aurora Case, upholding delegation, 69; referred to, 70, 72, 78, 119, 120
Britt, prohibition counsel, quoted, 260
Brown, R. A., referred to, 40-41
Bruce, Andrew A., referred to, 117
Bryce, James, on American committee system, 194
Bureau of Internal Revenue, interpretative regulations in, 145
Buttfield *v.* Stranahan, quoted, 40

Caha *v.* U. S., quoted, 42
Carr, Cecil T., referred to, 15, 194
Chamber of Commerce, New York, quoted, 147
Chamber of Commerce, U. S., quoted on delegation, 104
Cheadle, John B., quoted, 117
Collectivistic philosophy, 13-14
Committee hearings, on bills, 189-90; on administrative acts, 190-93; results, 192-93
Committee on Appeals and Review, 154, 159, 167
Consolidated Gas Company of New York, referred to, 244-45
Contingent legislation, nomenclature 32, *see* Administrative legislation
Control of administrative legislation, general, 170-71; judicial: President exempted personally, 171-73; other officers acting with discretion usually exempted, 173-74; general political: appointment and removal, 182-84; impeachment, 184-85; congressional: withdrawal of delegation, 185-86; withholding of funds, 185; reports, 187-89; committee investigations, 189-94; official publications, 194-97; group pressures: general, 198-201; procedure in Department of Agriculture: gen-

eral, 202; forest reserves, 204-11; plant quarantine, 212-19; cotton futures, 219-23; grain standards, 223-26; other agricultural standards, 226-27; livestock quarantine, 227-30; naval stores, 231-32; migratory birds, 232-36; packers and stockyards, 237-38; procedure in Water Power Commission, 239-46; procedure in Department of Interior: mineral leasing, 250-52; national parks, 252-55; procedure in Treasury Department: revenue laws (*1916-17*), 257-58; revenue laws (*1918*), 258-59; prohibition, 259-60; tariff (*1922*), 261-70

Cooley, Judge, quoted on separation of powers, 114-15

Coolidge, President, quoted, 107-8

Couzens, Senator, referred to, 143, 150, 151

Culbertson, W. S., quoted on delegation, 96-97, 106

Dakota Central Telephone *v.* S. D., quoted, 39

Daniel, Senator, on delegation, 88-89

Delegated legislation, *see* Administrative legislation

De Vries, Marion, on delegated legislation, 105-6; quoted, 113

Dicey, quoted, 12-13

Discretion, implications of, 33-34

Electric Bond and Share Company, pressure group, 240, 244, 246

Elliott *v.* Swartwout, quoted, 166, 179-80

Empire State Gas and Electric Association, pressure group, 242

Engineering Council of America, pressure group, 240-41

Erskine *v.* Hohnbach, referred to, 180; quoted, 181

Executive leadership, growth of, 14

"Expertise", 18

Evarts, Senator, opposes delegagation, 76-77; favors delegation, 75; referred to, 90

Fairlie, John A., on publication, 197

Field, Fred T., referred to, 156

Field *v.* Clark, upholding delegation, 78-80; referred to, 81, 82, 84, 88, 105; quoting Locke's *Appeal*, 121

Fisher, Secretary of Interior, referred to, 254

Flying Fish, quoted, 178

Freund, Ernst, referred to, 15

Goodnow, Frank J., quoted, 115

Greeley, W. B., Chief Forester, referred to, 210

Gregg, Solicitor, testimony, 156-57; on publicity, 163

Gulf Oil Company, referred to, 162

Hale, Senator, favors delegation, 75

Harding, President, quoted on delegation, 94

Hart, James, referred to, 15, 19, 118, 171

Hearings, compulsory, 200; voluntary, 200

History of administrative legislation, general, 50-51; supplementary class: *1789-1824*, 51-56; *1825-1860*, 56-59; *1861-1890*, 59-64; *1891-1926*, 203-46, 250-60; contingent class: *1789-1824*, 64-71; *1825-1860*, 71-72; *1861-1890*, 72-73; *1891-1926*, 73-112

Holmes, Justice, quoted, 47, 177

Illinois Central Railroad *v.* McKendree, referred to, 176

Impeachment, political control, 184-85

Interpretative regulations, nature, 137-38; distinguished from administrative regulations, 28-29, 137-38; necessity of: according to Congress, 139-40; according to courts, 140; according to officials, 140-41; general class: definition, 145; examples, 146-52; particular class: definition, 152; varied nomenclature, 153; novel cases, 152-53; examples, 154-55, 158-62; dangers: retroactivity, 150-51, 164-66; secrecy, 156-57, 162; checks: organization, 163; publicity, 163-64; Congress, 166; courts, 166-67; special boards, 167-69; group pressures, 241-42, 245, 256, 258-59

Interpretative regulations, retroactive effect, 150-51, 164-66; sanctioned by Congress, 165-66
Interstate Manufacturing Association, pressure group, 260
Iselin *v.* Hedden, quoted, 175

Jardine, Secretary of Agriculture, quoted, 186
Johnson *v.* Maryland, referred to, 43

Kendall *v.* Stokes, quoted, 171-72
Key, Philip B., opposes delegation, 70-71; theory of delegation, 76; referred to, 90
King, Senator, referred to, 144

Laissez-faire ideal, 10
Lane, Secretary of Interior, policy of, 252-53
Legality of administrative legislation, constitutional provisions, 114; separation of powers theory, 114-17; Constitutional Convention debates, 118; early court decisions, 119-20; early delegations, 120-21; *stare decisis* cases, 121-22; scope of discretion, 122-25; clear intent necessary, 126-31; subject matter included, 132; conditions of: procedural observance, 132-33; within terms of delegation, 133; reasonable relation to purpose of law, 134-35; conclusion, 135-36
Liverpool Cotton Association, foreign pressure group, 222
Lowden, Representative, quoted, 88
Luce, Robert, on American, committees, 189
Lynch *v.* Tilden, referred to, 149

McClure, Wallace, quoted, 95
McCulloch *v.* Maryland, referred to, 132
McCumber, Senator, remarks on delegation, 93
McGuire, Representative, quoted, 88
McVeagh, Secretary of Treasury, letter of, 147-48

Madison, James, quoted, 118
Marlatt, C. L., quoted, 215-16
Marshall, Chief Justice, quoted, 123
Martin *v.* Mott, referred to, 120; quoted, 170-71
Marvin, Thos. O., of Tariff Commission, quoted, 107; referred to, 108, 112
Mellon, Secretary of Treasury, referred to, 142
Merrill, O. C., of Water Power Commission, referred to 240, 241, 244
Morgan, Senator, quoted, 74-75, 84; referred to, 85

National Association of Fish and Game Commissioners, referred to, 234
National Association of Railway and Public Utilities Commissioners, referred to, 242
National Electric Light Association, pressure group, 240-41, 242, 243, 244
National Park Conferences, *1911*, 254; *1912*, 254; *1915*, 254; *1917*, 255
National Wholesale Druggists, pressure group, 260

Ohio Valley Water Co. *v.* Ben Avon Borough, referred to, 40
Order, *see* Administrative legislation

Page, Thos. W., formerly of Tariff Commission, referred to, 106
Parliamentary system, compared with presidential, 183, 184
Philadelphia Co. *v.* Stimson, referred to, 43
Pink Bollworm Quarantine, *No. 46*, 217-19
Plant Quarantine, *No. 37*, 215-16, 217
President, independent law-making power of, head of Army and Navy, 23; power of recognition, 24; executive orders, 24
Presidential system, theoretic responsibility of, 182-83; actual responsibility of, 183, 184
Pressure groups, 104, 147, 234, 240-46, 256, 258-60. *See also* Control of administrative legislation

Proclamation, *see* Administrative legislation; President, independent law-making power of
Publication of administrative legislation, official, 194-97
Publicity, as a safeguard, 186-97. *See also* Reports to Congress; Committee hearings; Publication of administrative legislation; Control of administrative legislation

Quasi-legislative power, *see* Administrative legislation
Quincy, Josiah, favors delegation, 71

Rachford, C. E., Forest Service, referred to, 208, 211
Rainey, Representative, quoted, 86, 88
Randolph, John, opposes delegation, 70
Reed, *Ex parte*, referred to, 60
Regulation, *see* Administrative legislation
Report of Joint Committee on Postage, etc., quoted, 9
Reports to Congress, as safeguards, 187-88; annual, 188; special, 189
Retroactivity of interpretative regulations, 150-51, 164-66
Rule, *see* Administrative legislation

Safeguards, definition, 170
Secondary legislation, *see* Administrative legislation
Senate Finance Committee, quoted, 168
Senate Select Committee on Investigation of Bureau of Internal Revenue, 140, 144, 152, 154, 155, 157, 159, 160, 162, 193
Sherman, Secretary of Treasury, referred to, 146
Simmons, Senator, on delegation, 91
Smith, Secretary of Interior, referred to, 248
Standard Oil Company, referred to, 160-61
Standards, cotton, 219-23; grain, 223-26; other agricultural products, 226-27; naval stores, 231-32
Subordinate legislation, *see* Administrative legislation
Subsidiary legislation, *see* Administrative legislation
Supplementary legislation, nomenclature, 27; *see* Administrative legislation
Swendig *v.* Power Company, referred to, 181

Taft, Chief Justice, quoted, 132-33
Taft, President, referred to, 85
Tallman, Clay, of Land Office, referred to, 250
Tariff Commission, quoted on delegation, 94-95, 103
Taussig, F. W., on delegation, 106
Tax Simplification Board, Bureau of Internal Revenue, 163, 167-68
Tracy *v.* Swartwout, quoted, 179

Underwood, Senator, on delegation, 91
U. S. *v.* Breen, referred to, 64
U. S. *v.* George, referred to, 176
U. S. *v.* Grimaud, referred to, 45; as leading case, 127, 176
U. S. *v.* Sing Tuck, referred to, 176-77
U. S. Steel Corporation, referred to, 151

Vest, Senator, on delegation, 83
Viner, Jacob, quoted, 98

Waite *v.* Macy quoted, 148
Wallace, Secretary of Agriculture, quoted, 202-3, 217, 228
Walsh, Senator Thos. J., on delegation, 105
Wayman *v.* Southard, referred to, 120, 124, 125; quoted 123
Willman, *Ex parte*, referred to, 43
Wilson, Woodrow, on American committees, 194
Work, Secretary of Interior, quoted, 250
Wrenbury, Lord, quoted, 9

Bei Fragen zur Produktsicherheit wenden Sie sich bitte an:
If you have any questions regarding product safety,
please contact:

Walter de Gruyter GmbH
Genthiner Straße 13
10785 Berlin
productsafety@degruyterbrill.com